SUPREME CHAOS

Stroud & Hall Publishers
P.O. Box 27210
Macon, Ga 31221
www.stroudhall.com

The paper used in this publication meets the minimum requirements
of American National Standard for Information Sciences—
Permanence of Paper for Printed Library Materials.
ANSI Z39.48–1984. (alk. paper)

Library of Congress Cataloging-in-Publication Data

Pickering, Charles Willis, 1937-
Supreme chaos : the politics of judicial confirmation and the culture war /
by Charles Pickering, Sr.
p. cm.
ISBN 0-9745376-5-9 (hardcover : alk. paper)
1. Judges--Selection and appointment—United States. I. Title.

KF8776.P53 2006
347.73'14—dc22

2005035096

SUPREME CHAOS

The Politics of Judicial Confirmation
& the Culture War

BY JUDGE CHARLES PICKERING, SR.

STROUD & HALL

This book is dedicated to my twenty-one grandchildren—Aubrey Ruth Dunkerton, Jeremy Grimes Dunkerton, Charles Willis "Will" Pickering III, John Abraham Montgomery, Anna Elise Dunkerton, Thomas Rossyn "Ross" Pickering, Mary Ivon Montgomery, Sarah Joy Dunkerton, Jackson "Jack" Brake Pickering, Hanna Grace Dunkerton, Robert Pickering Montgomery, Robert Asher Pickering, Emily Hope Dunkerton, Margaret Anne Montgomery, James Harper Pickering, Allison "Alli" Elizabeth Chapman, Thomas Hudson Dunkerton, Emma Gail Chapman, Mary Lucile "Lucy" Chapman, Joanna Christine Dunkerton, and Ann Katherine "Kate" Dunkerton—all for whom I have the greatest love.

I sincerely hope the America in which they live out their lives will be as great as the America in which I have been blessed to live my life. I hope the rule of law will be strengthened and that they will come to appreciate it as much as I.

Contents

Foreword

BY EDWIN MEESE III

TWENTY YEARS AGO I delivered a speech to the American Bar Association calling for a "Jurisprudence of Original Intention." That I would discuss a principle of constitutional fidelity rather than deliver platitudes and make lawyer jokes caused a stir among those in attendance. The message I shared created quite a legal debate that was joined in subsequent months by Supreme Court Justice William J. Brennan, Jr. and then by his colleague, Justice John Paul Stevens. Judge Robert H. Bork of the United States Court of Appeals for the District of Columbia joined the discussion on the side of Constitutional fidelity. This dialog culminated in a speech by President Ronald Reagan at the investiture ceremony for Chief Justice William H. Rehnquist and Associate Justice Antonin Scalia.

Our debate involved complex judicial doctrines, intricate legal and moral philosophies, and detailed law and precedents reaching back two centuries to the founding of our country. But essentially the debate held in 1985 actually began as early as the 1920s and is the same debate we see in the confirmation proceedings before the United States Senate today. Will we be a country ruled by laws or ruled by men? Will we guard the sanctity of the rule of law and the separation of powers, or will we allow the agenda of a few to overcome the expressed will of the people? Will our laws be written, recognized and changed by the democratic process or altered and overruled by an elite group of unelected judges, based on their personal values and policy preferences?

Now, Charles Pickering Sr. has introduced this debate to the public in a way that only a nominee who faced the Senate confirmation battle can do. Following his unanimous confirmation by the United States

Senate to a lifetime appointment as a Federal District Court Judge, and his subsequent ten years on the bench, Pickering was chosen by President George W. Bush to sit on the Fifth Circuit Court of Appeals in 2001. For almost five years Pickering faced opposition and obstruction by the left wing groups, as they created mischaracterizations and dishonest representations of his record and reputation. Pickering fought through the slander, kept his dignity, and eventually took a recess appointment to the Fifth Circuit. That appointment expired when the Senate—still engaged in unprecedented filibusters at the urging of liberal special interest groups — adjourned in December 2004 without acting on his nomination.

No one can tell this story like Judge Pickering, who lived the battle, observed the arguments and knows the truth. He takes us behind the smoke screen to tell the real story of why liberals seek to defeat conservative judicial nominees. As a former federal judge, he understands the legal philosophies behind the partisan rhetoric and makes those agendas apparent to the reader.

This great contribution to the ongoing discussion of the future of American jurisprudence is valuable not only to the experienced constitutional attorney. It also provides a coherent and accessible presentation of the debate to all those who have a passion and commitment to the future of our judiciary and country. This book appeals to those of us in the legal community, but boils down the great philosophical debates so that everyone can see how they relate to their own lives. This book clearly describes and explains the partisan battles and culture war that occupies the national network broadcasts as well as the local weekly newspapers. Pickering's work shows how crucial the discussion of the culture conflict, judicial activism, the confirmation process and the makeup of our national courts is at this point in our nation's history.

In this book, Pickering takes us on a journey through the current state of the judicial confirmation process. He describes how it is "broken and badly needs to be fixed." Combining policy and legal research with his own experience, he goes behind the scenes of the current judicial confirmation debates to share with us not just the ideological divide, but a process failure which prevents fair treatment of nominations by either party or by any president.

Pickering shares with us the epic values struggle confronting our nation, showing how the movement of religious conservatives to the Republican Party coincided with a movement of secularists to the Democratic Party. He discusses how the collision of these two world views shape the political debates of our day on issues of religious expression, abortion, special rights, the definition of marriage and pornography. He tells how the commitment to faith shaped our country's early history and influenced the leaders who founded our nation and framed our Constitution. He provides case evidence of how secularists attempt to use the court to remove religion from the public square and challenge judicial nominees of faith.

Pickering outlines the players, identifies the culture warriors on both sides of the debate, and describes the beliefs of those opposing conservative judicial nominees. After mentioning their radical and extreme views, he notes that, ironically, it is these organizations that claim President George W. Bush's nominees are "outside the mainstream of America." Through news reports and their own words, he shows the unfettered control these special interest groups maintain over the Democratic Party.

Pickering notes that many of the media share the ideology of the liberal special interest groups and often do not challenge their assertions. Worse, too many journalists assume the accusations from the left are accurate and reverse the burden of proof on the judicial nominees: plaguing them as guilty until proven innocent. But he mentions that journalists committed to the truth can find facts when they look for them, and describes his own positive experiences when national reporters came to visit small town Mississippi.

His illustrative phrase "the Mystery Constitution" reminds us that when we abandon the written rule of law for a so-called "living Constitution," we are left with a justice system filled with doubt, one in which we only know what our law means once a majority of the Supreme Court so instructs us. Then he gives current and real cases on how it affects the lives of everyday Americans: from losing private property to outlawing the Pledge of Allegiance.

He diligently reviews the history of the filibuster in the Senate and documents in unbiased numbers the confirmation rate of the nominees of George W. Bush at the hands of obstructionist Democrats, in comparison with those of other recent presidents. He provides a historic and constitutional framework for the "advice and consent" responsibility of the United States Senate as well as the case for approval of nominees by majority vote.

Pickering's insightful review of the "Gang of 14" that broke the filibusters, as well as his perspective on the debates over John Roberts Jr., Harriet Miers and Samuel Alito provide not only enduring examples of the constitutional and cultural battles noted in the book, but also an insider's look at current events in the throes of national debate.

All of this sets the stage for his subsequent book which will describe his personal odyssey through the confirmation process, and how all these theoretical and legal principles collided with partisan rhetoric to create and then break a filibuster. That book will tell how his defeat but ultimate appointment to the Fifth Circuit Court of Appeals left him a stronger individual and one even more committed to speaking out and reforming the judicial confirmation process to ensure a more fair process for nominees, their families, the U.S. Senate and future American Presidents—both Republican and Democrat. While we will have to wait for the publication of these solutions, Pickering shares the basics with us in the epilogue of this book: a return to civility, electoral victory, procedural reform, a Senate rules change, and a Constitutional amendment.

The constitutional amendment is most intriguing. He suggests an amendment which would require judges to interpret the constitution according to the common meaning of the relevant provision at the time of its adoption. While I believe arguments, history, logic and the whole of the American experience sides with those of us on the originalist side of the debate, I do recognize that there are those of good faith who believe it is the judge's role to rule beyond the letter of the constitution. There is currently no explicit legal prohibition against judges ruling in this matter. Such an amendment as Pickering mentions in the closing of this book, and promises to expound upon in his coming book, would provide such a specific limitation on judges and restrain them to the literal and intended meaning of the Constitution as written and amended by the people through their elected representatives.

In recent debates over President George W. Bush's nominees to the circuit courts of appeal and the Supreme Court, those on the left have spoken publicly about the need to defeat what they describe as "activist judges." The truth of their opposition may actually reside in their opposition to judges who are faithful to the Constitution. The assistance of those who are sincere in wanting judges who are not activists—who do not seek to advance their own ideology above the law—is appreciated. Those who truly oppose activist judges should embrace Pickering's constitutional recommendation.

Charles Pickering's dedication to the improvement of a diverse, independent and qualified judiciary will protect the rights of all Americans and secure the rule of law for our posterity. I am grateful he has chosen to write this book and share his insights with the American electorate. The rule of law, the supremacy of the Constitution, must not be subjugated to the will of unelected judicial officials. I believe Judge Pickering's work will advance the understanding of the need for a jurisprudence of originalism and will increase the public's demand for judges who rule according to the Constitution rather than substitute their own political agendas.

Former U.S. Attorney General Edwin Meese was among President Ronald Reagan's most important advisors. As Chairman of the Domestic Policy Council and the National Drug Policy Board, and as a member of the National Security Council, he played a key role in the development and execution of domestic and foreign policy. During the 1970s, Mr. Meese was Director of the Center for Criminal Justice Policy and Management and Professor of Law at the University of San Diego. He earlier served as Chief of Staff for then-Governor Reagan and was a local prosecutor in California. Mr. Meese is a Distinguished Visiting Fellow at the Hoover Institution, Stanford University. He earned his B.A. from Yale University and his J.D. from the University of California, Berkeley. He currently serves as the Ronald Reagan Distinguished Fellow in Public Policy and Chairman of the Center for Legal and Judicial Studies at The Heritage Foundation in Washington, DC.

Acknowledgments

I OWE SO much to so many, it is difficult to know where to begin and impossible to name everyone. I am deeply, deeply grateful for every word, letter, statement, e-mail, travel to Washington, or other effort made on behalf of my confirmation, and for every word of encouragement and prayer made on my behalf and on behalf of my family.

My greatest debt of gratitude goes to my wife, Margaret Ann, who stood with me every step of the way. She is an inspiration, an encourager, and an awesome prayer partner. Margaret Ann is a wonderful mother to our four children—they could have no better mother, nor I a better wife. She has been my loving and faithful wife for almost forty-seven years and a significant contributor to anything good I have accomplished. Words cannot express the gratitude and appreciation I have for her.

My son, Congressman Chip Pickering, worked the hardest to secure my confirmation. He did everything he could honorably and humanly do. He would not give up. I can never express sufficient appreciation to Chip for his actions to defend my name and reputation. Our three daughters, Paige Dunkerton, Allison Montgomery, and Christi Chapman, were equally supportive with their words and prayers. The families of my children gave strength to us all as well. I appreciate my only brother, Gene, his wife, Karon, and my only sister, Ellen Walker, and her husband, Jimmy, for traveling to Washington for my second hearing.

Senators Trent Lott and Thad Cochran recommended my appointment to the District Court in 1990 and to the Fifth Circuit Court of Appeals in 2001. I appreciate their recommendations and am thankful for their warm friendship and strong support over the years. President

George H. W. Bush appointed me to the District bench. I have always had the highest respect for him and Barbara. President George W. Bush showed loyalty and determination by nominating me, re-nominating me, and giving me a recess appointment. For his confidence and support, I will always be grateful.

Ed Haddon served on the staff of the Senate Judiciary Committee for Senator Jeff Sessions. He worked tirelessly for my confirmation and was indispensable to my confirmation fight. I am grateful to Ed as well as Senator Sessions, who allowed him to work so hard on my behalf.

I am grateful to Senator Orrin Hatch, Chairman of the Judiciary Committee; all the Republican senators on the Judiciary Committee and their staff who worked and supported my nomination; Senators Zell Miller and John Breaux who both broke rank with the Democrats, supported my nomination, and voted to stop the filibuster; the only Independent in the Senate, Jim Jeffords, who also supported my nomination and voted to stop the filibuster; Senator Ben Nelson of Nebraska who supported my nomination; and for the Republican senators all of whom supported my nomination and voted to end the filibuster.

Thanks to the following who worked on my confirmation: Steven Wall and Brad Prewitt, assistants to Senators Lott and Cochran respectively; Susan Butler, Mike Chappell, and Brian Perry on Chip's staff; staffs in the Justice Department, White House, and at the Judiciary Committee.

Working with me over the almost five years I was facing confirmation, my staff took the brunt of the battle as they helped me prepare documents and materials to respond to the various requests of the Senate Committee and charges of special-interest groups—hard work for which I'm deeply grateful: Paul Walters, career law clerk; Sonja Gatlin, secretary; Margaret Seal, court reporter; Stephen King, Brian Petruska, Lorraine Walters Boykin, and Jeff Williams, law clerks; and Sharon Potin, courtroom deputy.

Thanks to my fellow district judges with whom I served for thirteen years; members of the Fifth Circuit Court of Appeals, who accepted me and worked with me during the eleven months that I had the privilege of serving on the Fifth Circuit; and the staffs and the other support personnel of both Courts as well as the leadership and personnel at the Administrative Office for the Courts.

I was humbled by the editorial endorsement of every major newspaper in Mississippi, my local television station WDAM, and numerous columnist and editorial writers inside and outside Mississippi. I appreciate the near unanimous support of past presidents of the Mississippi Bar, and the broad base of support I received from Mississippians with whom I have lived and worked over the years, both Democrat and Republican, both black and white.

The Democratic support included former governor William Winter; Frank Hunger; all of the state-wide elected Democrat officials in Mississippi; former governor Bill Waller; former lieutenant governor Brad Dye; former lieutenant governor Evelyn Gandy; Wayne Dowdy, chairman of the Mississippi Democrat Party; Danny Cupit, chairman of the Democrat Party in the 1970s when I was chairman of the Mississippi Republican Party; Mayor Phillip West; former state representative David Green; Mayor Melvin Mack; Mayor Johnny Dupree; city council members Anne Clayton, Reverend Arthur Logan, Johnny Magee, Henry E. Naylor; Forrest County Supervisor Charles Marshall; and numerous others who identified themselves as Democrats in their letters of support.

Two of my closest friends, James Huff and Wesley Breland, did so many things to be supportive in my confirmation battle. Charles Evers, Deborah Gambrell, Charles Lawrence, Judge Henry Wingate, Judge Johnny Williams, Mike McMahan, and Frank Montague were most helpful.

I am very appreciative of my partners, colleagues, and staff at Baker Donelson Bearman Caldwell & Berkowitz who have been my friends and encouragers since I left the Court.

Thanks to Craig Shirley and Dianne Banister of Shirley and Banister, who put me in contact with Stroud & Hall, gave me advice and counsel along the way, and who will handle the marketing of this book; Randy Evans, who represented me in negotiations; and Dr. Cecil Staton and the staff at Stroud & Hall. Thanks to Joe Maxwell, who served as research editor and ably assisted in writing; Brian Perry, who took a leave of absence for this project, helped research, write, and edit, and without whose capable assistance I could not have written this book; Cindy Hosey, who is my administrative assistant and who typed every page of this book numerous times with good cheer and efficiency; and to Magnolia State Bank (where I serve on the Board of Directors) and Thomas Brown.

A special thanks to former Justice Reuben V. Anderson; Robert (Bob) Anderson; Rev. Cecil Ashford; Patsy Aycock; Rev. George Barnes; Angela Barnett; Ken Bassinger; Charles Bolton; Lillian Breland; Tucker Buchanan; Mr. and Mrs. Stan Burton; W. O. "Chet" Dillard; Melvin Daniels; Gus DeLoach; Don Dornan; Jennifer Drawdy; James K. Dukes; Donnie Ray Fairly Sr.; Reverend Kenneth E. Fairley; Milton Gavin; Early M. Gray; Mr. and Mrs. Louis Griffin; Ellen Gunn; Dr. and Mrs. Eddie Hamilton; Charles Harrison; Mr. and Mrs. Carey Hauenstein; Dr. and Mrs. Gene Henderson; John Holiday; Dr. and Mrs. Mark Horne; Scott Howell; Marilyn Huff; Dr. and Mrs. Doug Jefcoat; Tammi Jenkins; Nora J. Jones; Rev. Nathan Jordan; Judge Damon J. Keith; Dr. and Mrs. Larry Kennedy; J. W. (Judy) King; James King; Dr. and Mrs. Eric Linstrom; Chris McDaniel; Dr. Joe McKeever; Dr. and Mrs. Charles Marsh; Rev. and Mrs. Jim Ormon; the late Judge Fred Parker; Dr. John Perkins; Justice Mike Randolph; Joy Roberts; Al Rosenbaum; Stephanie Schmitt; Rev. Arthur L. Siggers; Ralph Simmons; Raymond Swartzfager; Rena Pittman Temple; Larry Thomas; Ginny Traylor; Dr. and Mrs. Randy Turner; Jennifer Selby; Mayor Susan Vincent; Rev. Dolphus Weary; Mr. and Mrs. Williams Wells; Dr. and Mrs. Jimmy Waites; and others whose names I cannot list because of space limitations.

Prologue

FOR ALMOST FIVE years, I was involved in a battle to be confirmed to the U.S. Court of Appeals for the Fifth Circuit, which sits in New Orleans. The position was an elevation above my lifetime appointment to the Federal District Court for Southern Mississippi, where I served for more than a decade after unanimous Senate confirmation.

Democrats blocked my nomination in committee in 2002 and filibustered my nomination in 2003. President George W. Bush gave me a recess appointment to the Fifth Circuit on January 16, 2004. Following my recess appointment, I had eleven months for Republicans to muster sixty votes to break a filibuster before my commission would expire upon Senate adjournment. If the Senate adjourned in December 2004 without my confirmation, I would be forced into retirement.

In 2004, the Democrats were in no mood to stop filibustering President Bush's appellate court nominees. My son Chip Pickering, a congressman from Mississippi, had done everything in his power to talk Democratic senators into ending their filibuster. Mississippi senator Trent Lott made Herculean efforts to stop the filibuster. Mississippi's senior senator Thad Cochran had talked to senators he could influence. But their efforts were futile.

I was flying home to Mississippi from Washington D.C. on the night of December 8 as the Senate wrapped up its work for the year. Chip was on the floor of the Senate securing a compromise on telecommunications legislation on one hand and seeking to secure my nomination on the other hand. He was successful in one of those missions.

Senate Majority Leader Bill Frist, at Chip's request, made one final plea to the Democrats. He asked Senator Harry Reid, minority whip and soon to be minority leader, for unanimous consent that I be confirmed. Reid agreed to contact Senator Patrick Leahy, ranking Democrat on the Judiciary Committee, to see if he would agree. Leahy refused consent. The Senate adjourned and I retired.

The next morning I returned to the federal courthouse in Hattiesburg where I had held court for fourteen years. There, at a press conference before friends and family, I announced my retirement and then retrieved my personal belongings from my chambers. I had served as a federal district court judge for thirteen years and as a federal appeals court judge for eleven months. I counted each day an honor and an occasion for service to my state and nation.

President Bush offered to renominate me, but at nearly sixty-eight years old and facing the prospect of another committee hearing and a fight on the Senate floor, I respectfully declined. I appreciated President Bush's loyalty but felt he should have the opportunity to nominate someone younger. It was time for my wife, Margaret Ann, and me to move on with our lives.

Retirement opened up an opportunity. While on the bench, I could not participate in or speak on political matters. Under canons of judicial ethics, a judge can only speak on issues that will improve the courts—the administration of justice. Partisan politics blocked my confirmation, and speaking about that would walk too fine a line between advocating judicial reform and moving into the political arena. But after retirement, I was free to speak candidly about judicial confirmation and the partisan process, as well as my personal odyssey.

One cannot go through an experience like mine unless there is a feeling that somehow one can accomplish something good. I decided if I was not confirmed, I would speak out and advocate reform of the confirmation process. It was too late for me, but I could help future nominees and strengthen the judiciary by encouraging improvement. It would not be easy, but to do nothing was unthinkable.

Before I accepted the recess appointment, Jorge Rangel of Corpus Christi, Texas—a Clinton nominee blocked from confirmation to the Fifth Circuit—and I had drafted a joint bipartisan statement calling for reformation of the confirmation system. We reserved a room at the

National Press Club in Washington and made plane reservations. We agreed the process is broken and needs to be fixed. Failure to repair the system will threaten the quality, the independence, and even the diversity of the judiciary.

When the White House called to offer the recess appointment, I had to decide to go forward with the bipartisan statement or accept the president's offer. Though a difficult decision, I concluded the most effective way for me to fight was to accept the recess appointment and the challenge of confirmation. Now that chapter has concluded and I am back in the private sector, I can speak freely on the need to reform the process.[1]

In April 2005, I started preliminary work on this book, but it was not until August that I began writing in earnest. Then Hurricane Katrina came roaring through Mississippi and disrupted everything, including my writing. My original intention was to write one book with three or four different sections. In section 1 I would discuss the confirmation fight and its causes. I would describe my own odyssey in section 2. My reflections and observations gleaned from the experience would comprise section 3. The final section would advocate solutions.

Timing is not only critical in politics; it is also crucial in releasing books. I regretted my book was not finished and available for distribution during the nominations of John Roberts and Harriet Miers. When the Senate pushed Sam Alito's confirmation into January 2006, my publisher and I made a joint decision to divide the material into two books and rush the first book to publication. Certainly, there is a marketing aspect to the decision, but I believe the wider the readership, the better the chance my story will contribute to the improvement of the confirmation process. Another book, which will discuss my personal odyssey and elaborate on solutions, will follow this one.

If a long-term, permanent solution is to be found to the judicial confirmation quagmire, it must be something that is fair and reasonable to both Democrats and Republicans; both sides must have meaningful input. The continued escalation of this battle will do good to no one, especially the American people. I hope you find this book informative on the confirmation struggle and its causes, as well as an interesting read.

The Problem

J U D I C I A L   C O N F I R M A T I O N , A   P R O C E S S   I N   C H A O S

THE JUDICIAL CONFIRMATION process is broken and badly needs to be fixed. Nominees endure a partisan conflict rather than a dignified and respectful legislative proceeding. This epic partisan fight leaves the reputations of nominees wounded on the battlefield from personal, bitter, and mean-spirited character assassinations. But the true casualty of the confirmation wars will be the quality, independence, diversity, and integrity of the American judiciary. The true victim is the American people.

Our Founding Fathers intended the third branch—the branch of government comprised of the courts—to secure and protect the rights of all Americans. This institution must be strengthened, yet the very method of continuing the structure of the Court—that is, the confirmation of judges—now undermines public trust in the system and its judges. Unless we find a solution, we run the risk of future presidents picking lackluster nominees who have little record to scrutinize but who are invulnerable to criticism and attacks, rather than choosing the best qualified and most experienced candidates with proven legal minds.

The frontline of the confirmation conflict is fought in the halls of the Capitol and on the floor of the U.S. Senate. Here the ravages of the clash over the judiciary threaten the legislative process as well. Special-interest groups and a downward spiral of rhetoric hold Senate comity and collegiality hostage. America must have judges. But the current confirmation conflict weakens both the judicial and legislative branches of government and does not benefit the American people. This problem cries out for a practical and reasonable solution fair to all sides.

I was a participant in this battle. I watched the Senate transform from the time of my unanimous confirmation to the Federal District Court for Southern Mississippi in 1990 to the past four years when a minority even refused to allow a vote on my nomination. I saw the inside of the process: its failings, shortcomings, and weaknesses. As a judge, I held my tongue while facing slanderous attacks. As a nominee, I remained quiet and allowed the parties involved to hammer out their political agendas. Now as a private citizen I can share my thoughts and suggestions, help create an awareness of the source and nature of the conflict, and present solutions to improve the process.

I love and respect the third branch of government; I served it as an attorney or judge all of my adult life. Our Founding Fathers created the judiciary as an institution to protect the life, liberty, and property of all our citizens. We must strengthen the judicial branch, not weaken it. This is the goal of my book.

Had I known what would happen to me, my family, and my state during the confirmation process, I'm not sure I would have agreed to be nominated. But once the fight started I could not withdraw or back down without giving perceived credibility to the charges and emboldening the opposition. The battle was far greater than me and my confirmation to the U.S. Fifth Circuit Court of Appeals. This war involved other nominees, and the outcome holds the future of the federal judiciary and the Supreme Court in the balance.

What provoked this battle? Why do special-interest groups passionately fight over something as dry as judicial confirmations? Who calls the shots? Is there a solution, and where do we go from here? I experienced the questions firsthand, and the answers impact us all.

Nan Aron, president of the liberal Alliance for Justice—which opposes conservative judges like me and helps lead the fight against President Bush's judicial nominees—divulged the truth to a National Public Radio audience: "Because the Republicans now control the House, the Senate, and the White House for the first time in basically a hundred years, there is obviously no way we're going to get any new rights created by the Congress. So now we have to look to the courts to create new rights that we won't be able to get from the legislature."[1] Her agenda is clear: liberal activist judges should legislate from the bench because the left wing failed to win support from the American people at the ballot box.

When a nation of destiny declared independence from the British Empire, revolutionary leaders and patriots proclaimed that "all Men are created equal, that they are endowed by their Creator with certain unalienable Rights, that among these are Life, Liberty, and the Pursuit of Happiness—That to secure these Rights, Governments are instituted among Men, deriving their just Powers from the Consent of the Governed." A few years later, men of vision designed the Constitution of the United States not to create rights, but to secure them.

The Framers of the Constitution never intended for courts to "create new rights." When the Constitution as originally drafted failed to secure fundamental rights, corrective amendments were successfully initiated and adopted. Two of the most significant among these amendments are the Thirteenth Amendment abolishing slavery and the Nineteenth Amendment granting women the right to vote. These changes were brought about through the amendment process involving the people and their elected representatives. Our Founders intended constitutional rights to be secured through the amendment process, not created through the judicial process. The American people overwhelmingly want judges to interpret the law, not to make law from the bench. Judges should protect rights, not create new rights.

Left wing special-interest groups want liberal activist judges to create new rights that neither the people nor the elected representatives of the people will approve. By definition and by her own admission, the ideology of those like Nan Aron is outside the mainstream. Those espousing her views lost in the 2004 senatorial elections and in the election for president. The American people employed the democratic elective process to reject her policies and candidates. So now she seeks to circumvent the results of the election and advance her agenda by court order. She seeks an activist liberal judiciary to create rights. She desires five members of the Supreme Court to author rights not granted by the Constitution and impose her beliefs upon the American people by judicial pronouncement.

This agenda of judicial supremacy, using the concept of a living Constitution, is the primary cause of the confirmation battles. The battle for the judiciary holds in balance the outcome of the current culture war raging in America. The Far Left special-interest groups crave a whole set of new rights not only unnecessary (since current law and the U.S. Constitution already protect the rights of all Americans), but also contrary to the views of most Americans.

The Far Left wants new rights for transgender people, rights for same-sex couples seeking marriage, and rights that guarantee abortion on demand. This promotion of abortion—including partial-birth abortion, abortion for teenagers without parental consent, and even abortion without parental notification—is the primary thrust of the Far Left's agenda in the culture war. Additional matters include radical secularism—removing references to God at public institutions, at public ceremonies, and in the Pledge of Allegiance—as well as the promotion of unfettered access to pornography, even when it exposes children to obscene material or exploits kids through the sex industry.

The culture war is not new. But the dramatic impact on the judicial confirmation process is comparatively recent. When George H. W. Bush, the first President Bush, exited office in January 1993, he left more than 125 vacancies in the federal judiciary.[2] In reality, some of these vacancies occurred late in his term and so near the time of the election they realistically could not have been confirmed. But had the administration felt a greater sense of urgency and known there would be no second term, they might have expedited filling many of these vacancies.

When the second President Bush—George W.—came to office, he determined his administration would vigilantly address the matter of filling judicial vacancies. At the end of his initial term, he wanted all vacancies on the federal bench to be occupied by conservative judges committed to interpreting the Constitution and not making law.

After his inauguration in January 2001, President Bush faced the opportunity of filling twenty-nine vacant seats on the U.S. Circuit

Courts of Appeal and sixty-two vacant U.S. Federal District Court judgeships.[3] President Bush chose to fill the appellate court vacancies first, because those courts function just beneath the Supreme Court and above the district courts (binding by precedent the district courts in that particular circuit).

On May 9, 2001, at a White House ceremony, President Bush announced his administration's first slate of nominees to the federal judiciary: eleven appointees to the appellate courts.[4] Over the next few weeks he submitted additional nominations, including mine, to fill the other appeals court vacancies. President Bush nominated more judges, more quickly, than any president in history during his first year: nearly one hundred.[5]

This was no surprise. President Bush campaigned and won on the issue of judges in 2000, and would win again in 2004. During his first campaign he promised to nominate judges in the tradition and mold of Supreme Court justices Antonin Scalia and Clarence Thomas, declaring, "I'll put competent judges on the bench, people who will strictly interpret the Constitution and will not use the bench to write social policy." He said of potential nominees from his Democratic opponent Vice President Al Gore, "I'll tell you what kind of judges he'll put on there. He'll put liberal, activist judges who will use their bench to subvert the legislature." Gore responded by saying, "In my view, the Constitution ought to be interpreted as a document that grows with our country."[6]

President Bush kept his campaign promise when he made his judicial nominations. With Republicans in control of the Senate, the administration assumed these nominees would be confirmed reasonably quickly. But on May 24, 2001, Senator Jim Jeffords of Vermont left the Republican Party and became an independent, voting with the Democrats to organize the Senate and throwing the Republicans into the minority. Vermont's other senator, Democrat Patrick Leahy, became chairman of the Judiciary Committee, replacing Republican senator Orrin Hatch of Utah. Senator Leahy would now set the pace and schedule the hearings for President Bush's nominees. This happened just one day before President Bush submitted my nomination for the U.S. Fifth Circuit Court of Appeals.

There was a confirmation slowdown. Senator Leahy made it plain there would be no hurry in confirming nominees. Extreme left wing special-interest groups immediately attacked many of the Bush appellate nominees, though I was not initially among them and was not opposed until some five months later.

Under Chairman Leahy the Senate would take up only one appellate court nominee per three or four district court nominees. Now the Bush administration sped up choices for the federal trial bench. Unlike the appeals court nominees, Democrats did not single out district court nominees for massive resistance (with the exception of J. Leon Holmes of Arkansas).

By the end of September 2001, only three of President Bush's appellate nominees had been confirmed; two of those were previously unconfirmed Clinton appointees re-nominated by President Bush. But the Senate Democrats did not return Bush's token of bipartisanship. Senator Leahy had not even held hearings on the remaining original eight. They would not see a hearing within a year of their nomination.[7]

Senate Republican Minority Leader Trent Lott of Mississippi pressured Senator Leahy to expedite the hearings. In response, Leahy scheduled a hearing on my nomination for October 18, 2001. I moved to the head of the line, ahead of many of the nominees announced earlier. I was ready to present my credentials, my decade of experience as a district court judge, and my good rating from the American Bar Association to the United States Senate.

Over the years many conservatives believed the American Bar Association (ABA) inappropriately used political philosophy as criteria for rating judicial nominees. So in a February 24, 1997, letter to the ABA, Senator Hatch, then chairman of the Senate Judiciary Committee, wrote,

> When the Chairman of the Judiciary Committee decided in 1947 to invite the ABA to advise the committee on the qualifications of judicial nominees, the ABA could be said to have been a neutral, objective representative of the legal profession as a whole. Since the 1980s, however, the ABA as a whole has taken stands on a series of political issues on which the bar has little, if any, special expertise or

experience. For example, the ABA has taken positions on abortion, affirmative action, flag desecration, religious liberty, habeas corpus reform, funding for the arts, welfare reform, deportation of criminal aliens, and medical liability reform, just to name a few among many. One cannot seriously dispute that the ABA has become a political interest group. . . . Since it was the Chairman of the Judiciary Committee who first invited the ABA to advise the Committee regarding the qualifications of judicial nominees, I believe it is now my responsibility to withdraw this invitation. Individual Senators are, of course, free to give the ABA's ratings whatever weight they choose.[8]

Consistent with Senator Hatch's letter to the ABA in 1997, the second President Bush decided not to utilize the ABA to vet his judicial nominees. After Bush announced that he would not ask the ABA to evaluate his nominees, Democratic senators praised the ABA evaluation and quickly and clearly made known what weight they felt should be given to the ABA ratings. Senator Tom Daschle of South Dakota said what the "ABA is simply telling us, and has historically, whether or not a prospective judge is competent."[9] According to Senator Leahy, "We've always used the ABA, used them for fifty years . . . because they're objective, they're outside the loop. They don't have a political axe to grind."[10] Wisconsin's Senator Russ Feingold said, "The ABA, with its extensive contacts in the legal community all across the country, is the best organization to evaluate the integrity, professional competence and judicial temperament of potential nominees."[11] And New York's Senator Chuck Schumer called the ABA's ratings the "gold standard by which judicial candidates are judged."[12] But the Democrats would soon reverse course—180 degrees—and totally ignore the ABA findings, with no explanation, no justification, no apology, and no shame.

The Justice Department told nominees they could choose to cooperate or not cooperate with an ABA investigation. Since the Democrats on the Judiciary Committee insisted they be given an ABA report before voting on a nominee, and because I had no fear of an ABA evaluation, I elected to cooperate with the ABA Standing Committee on the Judiciary. The ABA assigned Pike Powers, a Texas attorney from Dallas, to conduct my ABA background check.

The ABA procedure for evaluating nominees requires the investigator to contact the nominee's professional associates, and, in my case as a sitting judge, to talk with attorneys who appeared before me in various cases, including civil rights matters.

Before my unanimous confirmation by the Senate in 1990, there had been a couple of civil rights issues raised: one related to a law journal article I had been assigned to write as a student in 1959 relating to interracial marriage and the other regarding a vote I cast in the Mississippi Senate in the 1970s to abolish the defunct Sovereignty Commission (a state-sponsored segregation watchdog during the 1950s and early 1960s) and to seal and protect its records. I made the progressive vote; the alternative was to destroy the records and erase the evidence of the past. Nevertheless, that issue had been raised, and following investigation, the Senate Judiciary Committee unanimously recommended my confirmation in 1990. The full United States Senate agreed and unanimously confirmed me.

Pike Powers inquired of civil rights attorneys who had appeared before me whether I respected and protected civil rights as a federal judge. The rules of procedure for the ABA Committee require the ABA representative to advise a nominee of any criticisms in any area so the nominee can respond. After all his investigations, Pike Powers told me there were no issues raised in criticism of me in regard to civil rights during my ten years on the district court.

Because there was no public opposition in the first five months following my nomination, because the Senate Judiciary Committee had unanimously given me a favorable recommendation for confirmation in 1990, and because the Senate then unanimously confirmed me, I naïvely told people I was a non-controversial nominee. My optimism was further bolstered when the ABA increased my rating from their 1990 evaluation of "qualified" (their median recommendation given when I had no judicial experience and came from a political background) to their 2001 highest rating of "well qualified" following my ten years on the federal bench. I met the Democrats' "gold standard." I thought I would be confirmed.

Political reality soon demolished my naïveté. Two days before my scheduled hearing, Senator Leahy requested a list of all my unpublished opinions (some 4,000 or 5,000 cases), many of which were already archived. This was my first inkling something was amiss. I arrived in Washington D.C. the day before my October 18 committee hearing to learn that the People for the American Way and other left wing groups had distributed an e-mail opposing my nomination. They were incensed my hearing had even been scheduled, claiming they had been assured—due to September 11—that no "controversial" nominees would be considered for the balance of the year. Until then, I did not know I was a controversial nominee. The interest groups demanded Leahy either cancel my hearing and reschedule it, or that my hearing be recessed for a second hearing. The Republicans objected to a second hearing on my nomination. Second hearings are rare and scheduled only with a specific and compelling reason. Yet Leahy ordered a second hearing on my nomination for February 2, 2002.

The intensity and virulence of the left wing attacks ambushed both the Bush administration and me. During the three-and-a-half months between my two hearings, we realized the assault on me was the test case, model, and rehearsal for future left wing attacks.

Special-interest groups would use nominees like myself as cannon fodder in a warm-up exercise for their ultimate target: an anticipated Supreme Court nominee. A new generation of left wing staff and volunteers were hunting for George W. Bush's "Bork." They would cut their teeth researching our records to distort, mischaracterize, and misrepresent our statements in an attempt to destroy reputations and deny confirmations.

The groups were firing a shot across the bow of the Bush administration. The messages: do not send us conservative judges, and know this is just a taste of what your potential Supreme Court nominees will face. I received a portion of that message at my hearing and the vote that followed.

On March 14, six weeks after my contentious second hearing, the Democrat controlled Senate Judiciary Committee voted three times 10-9 not to send my nomination to the floor: not with the recommendation I be confirmed; not with a neutral recommendation; not with the recommendation I not be confirmed—not at all. They effectively voted to kill my nomination and prevented the Senate from giving President Bush advice and consent. Even though a majority of the full Senate supported me, the committee Democrats would not allow an up-or-down vote. I became the first casualty in the battle over confirming the Bush nominees to the courts of appeal.

I did not choose to be a flag bearer for the Bush nominees. I did not choose to be a symbol in the culture war. I did not choose to be a part of this fight. As a judge, I had no agenda in going to the U.S. Fifth Circuit other than to follow the rule of law and to base my decisions on Supreme Court precedents, prior Fifth Circuit precedents, and in cases where there were no controlling precedents, the Constitution according to its meaning at the time it was adopted. Far Left special-interest groups—determined to maintain an unrestricted right of abortion and fearing conservative nominees who openly speak of their religious faith—thrust this role upon me and other nominees.

It is obvious to me these groups didn't really know me or the Bush administration. They thought turning up the political heat would lead me to back down and the Bush administration to choose someone else. After all, at sixty-four years of age I could have withdrawn and continued to serve on the district court for many years, giving the Bush administration an opportunity to appoint someone younger to the Fifth Circuit. But the Pickering family doesn't back down from a fight when the cause is just, and the Bush family is loyal to their people.

I was not the only one to encounter opposition. In September 2002, Priscilla Owen suffered my same fate before the Judiciary Committee: a straight party-line vote denying a vote before the full Senate. Miguel Estrada was also given a hearing in September, but no vote. He was Hispanic, and for the Democrats, it was too close to the election.

Democrats confirmed only fourteen of President Bush's thirty-seven circuit court nominees during his first two years in office. By contrast, "in his first two years in office, President Clinton nominated twenty-two circuit judges, with nineteen confirmed . . . the elder President Bush nominated twenty-three circuit judges with twenty-two confirmed . . .

President Reagan nominated twenty circuit judges with nineteen confirmed . . . ."[13] The confirmation of judges became a campaign issue in the mid-term senatorial elections in 2002. President Bush "hammered the issue of nominees being blocked by Democrats in a final campaign swing for Senate Republicans."[14] The Republicans won and regained control of the Senate. Republicans credited the obstruction of judicial confirmations "with helping to win South Carolina, Georgia, Texas and Minnesota."[15] A spokesman for Senator Lott agreed: "Clearly, it did not help the Democrats' chances of either retaining control or gaining control of the Senate . . . it backfired completely."[16] Senator Hatch again became chairman of the Judiciary Committee.

Conventional Republican wisdom held that the election and transfer of power in the Senate sent a message to Democrats not to obstruct the confirmation process. In January 2003, President Bush renominated his blocked nominees. But conventional wisdom was wrong. The Democrats escalated the conflict from committee obstruction to full Senate filibuster.

When the new congress convened, Senator Hatch recognized that I did not again wish to be the first challenged nominee to come up for a hearing. On January 15, the Judiciary Committee (now under Republican control) sent Miguel Estrada to the full Senate on a party-line vote 10-9. The Republicans moved Priscilla Owen the same way on March 27.

Now under intense pressure from the left wing special-interest groups, the Democratic leadership filibustered these nominations on the floor of the U.S. Senate. This was not a "Mr. Smith Goes to Washington" filibuster. There was no desire to change minds through debate. There was no desire to debate at all. A minority in the Senate prevented the process from moving forward. The cloture motion to stop this filibuster required sixty votes to pass.

Miguel Estrada and Priscilla Owen both had the support of a majority of the Senate. But on March 6, 2003, Estrada lost his first of seven cloture votes 55-44. Then on May 1, Owen was denied cloture by a vote of 52-44, with Democrats blocking her three additional times. Each of these eleven votes denied the Senate an opportunity for an up-or-down vote on these two nominees. A minority manipulated Senate procedure eleven times between these two nominees to prevent the full Senate from exercising its advice and consent role in the judicial confirmation process.[17]

There would be no treat for me during Halloween 2003. On October 30 I joined Estrada and Owen in being denied an up-or-down vote. The Democratic minority—frightened by the specter of their left wing special-interest groups—defeated my cloture vote 54-43.[18] But their obstruction would again come back to haunt the Democrats during the 2004 election.

I had enough votes to win confirmation but no super-majority to break the filibuster. I had the support of all the Republican senators, plus the Senate's only independent member Jim Jeffords and two Democrats: Senator John Breaux of Louisiana and Senator Zell Miller of Georgia. Other Democratic senators had personally indicated their support, but when the moment of truth arrived, their votes were not there.

Filibustering nominees to the appellate courts was unprecedented. Never before had the philosophical debate on the Senate floor reserved for Supreme Court nominees reached the lower appellate level. Never before had a filibuster been used to block the confirmation of a judicial nominee enjoying majority Senate support. Never before had the leadership of either party supported a filibuster against a judicial nominee—never in the entire 214-year history of the United States Senate.

As the 2004 election approached, the Democrats, captured by Far Left special-interest groups, had filibustered ten Bush nominees to the appellate courts and threatened six more with the same fate. During the final two years of President Bush's first term, the Senate confirmed only eighteen of his thirty-four appellate nominees, failing even to consider 47 percent of his nominees to the circuit courts of appeal.[19]

Blocking judicial nominees was a potential victory for Democrats. Had John Kerry won the presidency, he would have nominated these lifetime federal appointments instead. But Republicans used the Democratic obstruction of judges as a campaign issue. President Bush won, and in the Senate, Republicans replaced Democrats in Florida,

Louisiana, South Carolina, North Carolina, and South Dakota. I recall watching Democratic senator Bob Graham of Florida on national television answering why the Democrats lost every hotly contested Senate election in the South. His response: one issue—filibustering judges.

The Democrats' price for obstruction: Senate seats lost; for only the second time this century a party leader in the Senate defeated for reelection; and George W. Bush reelected president. Although the Democrats paid a tremendous price for blocking judicial nominees, the confirmation process remains in chaos, in serious need of repair. But before a solution can be found, the causes for the battle must be identified.

CHAPTER TWO

The Cause

PROCEDURAL, POLITICAL, AND CULTURAL COLLISION

A THREE-PART COLLISION—procedural, political, and cultural—caused the current battle over judicial confirmations. (1) There is no detailed binding and controlling process for the confirmation of federal judges. (2) Democrats are retaliating against Republicans for not confirming some of President Bill Clinton's judicial nominees. (3) The liberal philosophy of a "living Constitution" transfers hot-button social issues from the legislative forum to the judicial arena.

The first cause and logistical root of the judicial confirmation battle is the lack of clearly defined procedures. This systemic failure permits and even encourages abuse. But because the remedy is ideologically neutral and independent from partisanship or passion, it may be the easiest of the three to reform.

Article II, Section 2 of the Constitution sets out the power of a president to appoint judges of the Supreme Court with the "Advice and Consent of the Senate." The Constitution clearly intends the Senate to perform this function by a majority vote.[1]

Article III, Section 1 of the Constitution empowers Congress to ordain and establish "inferior Courts" to the Supreme Court. Article II, Section 2 provides that judges to the inferior courts may be confirmed or Congress may vest the appointment "of such inferior Officers . . . in the President alone." Thus, under constitutional authority, Congress created by statute the district courts and the courts of appeal and required Senate confirmation of those judges.[2] However, Congress has not prescribed a framework for confirming judges. To remedy this omission, Congress should pass a Judicial Confirmation Improvements Act delineating the process for judicial confirmations.

There are also no Senate rules detailing the confirmation proceeding. Instead, the Senate developed nonbinding historical precedents and traditions. An evolving senatorial courtesy produced "holds" and "blue-slips" allowing senators to delay or block nominees from their home state and sometimes nominees from other states.

Each chairman of the Senate Judiciary Committee interprets differently these precedents, traditions, and senatorial courtesies. This lack of consistent procedural rules has allowed each party to accuse the other side of unfair treatment. As power shifts, the confirmation battle escalates. Abuse is natural when power is subjective. Escalation is inherent to the absence of restraint. A Judicial Confirmation Improvements Act would alleviate this cause of conflict.

The second cause for the judicial confirmation battle is political revenge. Though often denied, Democrats seized the opportunity to retaliate against Republicans for not confirming some of President Bill Clinton's nominees.

Over his eight years in office, the Senate confirmed 372 of President Clinton's courts of appeal and district court nominees.[3] However, twenty-five nominees to the courts of appeal and forty-five nominees to the district courts were never confirmed.[4] The Judiciary Committee under Republican control failed to hold hearings on a number of President Clinton's nominees. In fact, during Clinton's last two years, nineteen of his thirty-four appellate nominees failed confirmation.[5] Whether blocked in committee or filibustered on the floor, the outcome is the same: these nominees were not confirmed and did not serve.

In context, while President Clinton's nominee confirmation rate was low compared to the Carter and Reagan administrations, it was still higher than those of his Republican predecessor and successor. Each President Bush had lower confirmation rates than President Clinton.

Combining district and appeals court judges, Jimmy Carter's confirmation rate was 91.9 percent, Ronald Reagan's was 93.1 percent, George

H. W. Bush's was 79.3 percent, and Bill Clinton's was 84.0 percent. In contrast, George W. Bush's first term produced a 78.1 percent nominee confirmation rate.[6] Further, Democrats completely ignored Republican responses to Bill Clinton's two Supreme Court nominees, Justice Ruth Bader Ginsburg and Stephen Breyer, both very liberal. Ginsburg was counsel for the ACLU and had taken a liberal stance on just about every hot-button social issue. Breyer's record was likewise liberal. But Republicans did not bottle up these nominations, did not filibuster them, and they were confirmed with overwhelming Republican support: 97-3 and 87-9 respectively. Democratic partisans who attempt to vindicate their retaliatory actions by pointing to the treatment of President Clinton's nominees by Republicans ignore historical context.

Two additional issues distinguish the Democratic nominees from the Republican nominees. First, Republicans did not block President Clinton's nominees by filibuster. The filibuster is the latest, greatest escalation in the conflict.

Second, in most cases President Clinton's candidates did not experience the vilification and character assassination that went along with the attack on President Bush's nominees. Interest groups did not engage to the same extent under President Clinton because the issue of judicial confirmations was not made the high-profile matter it became during the Bush campaigns and administration. President Clinton's political strategy of triangulation prevented him from appealing to liberal activists in a way that President Bush now engages conservative enthusiasts on the judiciary issue. Furthermore, President Clinton's personal distractions encouraged him not to draw additional attention to the courts and legal proceedings. But from the beginning, after President Bush announced his first appellate nominees, left wing special-interest groups made it clear there would be confirmation fights over the Bush nominees and these battles would be high profile.

The accusation from the Left that "turnabout is fair play" dictates this chapter's consideration of President Clinton's judicial nominees. But our motivation in improving the system should not be based on revenge for the past, but rather doing the right thing in the future. Democrats direct their anger toward the past behavior of Senate Republicans. But their anger's ramifications impact others: nominees around the country and their families, and ultimately the judiciary. Even schoolchildren know two wrongs do not make a right. Unless the cycle of retaliation stops, the battle will continue to escalate.

The third major cause of the confirmation fight is the transfer of the battle over controversial social issues (like abortion, same-sex marriage, references to God in the public square, and pornography) from the election of state legislators, congressmen, and senators to the confirmation of judges.

During the 1960s and 1970s, the concept of a "living Constitution"—a Constitution that changes meaning in a changing society—spread from academic theory to judicial implementation. Since then, many federal judges have exercised their "independent judgment" to look for what offends society's "evolving standards of decency."

Unable to justify their decisions with the text or original intent of the Constitution, these activist judges look to trends in state law or even Europe or other foreign law to rationalize their in-vogue political view. We are not Europeans; we are Americans. Most Americans do not want to be governed by the laws of Europe; they want to be governed by the rule of law as established by the Constitution and the people they elect to represent them. We fought the American Revolution to be governed by our own laws and representatives.

About the time I graduated from law school at the University of Mississippi, I heard the story of a Supreme Court justice who was hearing arguments in a case. A young lawyer was arguing strenuously that the Court had to rule in his favor based on *stare decisis*: the legal doctrine that rules and principles established by prior controlling case law must be followed. The justice leaned forward and asked the young lawyer, "But is it right?"

There was a time when I might have thought this was a great question: a judge concerned about what is right rather than the niceties of the law. But who will we give—for the rest of their life and regardless of how they might decide—the power to determine what is right or wrong for America? Will it be a Democrat or a Republican? A conservative or a liberal? Will it be a Christian, someone of the Jewish faith, someone of another belief, or an atheist? Will it be someone from the Christian Coalition, or will it be a member of the ACLU or the People for the American Way? These rhetorical questions answer themselves. We should fight to uphold the principle that we have: "A government of laws, and not of men."[7]

Unlike the leaders of England or Rome, our Founding Fathers gave us a written Constitution so we would not be compelled to rely on the sense of justice or the sense of decency of a particular judge, or even five judges, for our life, liberty, or property. Instead, we could rely on our Constitution as written and ratified by the people through their duly elected representatives.

Most judges over the course of our history interpreted the meaning of the Constitution consistent with its language and precedents at the time it was adopted. Thus when the nomination of judges came before the Senate, the consideration was direct and basic: did the nominee have ability and integrity?

Historically, no nominee to the Supreme Court appeared before the Senate until Harlan Fisk Stone in 1925. Judicial nominees did not regularly appear before the Senate until John Marshall Harlan in 1955, shortly after television penetrated half the homes in America. Today, a suggestion that a Supreme Court nominee need not appear for a Senate Judiciary Committee hearing seems ridiculous. Everyone wants to know what the nominee personally believes because the media and Washington elite have embraced the idea of a living Constitution as a matter of course. Personal beliefs become relevant to them because they believe the nominee and not our Constitution will dictate the future laws of our country.

This overreach by judges committed to a living Constitution threatens the carefully crafted system of checks and balances between the three branches of government. The concept of a living Constitution propels the judicial branch into areas reserved by the Founders to the legislative branch or to the people themselves. This trespass seriously erodes the rule of law enshrined in our Constitution as envisioned by our Founders.

Why not allow a living Constitution with a judiciary empowered to impose values on the nation? Consider the American model in historical context.

Though near in time, the French Revolution diverged far from our American experience. The "essential difference between the American Revolution and the French Revolution is that the American Revolution . . . was a religious event, whereas the French Revolution was an anti-religious event."[8] The French Revolutionists submitted to no faith outside of themselves. They possessed no moral constraints to curb their vengeance, and blood ran like a river through the streets of Paris with Napoleon Bonaparte emerging to devastate Europe. The French Revolution established no rule of law, no checks and balances. Their failure bred a disaster.

In 1917, the Communist Bolsheviks revolted in Russia. Their philosophy espoused materialism and atheism. They rejected the rights of individuals and derided the importance of the human spirit. They instituted a totalitarian regime, murdering millions in the Soviet Union. Like the French, the Soviets permitted no checks and balances for their leaders and thus established no rule of law. Their imprudence spawned a catastrophe.

These examples illustrate the importance of moral constraints woven into a system of government, the necessity of a clearly established rule of law, and the wisdom of checks and balances among the three branches of government.

We Americans are fortunate indeed. Our Founders gave us a government deeply committed to the rule of law. They formed our government based on two premises: the worth of each individual person—"all Men are created equal"—and the imperfection of man, even a king.[9] The tyranny of King George III taught them what Lord Acton would verbalize years later: "Power tends to corrupt and absolute power corrupts absolutely."[10] They recognized the necessity of checks and balances to prevent the three independent and co-equal branches of our government from engaging in excesses. The Founders carefully limited the powers of each branch but worried that the judiciary was the weakest of the three. Hence, they gave federal judges lifetime tenure.

A violation by any branch of this carefully crafted system of checks and balances threatens the stability and vitality of the system. The concept of a living Constitution does not comport with these principles: specifically, it does not provide a clearly established rule of law and is in conflict with the system of checks and balances. To allow the judicial branch to cross over into the jurisdiction of the legislative branch increases the power of judges, but violating the separation of powers over time will erode confidence in the courts and thus ultimately weaken the judiciary—indeed it will decrease the power of all branches of our government.

Our Founders recognized that, over time, additions or changes to the Constitution would be necessary. They adopted and included in the Constitution a sensible and logical way to alter, modify, amend, or add to it—the amendment process. Under the rule of law, this Constitution is the supreme authority of the land, and to alter the document should require wide and broad consensus among the people and their elected officials.

Today, those whose ideology cannot win the necessary popular appeal for an amendment seek another avenue to advance their agenda. Special-interest groups discover that under a living Constitution, it is easier to change America's laws by convincing five members of the Supreme Court than through the old-fashioned amendment process, where the people and their elected representatives can participate. This moves the fights over abortion, same-sex marriage, secularism versus religion, and other contentious values issues from the ballot box to judicial decisions. All of the issues of the culture war now politicize the judicial confirmation process in a way never before seen.

There is no wonder we have a battle over judicial confirmations. The confirmation process is subject to the wishes of whichever party is in control. The opposition party wants political retaliation for perceived unfairness in previous years. And the very nature of the process has shifted focus from the qualifications of the nominee to the ideology of the nominee. This collision only intensifies in the atmosphere of the culture war.

CHAPTER THREE

Culture War

AMERICA'S CULTURE WAR rages at the center of the judicial confirmation battle. The living Constitution thrust the confirmation process into the culture war by moving the fight over hot-button social issues from the legislative branch to the judicial branch. Now, the court directly impacts culture war issues including religion, abortion, special rights, marriage, pornography, and references to God in the public arena.

The culture war is a battle for the hearts, souls, and minds of the American people. University of Virginia sociologist James Davidson Hunter brought the term "culture war" into accepted vernacular in his 1991 book, *The Culture Wars*. Hunter described the two camps in the culture war as being the "Orthodox" and the "Progressivists."

Hunter writes,

> America is in the midst of the culture war that has had and will continue to have reverberations not only within public policy but within the lives of ordinary Americans everywhere . . . . [P]ersonal disagreements that fire the culture war [between the Orthodox and Progressivists] are deep and perhaps unreconcilable.[1]

The powerful clashes that play out in Washington, D.C., between the Left and the Right—which the media intensifies and exacerbates— are not "just flashes of political madness but reveal the honest concerns of different communities engaged in a deeply rooted cultural conflict."[2]

We encounter this conflict daily. Companies sanitize speech to be "politically correct." Schools teach children not merely to tolerate but to condone actions violating the Christian convictions of many. The media, the entertainment culture, and the intellectual elite ridicule traditional values. Religious denominations split along the same lines as the secular debates. This struggle affects every segment of our society.

Louis Bolce and Gerald De Maio,[3] two professors at Baruch College at the City University of New York, offer further insight into the two groups identified in Hunter's work:

> Orthodox morality, according to Hunter, adheres to an absolute standard of right and wrong and is based on universalistic principles. Progressivists, in contrast, embrace a humanistic ethic drawn from reason, science, and personal experience. Progressivists' moral standards are "loose-bounded," pluralistic, and relative to circumstance. This new cleavage cuts across the major American faith traditions and most denominations.

The "orthodox"—or traditionalists—tend toward the right of the political spectrum: conservatives, often Evangelical Christians, who believe their values based on faith in God and belief in Scripture should impact government and public policy. The "progressivists"—or secularists—tend to be politically left wing: liberals, often atheists or agnostics, who reject religion and metaphysical authority over earthly actions.

Certainly there are people of faith and atheists on both sides. Some individuals fight on different sides of the culture war depending on the specific issue. These are general categories of polar opposites whether we call them right and left, or conservative and liberal, or red state and blue state. Those in the culture war understand these teams as clearly as if everyone wore uniforms.

Originalists fight one side of the battle. These strict constructionists interpret our Constitution according to its original meaning and believe it should be changed only through the amendment process. On the other side of the battle are those who see the Constitution as a living document, subject to change and revision by a majority of the members of the Supreme Court.

As evidenced by the presidential elections of 2000 and 2004, America is closely divided in this battle. Conservative commentator Dennis Prager writes, there is probably more hatred between the opposing sides today than there was during the First Civil War. And I am not talking about extremists. A senior editor of the respected center-left New Republic just wrote an article titled "The Case for Bush Hatred," an article that could have been written by writers at most major American newspapers, by most Hollywood celebrities, and almost anyone else left of center. And the conservative hatred of former President Bill Clinton was equally deep.

Prager then lists the issues he sees dividing "liberals, leftists, and Greens" from "conservatives, rightists, and libertarians": references to God, capital punishment, cradle-to-grave welfare, secularism, European versus American values, national sovereignty and internationalism, capitalism, tort reform, multiculturalism, sex education, crime, war, abortion, poverty, taxation, environmentalism/conservationism, healthcare, education, foreign policy, and others. Certainly everyone is anti-crime and no one desires war; on many of these issues both sides agree. But the debate is one of public policy concerning implementation and priority.

Prager writes, "The fact is that this country is profoundly divided on virtually every major social, personal, and political issue. We are in the midst of the Second American Civil War. Who wins it will determine the nature of this country as much as the winner of the first did."[4]

Noah Feldman, writing on the culture war in the *New York Times*, recognizes the same cultural divide: "Talk of secession of blue states from red in the aftermath of the 2004 election was not meant seriously; but this kind of dark musing, with its implicit reference to the Civil War, is also not coincidental. It bespeaks a division deeper than any other in our public life."[5] This societal divergence appears acutely in discussions over abortion, special rights, marriage, and pornography.

Few issues stir the passions of American politics like abortion. Rightfully so, it is a debate over ultimate questions—life and living. What does our society treasure more: the sanctity of life or the quality of life? The preeminence of abortion in the culture war and its impact on the judicial confirmation battles cannot be ignored. Abortion is the engine that drives the opposition against conservative nominees. The day after President Bush announced his choice of John Roberts to replace Sandra Day O'Connor on the Supreme Court, the talk about abortion was already in the air. Katie Couric was not unusual among network talking heads as she cut through the debates and said on NBC's *Today Show*, "some liberal groups have already raised some concerns about his record on the environment, civil rights, and civil liberties. But of course the real question is his position on abortion."[6]

Before the left's victorious 1973 Supreme Court decision in which *Roe v. Wade* found "a right to privacy" in the Constitution,[7] the question of abortion was settled by voters determining whether each state would allow or restrict abortions. Rather than resolving the issue, the Court's decision increased political focus on abortion (a common consequence of judicial activism). More than thirty years after Roe, our nation still debates abortion and wrestles with some of the initial questions.

While many voters choose their candidates based on one issue (economy, security, party, education, healthcare, taxes), the abortion question is synonymous with the "single-issue voter." Many liberals disregard anyone's campaign deemed not "pro-choice." Many conservatives will under no condition vote for a candidate who is not "pro-life."

Progressivists support abortion as an individual woman's fundamental right to choose. For them—be it economic, relationship, or lifestyle reasons—this decision is a "quality of life" issue.

Traditionalists oppose abortion primarily from religious conviction. However, a growing number of abortion opponents come from the humanist camp usually associated with the Left in the culture war. The former believe Scripture teaches life is a sacred gift from God. The latter believe the highest tradition of the Left protects the weak and helpless and defends their individual rights.

For example, longtime writer, journalist, and activist Nat Hentoff writes,

> I'm regarded as a "liberal," although I often stray from that category, and certainly a civil libertarian—though the ACLU and I are in profound disagreement on the matters of abortion, handicapped infants, and euthanasia, because I think they have forsaken basic civil liberties in dealing with these issues. I'm considered a liberal except for that unaccountable heresy of recent years that has to do with pro-life

matters. It's all the more unaccountable to a lot of people because I remain an atheist, a Jewish atheist. (That's a special branch of the division.) I think the question I'm most often asked from both sides is, "How do you presume to have this kind of moral conception without a belief in God?" And the answer is, "It's harder." But it's not impossible.[8]

Hentoff cites another example in liberal author Mary Meehan:

It is out of character for the left to neglect the weak and helpless. The traditional mark of the left has been its protection of the underdog, the weak and the poor. The unborn child is the most helpless form of humanity, even more in need of protection than the poor tenant farmer or the mental patient. The basic instinct of the left is to aid those who cannot aid themselves. And that instinct is absolutely sound. It's what keeps the human proposition going.[9]

Whether the motivation for protecting the unborn is rooted in the image and creation of God or the fundamental principle that human beings—especially the helpless—should be protected, for this side of the culture war the "sanctity of life" is an ultimate matter.

The Left views the "right to abortion" as essential to the empowerment of women to control their own destiny. They claim restricting abortion would allow biological forces to relegate women to second-class citizens. They speak of abortion in terms of fighting poverty, ensuring all children are wanted, and maintaining a preferred lifestyle.

The Right views abortion as a human rights issue. They argue an abortion kills an innocent human being. The Right claims medical science supports their position. Life begins at conception, they would say; this is a scientific fact, not a theological question. Genetically the embryo is unique and different from both parents; it is something other than the mother. Today, ultrasounds show unborn babies in color video: smiling, laughing, kicking, and sucking a thumb. Children receive lifesaving operations before they are even born. Expectant mothers purchase prenatal music and vitamins to help a baby's intellectual and physical development.

Pro-life groups say a fetus is a person and nothing can justify abortion. Pro-choice groups argue that just because those cells constitute "life," it does not mean that "life" is a "person" who inherently possesses human rights.

In the face of prenatal science, even some members of the Left, such as feminist leader Naomi Wolf,[10] recognize the baby (or fetus or embryo) is life. Wolf, a senior advisor on Vice President Al Gore's 2000 campaign for president, believes the abortion rights movement must admit the facts of what it is advocating: "Clinging to a rhetoric about abortion in which there is no life and no death, we entangle our beliefs in a series of self-delusions, fibs and evasions . . . . [W]e need to contextualize the fight to defend abortion rights within a moral framework that admits that the death of a fetus is a real death."

The "slippery slope" of admitting yet accepting abortion as the death of a human being changed previously mentioned liberal activist, journalist, and author Nat Hentoff into a pro-life advocate. While researching articles on the deaths of infants suffering from physical or mental limitations, Hentoff was stunned at the natural conclusion of the Left's position on abortion.

Hentoff writes,

> You mentioned abortion and I would say, "Oh yeah, that's a fundamental part of women's liberation," and that was the end of it. But then I started hearing about "late abortion." The simple "fact" that the infant had been born, proponents suggest, should not get in the way . . . . I heard the head of the Reproductive Freedom Rights unit of the ACLU saying . . . "I don't know what all this fuss is about. Dealing with these handicapped infants is really an extension of women's reproductive freedom rights, women's right to control their own bodies." That stopped me. It seemed to me we were not talking about *Roe v. Wade*. These infants were born. And having been born, as persons under the Constitution, they were entitled to at least the same rights as people on death row—due process, equal protection of the law. So for the first time, I began to pay attention to the "slippery slope" warnings of pro-lifers . . . .[11]

Peter Singer, professor of bioethics at Princeton University and author of the book *Unsanctifying Human Life*, says the "slippery slope" is true, but we should come down on the side of death:

> The pro-life groups were right about one thing, the location of the baby inside or outside the womb cannot make much of a moral difference. We cannot coherently hold it is alright to kill a fetus a week before birth, but as soon as the baby is born everything must be done to keep it alive. The solution, however, is not to accept the pro-life view that the fetus is a human being with the same moral status as yours or mine. The solution is the very opposite, to abandon the idea that all human life is of equal worth.[12]

Both sides of the debate are dominated by absolutists. Absolutists on the Left contend there should be no limitations on a woman's right to choose. They oppose any limitation on abortion, including partial-birth abortion and abortions by teenagers without parental consent or even parental notification. Meanwhile, absolutists on the Right oppose not only "abortion on demand" but abortion for any reason including rape, incest, or when the mother's life is in danger.

Moderate voices on both sides find common ground with the Left accepting some restrictions and the Right allowing some exemptions. The Left calls this the "legal but rare" position; the Right calls this the "pro-life with exceptions" position.

Most Americans seem conflicted on the issue as well. A national USA Today/CNN/Gallup poll in July 2005 concluded that while 68 percent of Americans do not think the landmark abortion case *Roe v. Wade* should be overturned, 60 percent also believe abortion should be illegal in all or most circumstances.[13]

The battle over the legalization of abortion for the time being seems to be at a standstill. But the cultural fight continues on related issues. Should partial-birth abortion be legal, or what restrictions should be placed on it? Should teenagers who may even require parental permission to take medicine at school be allowed to have a surgical abortion without telling their parents? What, if any, policies related to abortion should be promoted by the state? Should the state advocate contraception or abstinence? Can adoption policies for the baby's future as well as financial supports for the mother be improved to encourage women to give birth rather than choose abortion? The sanctity of life questions flow into the debates over cloning, embryonic stem cell research, and euthanasia.

The Left may maintain abortion is settled law, but in the hearts of the American people, the debate continues and the issue splits the country into two sides of the culture war. While abortion excites political passions, the fight over new special rights for groups is another controversial front in the culture war.

In recent years, the Left has sought to make sexual orientation a civil right upon which protections must be granted. These are exactly the types of rights of which Nan Aron spoke in the first chapter—the kind created by the courts and not representatives of the people.

In 1992, conservatives in Colorado pushed against liberal activism in the culture war. They drafted, put on the ballot, and watched as the voters of Colorado approved an amendment to their state Constitution that would prevent state or local government from using "homosexual, lesbian, or bisexual orientation, conduct, practices or relationships" to "constitute or otherwise be the basis of or entitle any person or class of persons to have or claim any minority status, quota preferences, protected status, or claim of discrimination."

Defeated in the democratic process, the Left turned to the federal courts. The United States Supreme Court found 6-3 in 1996 (*Romer v. Evans*) that the Colorado amendment violated the U.S. Constitution's Equal Protection Clause. Justice Anthony Kennedy, writing for the majority, said this amendment "classifies homosexuals not to further a proper legislative end but to make them unequal to everyone else. This Colorado cannot do. A State cannot so deem a class of persons a stranger to its laws."[14]

Justice Antonin Scalia wrote for the minority (joined by William Rehnquist and Clarence Thomas),

> No principle set forth in the Constitution, nor even any imagined by this Court in the past 200 years, prohibits what Colorado has done . . . . [the amendment] put directly, to all the citizens of the State, the

question: Should homosexuality be given special protection? They answered no. The Court today asserts that this most democratic of procedures is unconstitutional. Lacking any cases to establish that facially absurd proposition, it simply asserts that it must be unconstitutional, because it has never happened before . . . . The people of Colorado have adopted an entirely reasonable provision that does not even disfavor homosexuals in any substantive sense, but merely denies them preferential treatment. [The amendment] is designed to prevent piecemeal deterioration of the sexual morality favored by a majority of Coloradoans, and is not only an appropriate means to that legitimate end, but a means that Americans have employed before. Striking it down is an act, not of judicial judgment, but of political will.[15]

A few years after the Colorado case, the Left achieved another victory in the culture war in *Lawrence v. Texas*, which struck down that state's anti-sodomy statute.[16] Jamin B. Raskin, a professor of constitutional law at American University, says this ruling in the homosexual rights movement ended the culture war and that the liberals won: "In case you didn't notice, America's 20th century 'culture war' ended yesterday. Liberalism won . . . Justice Kennedy's magisterial opinion for the Supreme Court striking down anti-sodomy laws in *Lawrence v. Texas* will come to mark the end of 30 years of political strife fueled by right-wing rage against sexual modernity. Liberalism has won the final battle."[17]

Justice Scalia wrote in his dissenting opinion in *Lawrence v. Texas*,

the Court has taken sides in the culture war, departing from its role of assuring, as neutral observer, that the democratic rules of engagement are observed. Let me be clear that I have nothing against homosexuals, or any other group, promoting their agenda through normal democratic means. Social perceptions of sexual and other morality change over time, and every group has the right to persuade its fellow citizens that its view of such matters is the best . . . . But persuading one's fellow citizens is one thing, and imposing one's views in absence of democratic majority will is something else . . . . But it is the premise of our system that those judgments are to be made by the people, and not imposed by a governing caste that knows best.

I firmly believe that homosexuals have the same rights as all other Americans, but no more. I believe all people should be respected as individuals. I dealt with the homosexual issue in three different cases while I was on the federal trial bench. I presided over a trial that involved an extensive scam directed at homosexuals, depriving the victims of hundreds of thousands of dollars. It was evident the defense team was going to engage in "gay bashing." After they emphasized several times the homosexual nature of the victims' relationship, I stopped the proceeding. Turning to the jury, I specifically instructed them, "Jurors are not to consider sympathy or bias, and I would say to you that the issue of homosexuality has nothing to do with whether or not these defendants were defrauded of money . . . . [T]he fact that this man is homosexual has nothing to do with whether or not he was defrauded."[18] I turned back to the defense attorneys and told them they could proceed. They got the point. That ended gay bashing in the case.

Another case that came before me was a female plaintiff suing for personal injuries. The jury found in her favor but returned a verdict for less than her medical bills. I felt the testimony and demeanor of one of the witnesses created the impression of a lesbian relationship, and I concluded this had biased the jury. In my thirteen years on the federal trial bench, I only set aside two jury verdicts, and this was one of them. I ordered a new trial for the plaintiff.

In a third case, a lesbian group established a colony called Camp Sister Spirit on a farm in Jones County, Mississippi. This was not only in my jurisdiction, but also my family's home county for generations. Some local citizens protested vigorously. U.S. attorney general Janet Reno criticized these local citizens and attempted to force mediation. The local citizens sued Janet Reno personally as well as Camp Sister Spirit.

At the pretrial conference, I encouraged both sides to resolve the conflict and suggested ways this could be accomplished. Attorney General Reno stipulated the United States did not contend that the Civil Rights Act covered sexual orientation, that the plaintiffs were not under any compulsion to mediate, and that they could exercise their First Amendment right to freedom of speech. I advised the plaintiffs they could not violate the constitutional rights of those at Camp Sister Spirit.

The plaintiffs agreed to dismiss their lawsuit. Attorney General Reno expressed her appreciation for the manner in which I handled this case.

When the court steps in to grant special status to people because of a lifestyle they share in common, it essentially is promoting or condoning that behavior. The above cases show such judicial activism is unnecessary. Homosexuals do not require special rights; they have the same rights as all Americans already and receive justice without seeking special status.

The Massachusetts Supreme Court would cite the *Lawrence v. Texas* decision in its redefinition of marriage, which energized another front in the culture war. This battle concerns a foundational institution in our society: marriage. This is not merely an aggressive assault on this institution by the media and Hollywood, but an attempt to redefine it to include a union between same-sex individuals.

The definition of marriage is "not white or black; it is not liberal or conservative; it is not Republican or Democrat. Marriage is not for everyone; many choose singleness for their life. But by tradition and custom and law, marriage partners a man and a woman in love for their mutual edification" and as the traditional structure for raising a family.[19]

In 1775, in Massachusetts, a shot heard around the world was fired, launching the American Revolutionary War. In November 2003, a shot was again fired in Massachusetts, this one leading to a new round of fighting in the culture war: a battle for the redefinition of marriage. This shot would be heard around the world, too, as the following year this decision contributed to the reelection of President George W. Bush as well as Republican gains in the House and Senate.

Four judges on the Massachusetts Supreme Court, over the strong dissent of their three colleagues, redefined marriage. By judicial decree, the court determined legal marriage could occur between any two people. Same-sex marriages in Massachusetts were made legal not by an act of the legislature but by judicial decision. The majority concluded there was "no rational basis" for the Massachusetts State Legislature to limit marriage to a relationship between a man and a woman. The court called 375 years of Massachusetts history and the views of the majority of Americans irrational.

The Left supports the Massachusetts decision and claims homosexuals denied the right to unite in marriage are denied equal rights guaranteed by the Constitution. The Right opposes same-sex marriage and contends marriage between one man and one woman is an institution ordained by God with a long historical tradition. The legitimate state interest in traditional marriage is to support an institution for conceiving and rearing children, a result not present in a same-sex relationship.

In writing the decision for the majority, Chief Justice Margaret Marshall acknowledges, "Marriage is a vital social institution. The exclusive commitment of two individuals to each other nurtures love and mutual support; it brings stability to our society."[20] She continues, "Barred access to the protections, benefits, and obligations of civil marriage, a person who enters into an intimate, exclusive union with another of the same sex is arbitrarily deprived of membership in one of our community's most rewarding and cherished institutions." She claims marriage—defined as the union of a man and woman—excludes and thus discriminates against homosexuals.

Justice John Greaney, concurring with the majority, claims the value of the institution of marriage is too great to deny to same-sex couples: "Because marriage is, by all accounts, the cornerstone of our social structure, as well as the defining relationship in our personal lives, confining eligibility in the institution, and all of its accompanying benefits and responsibilities, to opposite-sex couples is basely unfair." Thus the reason, the purpose, of redefining marriage is to be fair and allow same-sex couples to participate in an institution of widespread historic and social importance.

The three judges dissenting in the case write,

> While the institution of marriage is deeply rooted in the history and traditions of our country and our State, the right to marry someone of the same sex is not. No matter how personal or intimate a decision to marry someone of the same sex might be, the right to make it is not guaranteed by the right of personal autonomy. . . . Unlike opposite-sex marriages, which have deep historical roots, or the parent-child relationship, which reflects a "strong tradition" founded on "the

history and culture of Western civilization" and "is now established beyond debate as an enduring American tradition," . . . or extended family relationships, which have been "honored throughout our history," . . . same-sex relationships, although becoming more accepted, are certainly not so "deeply rooted in this Nation's history and tradition" as to warrant such enhanced constitutional protection.

In redefining marriage, the majority declares "that barring an individual from the protections, benefits, and obligations of civil marriage solely because that person would marry a person of the same sex violates the Massachusetts Constitution." But until now when this court decided otherwise, "marriage" meant one man and one woman. A court with the power to change the definition of a word has the power to render any law meaningless.

As noted by the minority, society recognizes and rewards marriage as the proper convention to conceive and then rear children. A same-sex marriage has no internal potential for this function. Both federal public policy and the attention of many states are focused on the problem of teenage pregnancy or, more specifically, out-of-wedlock pregnancy. The dissent argues,

> So long as marriage is limited to opposite-sex couples who can at least theoretically procreate, society is able to communicate a consistent message to its citizens that marriage is a (normatively) necessary part of their procreative endeavor, that if they are to procreate, then society has endorsed the institution of marriage as the environment for it and for the subsequent rearing of their children; and that benefits are available explicitly to create a supportive and conductive atmosphere for those purposes. If society proceeds similarly to recognize marriages between same-sex couples who cannot procreate, it could be perceived as an abandonment of this claim, and might result in the mistaken view that civil marriage has little to do with procreation . . . .

As noted by the minority in the Massachusetts case, the court majority ignored the testimony and research brought before them that there is a state interest in the traditional family structure. The majority further rejected the studies showing children of a traditional family tend to engage less in risky behavior. But the dissent notes,

> studies to date reveal that there are still some observable differences between children raised by opposite-sex couples and children raised by same-sex couples . . . . Statistics continue to show that the most stable family for children to grow up in is that consisting of a father and a mother . . . concluding results of limited study consonant with notion that children raised by homosexuals disproportionately experience emotional disturbance and sexual victimization.

Children who develop with a father and mother are less likely to engage in risky behavior; same-sex marriage produces a situation where girls may grow up without a mother figure and boys may grow up without a father figure.

The role of traditional marriage in regard to children then is also threatened by the same-sex marriage ruling. The dissent suggested, "Paramount among its many important functions, the institution of marriage has systematically provided for the regulation of heterosexual behavior, brought order to the resulting procreation, and ensured a stable family structure in which children will be reared, educated, and socialized." This decision by Massachusetts judges sets the stage for an expansion and eventually a federal ruling that could extend same-sex marriages to every state in the union.

On October 6, 2005, an out-of-state gay couple argued before the Massachusetts Supreme Court that the 1913 law prohibiting out-of-state couples from marrying in Massachusetts "if their marriage would be 'void' in their home state" is unconstitutional. "Members of the state's highest court raised some tough questions . . . and expressed new doubts about an old law that bans out-of-state gay couples from marrying in Massachusetts." The court is expected "to rule on the case within several months."[21]

If this challenge is successful, you will then see a federal lawsuit attempting to force states that do not approve of same-sex marriage to recognize same-sex marriages performed in Massachusetts. If the Massachusetts court does allow out-of-state residents of the same sex to marry in Massachusetts, no one can predict what the outcome will be when the case reaches the U.S. Supreme Court under the provision of the Constitution requiring "full faith and credit shall be given in each state to the public acts, records, and judicial proceedings of every other state."[22]

While liberal groups seek to change the definition of marriage by judicial decision, conservatives and others seek to promote traditional marriage legislatively with an amendment to the U.S. Constitution that would prevent a federal court from using the "full faith and credit" clause to impose one state's same-sex marriages upon another state. If the Massachusetts court allows same-sex couples from out of state to marry in Massachusetts, this could reenergize the push for a Federal Marriage Amendment.

One group, the Alliance for Marriage, represents millions of Americans of faith: African-American denominations, Hispanic denominations, Catholic bishops, evangelicals, Jews, Muslims, and more. They cover a broad ideological and racial spectrum of individuals who believe traditional marriage has provided the primary moral compass and practical example for children for centuries. They believe preservation of marriage as an institution between one man and one woman is essential to our future prosperity and success. Civil rights activist Walter Fauntroy, organizer of Martin Luther King Jr.'s 1963 March on Washington, said in announcing his support of the Federal Marriage Amendment, "Marriage is the classroom where children, in interaction with their male and female parents, learn the most important lessons of civil society. When you lose that glue, the fabric of your society begins to unravel."[23]

While the Right has not yet succeeded in passing the Federal Marriage Amendment, it did succeed in an earlier attempt to preserve the traditional definition of marriage. Congress passed the Defense of Marriage Act overwhelmingly in 1996. President Bill Clinton signed it into law. This act denied federal recognition of "same-sex marriages" and gave states the right to refuse recognition of "same-sex marriage" from other states.

In addition to this federal law, forty-four states have a statute or a provision in their state constitution making marriage an institution between one man and one woman. Only five states (plus the District of Columbia) have no explicit provision prohibiting "marriages" between individuals of the same sex: Connecticut,[24] New Jersey, New Mexico, New York, and Rhode Island. Only Massachusetts issues "legal" marriage licenses to same-sex couples and that because of court decree.[25]

In 2004, in response to the Massachusetts case, eleven states had some type of initiative on the November ballot to validate the traditional one man and one woman definition of marriage. Steven Fisher spoke for the nation's largest gay and lesbian lobbying group, the Human Rights Campaign: "It's no accident that many are battleground states and are being put on the November ballot at a time when President Bush is desperately trying to energize his extremist base."[26]

The Massachusetts Court—not George W. Bush—energized his base in the 2004 election. The Left may have succeeded in moving the debate over these issues to the court, but the culture war continues and the Massachusetts ruling, rather than being a complete victory for the Left, energized the Right in the political process. Certainly President Bush's reelection benefited from this energy, but had the Left not sought to change the definition of marriage, the Right would not have reacted.

Not only the right wing turned out to vote on the marriage initiatives that could easily be characterized as a landslide for pro-family groups. Fisher called them Bush's "extremist base." Few in the mainstream would characterize 70 percent of the electorate as extremist. Each state that carried this measure on their ballot in 2004 overwhelmingly voted to ban "same-sex marriage." Those voting for a definition of marriage as being between one man and one woman: Arkansas 75 percent, Georgia 76 percent, Kentucky 75 percent, Mississippi 86 percent, Michigan 59 percent, Montana 67 percent, North Dakota 73 percent, Ohio 62 percent, Oklahoma 76 percent, Oregon 57 percent, and Utah 66 percent.[27] The Massachusetts court's ruling effectively says these majorities acted with "no rational basis" with their votes.

When the Left claimed they won the culture war with *Lawrence v. Texas* in June 2003 (followed by the Massachusetts ruling in November of that same year), they spoke too soon. As the 2004 election demonstrated, the struggle continues.

Another battle in the culture war affecting marriages and relationships is pornography. This battle in the culture war is between those who see child and hard-core pornography as dangerous to society and those who believe the freedom of speech is absolute, even when it comes to obscenity.

NBC News recently reported that there are an estimated 420 million porn web pages, and the largest group of consumers of these pages is children ages twelve to seventeen with the average age of first exposure being eleven. These children are not always seeking porn; sometimes they are lured there. Some porn pages embed phrases like "Disneyland," "Pokémon," and "Sleeping Beauty" into the website so children seeking those terms with a search engine will be invited to the sites by strangers, no different than with candy into a nondescript van. Pornographers generate more income than ABC, CBS, and NBC combined.[28] One in five children is sexually solicited online.

While most agree that involved and engaged parents continue to be the strongest safeguard against pornographic intrusion into the home, the political Left argues that parents do not have the same authority in our public libraries or even our public schools. With the digital drive to connect these institutions to the massive data and information found on the Internet, Congress passed the Children's Internet Protection Act (CIPA), signed into law by President Bill Clinton. This legislation requires any public library or school that receives federal funds to install filtering software on Internet-accessible computers open to the public. These public institutions are welcome to refuse, but the federal government will not supply them with federal tax dollars if they do not offer this basic protection.

The American Civil Liberties Union, the People for the American Way, and the American Library Association were joined by organizations like the Association of American Publishers and the Gay Lesbian Straight Education Network to file suit against CIPA. Their lawyer, Theresa Chmara, equated obscenity and child pornography with speech: "The law requires libraries to block adults from access to visual depictions that are obscene or child pornography. The law requires libraries to block minors from access to visual depictions that are obscene, child pornography, or harmful to minors . . . . This law forces libraries to censor access to speech or forgo critical Internet funding."[29]

These groups feel so strongly that adults should have unfettered access to pornography—even child and hard-core pornography—that they are willing to risk damage to children. This is a philosophy that promotes "me" over everything else. If it feels good, do it, regardless of the consequences to others, even children. In a 6-3 decision, the Supreme Court disagreed and upheld CIPA.

A recent ruling by another court shows how far liberal judges will go to protect pornography in the culture war. On September 29, 2005, the Oregon Supreme Court found under the Oregon Constitution a constitutional right to perform live sex acts in public; ruled that requiring patrons to remain four feet away from nude dancers was an unconstitutional restriction on freedom of speech and expression; and declared unconstitutional "a state law against conducting live sex shows and a local ordinance regulating conduct of nude dancers." One of the performers was under the age of eighteen.[30]

The Oregon Constitution adopted in 1859 provides: "No law shall be passed restraining the free expression of opinion, or restricting the right to speak, write or print freely on any subject whatever." The state supreme court overruled a lower court that "contended that bans on sexual performance should be considered valid as 'historical exceptions' to free speech rights because there were restrictions on public nudity and sexual conduct when the constitution was adopted."[31]

Justice Paul J. De Muniz dissented from the high court ruling, saying "the idea that the Victorian-era drafters and ratifiers of the Oregon Constitution sought to bring public masturbation and sexual intercourse within the purview of constitutional free-speech protection is difficult to comprehend."[32] De Muniz wrote, "limiting proximity of the dancers is simply not limiting expression."[33]

Columnist David Reinhard writes:

CULTURE WAR | 41

It's hard to say what's more nauseating . . . [that these explicit live sex shows] . . . are now legal in Oregon, or that the state Supreme Court has reasoned its way into the view that the Victorian-era framers of our constitution would have held that their document's "free expression" clause extended to such shows[.] If forced, I'll choose the latter. Live sex shows are one thing, but it's another thing for the justices to tell us Oregon laws barring such degradation are unconstitutional and our framers somehow had this in mind when they pinned Article 1, Section 8. . . . [It] says something that it took 21 dense pages to show the framers really meant to protect onstage sex. . . . [The decision is the] high court's recent contribution to jurisprudence and decadence. . . . The opinion's length and density suggests we're watching very smart people do what they do best if they lack restraint or common sense: reason their way into anything they want.[34]

Reinhard refers to the majority opinion's graphic description of the alleged sex acts, "a description my editors won't allow me to quote . . . . You need not be a Victorian-era Oregonian to understand that such conduct demeans viewer and viewed alike—and victimizes the women who perform . . . and hardly constitutes 'free expression.'"[35]

It is hard for me to grasp, hard for me to understand how anyone can find a constitutionally protected right to perform live sex acts in public. But eight judges in Oregon, practiced in intellectual gymnastics and arguments of incredible sophistry, declared live, graphic sex acts to be "protected speech"—a constitutional right.

Pornographic images make a difference; otherwise the billion-dollar advertising industry is a sham and television, radio, and print media empires have been built on a false premise. Irving Kristol, one of the leaders of the neo-conservative movement, says if speech and images do not have the power to injure, then they cannot have the power to improve society: "After all, if you believe that no one was ever corrupted by a book, you have also to believe that no one was ever improved by a book (or a play or a movie). You have to believe, in other words, that all art is morally trivial and that, consequently, all education is morally irrelevant. No one, not even a university professor, really believes that."[36]

There is a strong contrast between an editorial in the *New York Times* and a pithy yet powerful point by columnist George Will. The *Times* suggested, "There is much in the movies and in hard-core rap music that is disturbing and demeaning to many Americans. Rap music, which often reaches the top of the charts, is also the music in which women are degraded and men seem to murder each other for sport. But no one has ever dropped dead from viewing *Natural Born Killers* or listening to gangster rap records." To this George Will responded, "No one ever dropped dead reading *Der Sturmer*, the Nazi anti-Semitic newspaper, but the culture it served caused six million Jews to drop dead."[37] The Left claims that those who do not like pornography should not buy it or watch it. George Will makes the point that in a community—a culture—no man lives in vacuum and there is societal health in addition to individual health.

David Amsden writes in the *New York Magazine* on the mainstreaming of pornography in our culture,

> After all, we live in a society that not only has embraced porn but giddily lavishes it with high-brow attention. Frank Rich "analyzes" adult entertainment in the *Times*. Writer Irvine Welsh revisits the *Trainspotting* crew as it makes a skin flick in his latest novel, *Porno*. Timothy Greenfield-Sanders offers a coffee-table book of photographs of porn stars—with essays by literary types—and it's snatched up by an A-list publisher. Porn is not merely acceptable; it's hip.[38]

For all the Left's talk about sex education, sexual liberation, and the freedom of pornography, today their dream has unfortunately arrived for many young people. Naomi Wolf says, "The whole world, post-Internet, did become pornographized. Young men and women are indeed being taught what sex is, how it looks, what its etiquette and expectations are, by pornographic training—and this is having a huge effect on how they interact." Wolf, a leading voice in the liberal women's movement continues,

> People are not closer because of porn but further apart; people are not more turned on in their daily lives but less so . . . . [W]hen I ask [college students] about loneliness, a deep, sad silence descends on

audiences of young men and young women alike. They know they are lonely together, even when conjoined, and that this [pornographic] imagery is a big part of that loneliness. What they don't know is how to get out, how to find each other again erotically, face-to-face.[39]

The Right says this is more than nude photographs in magazines, or even R-rated sex in movies. These are thousands of young people across the nation dealing with the ramifications of hardcore online pornography: perhaps not your child but maybe your children's friends or dates. Whether our elected representatives are able to restrict children's access to pornography depends on whether the federal judiciary will exceed the Constitution and further spread cultural permissiveness.

When judges, rather than legislators, began deciding cultural issues including abortion, special rights, marriage, and pornography, the battle over the confirmation of judges became part of the culture war. But the confirmation of judges is just the tip of the iceberg. The war is waged in the media, on television, in movies, in books and magazines, at colleges and universities, in academia, in high schools, and even in elementary schools across the nation. The impact in these other arenas has far more potential for dramatic change in American culture than does the judicial confirmation fight. But as we see, unchecked judges have immense power to affect these arenas.

When we dig to the culture war's root, we discover the clash of worldviews between people of faith and secularists. Extreme left wing groups seek to ensure pornography can come into our schools, but references to God and the Bible must stay out. We see little tolerance by secularists for religious tradition. Secularists challenge references to God in public and in the Pledge of Allegiance as well as historical representations of the Ten Commandments on public ground. They seek not only the separation of church and state; they also seek separation of God and country.

CHAPTER FOUR

Historical Religious Tradition Collides with Secularism

NOWHERE HAS THE clash over the culture war produced more intense feelings and passions than in the area of religion. It is impossible to understand the ramifications and implications of the impact of the collision between secularism and religious tradition without having an understanding of America's religious heritage. It is also impossible to comprehend the depth of feeling that this train wreck has created without a review of history and without knowing something of the results of the crash between these two giants.

Religion—Christianity in particular—played a prominent role in the political development of America; it played a prominent role in the educational development of America; and it played a prominent role in the cultural development of America. Today, America's historical religious traditions collide head-on with secularism to create a central front in the culture war; in truth, it may be the entire front. While the debate centers on "church/state" issues, the effects reach us through the removal of the Ten Commandments from the public square, the banishment of "God" from public discourse, and the rejection of America's religious history. As long as courts hold in the balance the outcome of this struggle, the religious and the secular will battle over the confirmation of judges.

Joel Belz, founder and CEO of *World Magazine*, writes,

> The secularist sincerely believes it is both possible and important to keep the idea of God out of public-policy discussions. A biblical

worldview affirms that it is both possible and important to include the idea of God in any and all public-policy discussions. . . . Whether God has a place in public life, and in the values debate, is a key part of what some people call the "culture wars." Indeed, it may be what the whole argument's about.[1]

In Noah Feldman's recent piece in the *New York Times Magazine*,[2] he describes the two sides in this aspect of the culture war:

Two camps dominate the church-state debate in American life, corresponding to what are now the two most prominent approaches to the proper relation of religion and government. One school of thought contends that the right answers to questions of government policy must come from the wisdom of religious tradition. You might call those who insist on the direct relevance of religious values to political life "values evangelicals." Not every values evangelical is, technically speaking, an evangelical or a born-again Christian, although many are. Values evangelicals include Jews, Catholics, Muslims and even people who do not focus on a particular religious tradition but care primarily about identifying traditional moral values that can in theory be shared by everyone . . . .

Feldman describes the Left on this issue as "those who see religion as a matter of personal belief and choice largely irrelevant to government and who are concerned that values derived from religion will divide us, not unite us. You might call those who hold this view 'legal secularists,' not because they are necessarily strongly secular in their personal worldviews—though many are—but because they argue that government should be secular and that the laws should make it so." He says of the values evangelicals, "the solution lies in finding and embracing traditional values we can all share and without which we will never hold together. Legal secularists counter that we can maintain our national unity only if we treat religion as a personal, private matter, separate from concerns of citizenship."

The media usually characterize this struggle in terms of the Republican Party's "religious right" but seldom mention the Democrat's self-avowed "secularist left": a Democratic constituency as large and loyal as organized labor.[3]

It was not always so. Louis Bolce and Gerald De Maio write in the Fall 2002 issue of *The Public Interest* that, until 1972, both parties remained religiously conservative.[4] Secularists became a political force inside the Democratic Party during the 1972 Democratic National Convention, making the Republican Party more acceptable to people of faith:

> Prior to then, neither party contained many secularists nor showed many signs of moral or cultural progressivism. Moreover, prior to the late 1960s, there was something of a tacit commitment among elites in both parties to the traditional Judeo-Christian teachings regarding authority, sexual mores, and the family. This consensus was shattered in 1972 when the Democratic Party was captured by a faction whose cultural reform agenda was perceived by many (both inside and outside the convention) as antagonistic to traditional religious values. These were the "secularists"—that is, self-identified agnostics, atheists, and persons who never or seldom attend religious services. Over a third of white delegates fit this description, a remarkable figure considering that, according to James Davison Hunter, only about 5 percent of the population in 1972 could be described as secularists. . . . The GOP platform that year merely reiterated cultural positions the party had endorsed in past platforms . . . . The Republicans, by default more than by overt action, became the traditionalist party.

Rather than being neutral toward religious values, these secularists aggressively oppose religious values and those on the Right who advance them. Bolce and De Maio reported on data from the American National Election Study (ANES), a national survey carried out each election year since 1948 by the Survey Research Center and the Center for Political Studies of the Institute for Social Research at the University of Michigan. In 2000, nearly a quarter of white respondents who were delegates to the Democratic convention were anti-fundamentalist. These individuals tend to be those who are "highly educated . . . living in big cities . . . favor legalized abortion and gay rights, oppose prayer in schools, and who, ironically, 'strongly agree' that one should be tolerant of persons whose moral standards are different from one's own." But for secularists who urge tolerance, tolerance is something for someone else.

Secularists have found a home in the Democratic Party, and while they are but one wing of the party, they have made themselves significantly valuable in elections: "over a quarter of Clinton's white supporters in 1992 said that they intensely disliked Christian fundamentalists: in both 1996 and 2000, about a third of the total white Democratic presidential vote came from persons with these sentiments . . . . Clinton captured 80 percent of these voters in his victories [in 1992 and 1996] . . . . Gore picked up 70 percent of the anti-fundamentalist vote in the 2000 election."

Bolce and De Maio claim this kind of intolerance of religious beliefs has been unseen since the early twentieth century: "One has to reach back to pre-New Deal America, when political divisions between Catholics and Protestants encapsulated local ethno-cultural cleavages over prohibition, immigration, public education, and blue laws, to find a period when voting behavior was influenced by this degree of antipathy toward a religious group."

The current secularism versus religion debate began over prayer in schools but moved on to include the public display of the Ten Commandments and references to God at public institutions, ceremonies, and buildings—even the Pledge of Allegiance. Those on the Left contend these expressions violate the wall of separation erected by our Founders between church and state, and these expressions violate the constitutional prohibition that "Congress shall make no law respecting an establishment of religion."

Those on the Right argue religion played an important role in the founding of Plymouth Colony and the founding of our nation; it played a significant role in the American Revolution and the Constitutional Convention. They say the establishment of religion clause only refers to state-sponsored denominations (the selection of a state religion and turning over tax dollars to the preferred denominations). They contend the establishment clause as originally understood by the Founders does not justify the recent decisions outlawing the display of the Ten

Commandments at public sites, prayer in school, and the reference to "one Nation under God" in the Pledge of Allegiance.

The secularists' attempt to remove religion from the public square stands in opposition to hundreds of years of American history. You cannot walk through our historic areas without discovering the profound role religion played in our nation's development. Sculpted around the chamber of the U.S. House of Representatives are the profiles of history's great lawmakers, and in the very center—the only one with his full face—is Moses. The law bringer Moses, who according to Jewish, Christian, and Muslim religions brought the Ten Commandments down from Mt. Sinai, can also be found above the entrance to the Supreme Court, where he stands holding the Ten Commandments, flanked on each side by other law givers. Inside the Supreme Court, above the justices, is another depiction of the Ten Commandments.

Engraved on the east face of the metal cap of the Washington Monument are the Latin words *Laus Deo,* which means "Praise be to God."[5] On the stairway of the Washington Monument are carved in memorial stones various biblical passages including "Bring up a child in the way he should go and when he is old, he will not depart from it" (Proverbs 22:6).[6] There are references to God at the Lincoln Memorial, the National Archives, Senate and House office buildings, the Jefferson Memorial, and the Library of Congress. Monuments to and statues of people of faith can be found throughout our nation's capital.

But America's most enduring monuments to history are our founding documents and the principle of the rule of law. America's first written plan of self-government, the Mayflower Compact, was drafted by the Pilgrims, a group of religious dissidents fleeing Europe in order to worship God as they saw fit. These devout Christians proclaimed they had written and adopted the Mayflower Compact "to the glory of God and the advancement of the Christian faith."

The first laws relating to public education were passed in Massachusetts in 1642 and 1647 for the purpose of educating children so that they could read Scripture.[7] Our earliest colleges and universities (Harvard, Yale, and Princeton) were created to teach Christian values and train ministers. *The New England Primer,* printed in America in 1690 by Benjamin Harris, was America's first schoolbook text and continued to be widely used in schools even through the nineteenth century. The primer contains the Shorter Catechism, the Lord's Prayer, the Apostles' Creed, and many questions and answers taken directly from the Bible.

Leading up to the American Revolution, pamphleteers used the Ten Commandments—specifically the commandment against idols—to argue the orders of Parliament and the edicts of the king were so wrong that to follow them would be an act of idolatry.[8] When it came time to declare our independence from Great Britain, many of the Founders proclaimed their faith and relied upon the teachings of the Bible for guidance and direction. The Declaration of Independence proclaimed, "We hold these Truths to be self evident, that all Men are created equal, that they are endowed by their Creator with certain unalienable Rights," and the authors held "a firm Reliance on the Protection of divine Providence." Revolutionary patriot Patrick Henry proclaimed, "It cannot be emphasized too strongly or too often that this great Nation was founded not by religionists but by Christians."[9]

During the time the Founders were meeting to draft the Constitution, the Congress under the Articles of Confederation passed one of its most significant pieces of legislation, the Northwest Ordinance of July 13, 1787. In it, the Congress proclaimed, "Religion, Morality, and Knowledge being necessary to good Government and the happiness of mankind, schools, and the means of education shall forever be encouraged."[10]

Where did the Framers find inspiration for the Constitution? What sources and what people did they quote? The Bible was quoted four times more frequently by our Founders than any other person or source. It was quoted four times more frequently than Sir William Blackstone, twelve times more than John Locke.[11]

James Madison—father of our Constitution—proposed the plan to divide the government into three equal branches at the Constitutional Convention of 1787. The concept mirrored that of Isaiah 33:22: "For the Lord is our Judge [judicial branch], the Lord is our lawgiver [legislative branch], the Lord is our King [executive branch]."

When the convention seemed hopelessly deadlocked by diverse interests of the Founders, Benjamin Franklin rose to the floor and gave this eloquent address:

> The longer I live, the more convincing Proofs I see of this Truth—that God governs in the Affairs of Men. And if a sparrow cannot fall to the ground without His Notice, is it probable that an Empire can rise without His Aid? We have been assured, Sir, in the Sacred Writings, that except the Lord build the House they labor in vain who build it. I firmly believe this—and I also believe that without His concurring Aid, we shall succeed in this political Building no better than the Builders of Babel . . . . In the beginning of the contest with Britain, when we were sensible of danger, we had daily prayers in this room for Divine protection. Our prayers, sir, were heard, and they were graciously answered . . . . Do we imagine we no longer need His assistance?[12]

The next day they opened the session with prayer, and each day thereafter until the Constitution was drafted and signed.

In his first inaugural address delivered on April 20, 1789, President George Washington made "fervent supplications to that Almighty Being who rules over the universe," which he further identified as "the Great Author of every public and private good."[13] Washington warned that "the propitious smiles of Heaven can never be expected on a nation that disregards the eternal rules of order and right which Heaven itself has ordained . . . ."

Chief Justice William Rehnquist, while arguing that the Ninth Circuit Court of Appeals should have been reversed in the Newdow Pledge of Allegiance case, reflects,

> The phrase under God in the Pledge seems, as a historical matter, to sum up the attitude of the Nation's leaders, and to manifest itself in many of our public observances . . . . At George Washington's first inauguration on April 30, 1789, he stepped toward the iron rail . . . put his right hand on the Bible, opened to Psalm 121:1: "I raise my

eyes toward the hills. Whence shall my help come." The Chancellor proceeded with the oath: "Do you solemnly swear that you will faithfully execute the office of the President of the United States and will to the best of your ability preserve, protect, and defend the Constitution of the United States?" The President responded, "I solemnly swear," and repeated the oath, adding, "So help me God." He then bent forward and kissed the Bible before him.[14]

During his first year in office, President George Washington issued a Thanksgiving proclamation. He began his proclamation, "Whereas it is the duty of all Nations to acknowledge the providence of Almighty God, to obey His will, to be grateful for His benefits, and humbly to implore His protection and favor." In his farewell address, President Washington identified two essential components of Democracy: religion and morality. He even went so far as to say that no person could claim to be a patriot who tried to subvert these two pillars of democracy. "Of all the dispositions and habits, which lead to political prosperity, religion and morality are indispensable supports."[15]

When Congress convened in 1789, both Houses opened the first sessions with prayer. Ever since that time, both Houses of Congress have opened each legislative day with prayer. John Jay, the first chief justice of the Supreme Court, said "Providence has given to our people the choice of their rulers, and it is the duty, as well as the privilege and interest of our Christian nation, to select and prefer Christians for their rulers."[16]

"On the very day Congress approved the wording of the First Amendment, its members resolved to request of President Washington a day of public thanksgiving and prayer."[17] Even Thomas Jefferson (who is alleged to have created the Wall of Separation between church and state) worked with James Madison to revise Virginia's law including "Bill Number 84: Bill for Punishing Disturbers of Religious Worship and Sabbath Breakers."[18] Jefferson said in his first inaugural, ". . . enlightened by a benign religion, professed, indeed, and practiced in various forms, yet all of them inculcating honesty, truth, temperance, gratitude, and the love of man; acknowledging and adoring an overruling Providence . . . ."[19]

Matt Kaufman writes that in 1835, Alexis de Tocqueville, a French historian and sociologist, came to America to study democracy. He was aware of what had happened in France and the terrible atrocities committed in the name of democracy during the French experiment. He wanted to know what made democracy in America work and why America was great. He knew European political authority came largely from monarchs and unelected leaders. He discovered a different social authority in America that prevented our Founders from behaving as the French had in their revolution. His conclusion: "Religion in America takes no direct part in the government of society, but it must be regarded as the first of their political institutions."[20]

De Tocqueville continued,

> . . . some profess the doctrines of Christianity from a sincere belief in them, and others do the same because they fear to be suspected of unbelief. Christianity, therefore, reigns without obstacle, by universal consent; the consequence is, as I have before observed, that every principle of the moral world is fixed and determinate, although the political world is abandoned to the debates and the experiments of men. . . . Thus, while the law permits the Americans to do what they please, religion prevents them from conceiving, and forbids them to commit, what is rash or unjust. . . . I do not know whether all Americans have a sincere faith in their religion—for who can search the human heart?—but I am certain that they hold it to be indispensable to the maintenance of republican institutions. This opinion is not peculiar to a class of citizens or to a party, but it belongs to the whole nation and to every rank of society.

De Tocqueville warned that confusion and ultimately tyranny would result from the destruction of religion in America: "When a people's religion is destroyed doubt invades the highest faculties of the mind and half paralyzes all the rest." People find they have nothing to rely on but continually changing personal opinions: "When there is not authority in religion or on politics, men are soon frightened by the limitless independence with which they are faced. They are worried and worn out by the constant restlessness of everything. With everything on the move in the realm of the mind, they want the material order at least to be firm and stable, and as they cannot accept their ancient beliefs again, they hand themselves over to a master."

John Adams, second president of the United States, understood this about both our government's structure and the nature of man when he said, "Our Constitution was made only for a moral and religious people, it is wholly inadequate for the governing of any other."[21]

In 1833, Justice Joseph Story wrote,

> Christianity is indispensable to the true interest & solid foundations of all free governments. I distinguish . . . between the establishment of a particular sect, as the Religion of the State, & the Establishment of Christianity itself, without any preference of any particular form of it. I know not, indeed, how any deep sense of moral obligation or accountableness can be expected to prevail in the community without a firm persuasion of the great Christian Truths.[22]

Justice John Paul Stevens, dissenting in the Texas Ten Commandments case and speaking of the early understanding of the First Amendment, reported, "one influential thinker wrote of the First Amendment that [t]he meaning of the term establishment in this amendment unquestionably is, the preference and establishment given by law to one sect of Christians over every other . . . . Many accepted this premise for nearly a century after the Founding."[23] In 1892, the Supreme Court declared, "This is a religious people. . . . This is a Christian Nation."[24]

Theodore Roosevelt, engaged in a fight against government corruption wrought by public officials without moral compasses, referred to a political rival who suggested that "the Ten Commandments and the Golden Rule have no part in political life." Teddy retorted that this implied the public had "dull" conscience and that if such leaders should continue in office, "the public has itself to thank for all shortcomings in public life."[25] Another president would say these principles were the birth heritage of our country. Woodrow Wilson stated, "America was born a Christian Nation. America was born to exemplify that devotion to the elements of righteousness which are derived from the revelations of the Holy Scripture."[26]

General Dwight D. Eisenhower concluded his "Great Crusade" speech ordering the invasion of Europe with these words: "let us beseech the blessing of Almighty God upon this great and noble undertaking." Today in Normandy, France, overlooking the beaches of Omaha, you will find white crosses and Stars of David marking the graves of the brave young men who gave their lives there in June 1944. The families and members of the greatest generation recognize that these religious symbols honor those who gave their lives for the cause of liberty and freedom in addition to honoring God whose blessings were invoked.

America's religious traditions were still recognized by the Court through the middle of the last century. As late as 1952, Justice William O'Douglas, one of the most liberal members of the United States Supreme Court, wrote,

> We are a religious people whose institutions presuppose a Supreme Being. We guarantee the freedom to worship as one chooses . . . . When the State encourages religious instruction or cooperates with religious authorities by adjusting the schedule of public events to sectarian needs, it follows the best of our traditions. For it then respects the religious nature of our people and accommodates the public service to their spiritual needs. To hold that it may not would be to find in the Constitution a requirement that the Government show a callous indifference to religious groups. That would be prefer- ring those who believe in no religion over those who do believe . . . but we find no Constitutional requirement which makes it necessary for Government to be hostile to religion.[27]

In 1954, Chief Justice Earl Warren attributed a foundational role in the development of our legal system not only to the Ten Commandments, but to the Bible in general, saying,

> I believe no one can read the history of our country without realizing that the Good Book and the spirit of the Savior have from the begin- ning been our guiding geniuses . . . . Whether we look to the first

Charter of Virginia . . . or to the Charter of New England . . . or to the Charter of Massachusetts Bay . . . or to the Fundamental Orders of Connecticut . . . the same objective is present . . . a Christian land governed by Christian principles. I believe the entire Bill of Rights came into being because of the knowledge our forefathers had of the Bible and their belief in it."[28]

Should we exercise religious values in the realm of public policy? It wasn't Dr. James Dobson who said, "God's work must truly be our own."[29] It was President John F. Kennedy. In his 1961 inaugural address, Kennedy said, "And yet the same revolutionary beliefs for which our forbears fought are still at issue around the globe—the belief that the rights of man come not from the generosity of the state, but from the hand of God."

Despite the fact each of the fifty state constitutions acknowledge God in one way or another,[30] a growing secularist movement is colliding head-on with traditional religious values. In 1962, the Supreme Court declared in *Engel v. Vitale*,[31] "the daily recitation of a voluntary twenty-two-word non-denominational prayer in New York's public schools violated the Establishment Clause, notwithstanding the fact that the Congress that had authored the First Amendment had itself begun its days with prayer." The Court's holding in Engel "ended a practice that had been part of the American experience since the outset of public education and that an overwhelming majority of American parents wished to have continued."[32]

Complaints were made in 2005 that cadets and faculty at the United States Air Force Academy were sending e-mails containing Scripture verses and encouraging fellow believers to trust in God for help. National Public Radio opined, "Not everyone is convinced the Air Force can fix this problem on its own," but did assure us the "Academy says it is addressing the problem."[33] The "problem" was Christian cadets exercising their First Amendment rights of speech and religion. After internal investigations as well as a Pentagon task force, "A military panel says it did not find evidence of religious discrimination."[34] One may not like to hear a Christian cadet express his religious convictions, but without question, he has the constitutional right to do so, both under the free speech and freedom of religion clauses. The same Christian cadet may be offended by songs or rap lyrics that denigrate women, espouse violence and rape, glorify the killing of policemen, and explicitly describe sex acts in detail. Some who would defend the rappers' constitutional rights would deny the right of freedom of expression to Christians.

In May 2005, the South Kitsap School District in Washington state decided to reverse "political correctness run amok" and voted to change "Winter Break" to "Christmas Break," returning to its pre-1984 standard. By August 2005, it was Winter Break once again following the threat of a lawsuit by the American Civil Liberties Union. "If everybody calls it Christmas, and calls it Christmas break, why is it these people insist on this political correctness that we must call it winter break? It's being dishonest," said Jim Huff, who was the president of the school board when Christmas was put back on the calendar.[35] If the ACLU would be willing to divert money from a school's education budget to defend a lawsuit over what the school calls a period of time when students are not even at school, imagine what they would do if the New England Primer were still a textbook.

There has also been a successful attempt to rewrite history. According to David Limbaugh, social studies textbooks used by 87 percent of public school students do not mention that religion played any role in the Pilgrims coming to America. The executive director of Mt. Vernon attests that the 1960s textbooks in Virginia had ten times more material on George Washington than do the current history textbooks in Virginia. One high school history textbook gives six lines to George Washington and six and one-half pages to Marilyn Monroe.[36]

Recently, to the outrage of people across the country, the Ninth Circuit Court of Appeals held that "one Nation under God" in the Pledge of Allegiance was unconstitutional. The U.S. Supreme Court held that the plaintiff, Michael Newdow, did not possess "standing" to file the suit and sidestepped resolving the issue. The Ninth Circuit held this was a violation of the Constitution's "establishment clause" and that the wall between church and state had been breached.[37]

It is not difficult to understand what our Founders intended in regard to separation of church and state. Their intent is clearly and easily discernable from what they said and what they did. In the Constitution, they wrote and adopted three requirements relating to religion.

First, there will be no establishment of religion. At that particular time in our history this terminology had an obvious meaning. England, from whom the colonies had just separated—as well as many of the colonies making up the new states—had established religions. Our new federal government would not favor one religion over another and it would not favor religion over non-religion.

Secondly, our Founders determined Congress should make no law prohibiting the "free exercise of religion." Any American citizen is free to choose whether he will or will not worship and the object or objects of his worship. Americans can choose their own religion, their own denomination, or their own non-religion. Americans are free to believe or not to believe. No government power can interfere with this right.

Third, our Founding Fathers provided that "no religious Test shall ever be required as a Qualification to hold office." Plainly one cannot be required to believe in God to hold office. One cannot be excluded from office because one does believe in God. Catholics cannot be preferred over Protestants, and Protestants cannot be preferred over someone of the Jewish faith. One cannot be excluded from office because of Hindu or Muslim faith. The Constitution prohibits religious tests as a qualification to hold office.

The language of the Constitution is clear and the actions of the Founders demonstrate their intentions as plainly as their words. They opened the first session of both Houses of Congress with prayer, a tradition continuing still today. They immediately hired a chaplain for both the House and the Senate. They appointed chaplains for the armed services. They placed religious symbols and words on public buildings and public monuments. They openly spoke of their faith and religion in public debate both in and out of government. They prohibited Congress from selecting a state religion. They prohibited Congress from favoring or supporting with tax dollars one church, religion, or denomination over another. They provided neutrality—not hostility—toward religion.

Even the phrase "a wall of separation between church and state" is from a letter written by then President Thomas Jefferson to some Connecticut Baptists who feared government's intrusion into free religious worship, not the impact of faith upon government.

As Larry Schweikart and Michael Allen wrote in their book, *A Patriot's History of the United States,*

> Few issues have been more mischaracterized than religion, and the government's attitude toward religion, in the early Republic. Modern Americans readily cite the "separation of church and state," a phrase that does not appear in the Constitution, yet is a concept that has become a guiding force in the disestablishment of religion in America. Most settlers had come to America with the quest for religious freedom constituting an important, if not the most important, goal of their journey. . . . At the same time, this generic Christian faith, wherein everyone agreed to disagree, served as a unifying element by breaking down parish boundaries. The Great Awakening had galvanized American Christianity, pushing it even further into evangelism, and it served as a springboard to the Revolution itself, fueling the political fire with religious fervor and imbuing in the Founders a sense of rightness of cause. To some extent, then, "the essential difference between the American Revolution and the French Revolution is that the American Revolution . . . was a religious event, whereas the French Revolution was an anti-religious event." John Adams said as much when he observed that the "Revolution was in the mind and hearts of the people; and change in their religious sentiments of their duties and obligations. Consequently, America while attaching itself to no specific variant of Christianity, operated on an understanding that the nation would adopt an unofficial, generic Christianity that fit hand in glove with republicanism."[38]

They conclude that "understanding that faith was indispensable, Americans have, more than any other place on earth, placed it at the center of the Republic. The American character and the American dream could never be disentangled, and ultimately the latter would go only as far as the former would take it."[39]

One cannot study the convergence of history and religion in America without concluding conclusively that religion—especially Christianity—was an important component of the founding of our nation and its development. For the secularists to attempt to rewrite history, to downplay the historical role of religion in America, to attempt to remove all religious symbols and references to God from the public square, disturbs those who have strong faith. They fear that next will be an attempt to regulate what can be proclaimed from the pulpit as has been done in other countries even in modern times. It is no wonder that feelings are so intense in this facet of the culture war.

Government can no more constitutionally take a position that is hostile to religion than it can take a position that favors religion. Any person in our country has a right to their beliefs and to determine their own lifestyle. But they do not have a right to force other people to condone their lifestyle or to accept it or to promote it. There should neither be conversion by the sword nor religious oppression by the sovereign.

Just as unbelievers have the right to reject Scripture, believers have a right to believe Scripture and accept its teachings. And those who hold a high view of Scripture and draw their moral position from that source—including judicial nominees—should not be disqualified from holding office or participating in the political process because of their values.

A Scripture reference on a public building should be no more threatening to a nonbeliever than a quote from a piece of literature. The right to share one's personal religious beliefs should be at least as permissible—as a freedom of speech issue—as the right to share political beliefs. This same protection extends to those individuals who wish to disprove or attack religious beliefs, but not to the government. Neither the Supreme Court nor any other branch of government can constitutionally promote secularism, non-belief, or religion.

Nowhere is the collision between historic religious traditions and secularism more evident than in Supreme Court decisions relating to the display of the Ten Commandments. The two most recent decisions—one from Texas and one from Kentucky—came to opposite conclusions, leaving local officials in confusion as to what they can and cannot do and exposing the strong feelings this issue generates among America's citizens and even among the justices themselves.

In the Texas case, the display of the Ten Commandments was a monument located on the state capitol grounds. On this twenty-two-acre tract between the state capitol building and the Supreme Court building are located seventeen monuments and twenty-one historical markers commemorating "The people, ideals, and events that comprise Texan identity." The monument in question stands six feet high and two and one-half feet wide. It was contributed by the Eagles, a national social, civic, and patriotic organization, in 1961. Five members of the Supreme Court concluded this display did not violate the establishment of religion clause in 2005—forty years after the monument was erected.

The Kentucky case involved the display of the Ten Commandments at two county courthouses. The governing boards of the two counties originally ordered display of the Ten Commandments on the walls within the courthouses responding to Judge Roy Moore's efforts to display a Ten Commandments monument in Alabama. The ACLU filed suit. Trying to avoid an adverse ruling, the governing bodies changed the displays to include other documents but clearly made the display religious and in conflict with previous federal cases. The counties changed attorneys and created a composite display including the Magna Carta, the Declaration of Independence, the Bill of Rights, the lyrics of the Star-spangled Banner, the Mayflower Compact, the National Motto, the preamble to the Kentucky Constitution, and a picture of Lady Justice. The collection was titled "The Foundations of American Law and Government Display." This attempt to conform to previous rulings succeeded in that neither the attorneys for the American Civil Liberties Union nor the majority of the Supreme Court contended the reconstructed display violated the Constitution. Instead, the ACLU argued the county's original motivation was to promote religion and thus the display should be taken down, even though it had been drastically changed. Five members of the Supreme Court agreed.

Four justices—John Paul Stevens, Ruth Bader Ginsburg, David Souter, and Sandra Day O'Connor—would have removed the displays in both the Texas and Kentucky cases. Four justices—William

Rehnquist, Antonin Scalia, Clarence Thomas, and Anthony Kennedy—would have found the displays consistent with the Constitution in both cases.

Justice Stephen Breyer found the Texas display constitutional but the Kentucky display unconstitutional. He based his decision largely on the time involved, suggesting that after forty years, few individuals would consider the Texas Ten Commandments to favor a particular religion, while the motive of those in the Kentucky case was to do just that, and thus unconstitutional.

Justice Breyer fearing that to order the removal of the Texas Ten Commandments display in addition to the Kentucky display would "lead the way to exhibit a hostility toward religion that has no place in Establishment Clause tradition," argues,

> Such a holding might well encourage disputes concerning the removal of long standing depictions of the Ten Commandments from public buildings across the Nation. And it could thereby create the very kind of religiously based divisiveness that the Establishment Clause seeks to avoid.

Significantly, even Breyer believed that had the minority prevailed in the Texas case, the ruling would have been hostile to religion.

The primary difference between the two cases was that the Ten Commandments display in Texas had been up for some forty years and was placed there by a national social, civic, and patriotic organization. There was no paper trail showing the original intent had been for religious purposes. The court found the local Kentucky officials expected the display to be understood in a religious manner.

Justice Stevens, who would have ordered the removal of the Texas monument, says in his dissent joined by Justice Ginsburg that the "monument is not a work of art and does not refer to any event in the history of the State." He maintains, "The message . . . is quite plain: This State endorses the divine code of the 'Judeo-Christian God,'" though he did note that "The donors were motivated by a desire to 'inspire the youth' and curb juvenile delinquency by providing children with a 'code of conduct or standards by which to govern their actions,'" which he recognizes "is both admirable and unquestionably secular."

Some could argue that the promotion of morality can be separated from the promotion of religion and that the Ten Commandments is so basic in Western law and historical tradition that their display can serve a secular purpose. In fact, the plaintiff in the Texas case noted the irony in his brief that those who support the display of the Ten Commandments are forced to "defend them as secular." He says, "This denigrates religion by denying the essential and profoundly religious nature of the Ten Commandments." And Justice Stevens dismisses the historic element, saying, "appeals to the religiosity of the Framers ring hollow."

In the Kentucky case, the majority concluded that since the first resolution authorizing the display was tainted by a desire to promote religion, their subsequent efforts to cure the constitutional defects were of no avail, it was the intent that controlled the case.

Justice Scalia argues in his dissent,

> Displays erected in silence (and under the direction of good legal advice) are permissible, while those hung after discussion and debate are deemed unconstitutional. Reduction of the Establishment Clause to such minutiae trivializes the Clause's protection against religious establishment; indeed, it may inflame religious passions by making the passing comments of every government official the subject of endless litigations.

Since 1973, there have been thirty reported federal cases in the country regarding the Ten Commandments. Seven of those were reported prior to 1999, a period of twenty-six years. Since 1999, a period of six years, twenty-three cases have been reported. Justice Stevens referred to the "deluge of cases flooding lower courts" relative to the Ten Commandments. But the confusion in these two cases that Justice Rehnquist says "point in two directions" will not solve the chaos.

Justice Thomas, in the Texas case, argues,

> [The Court adopts] an unhappy compromise that fails fully to account for either the adherent's or the non adherent's beliefs, and provides no principled way to choose between them. Even worse, the incoherence of the Court's decisions in this area renders the Establishment Clause impenetrable and incapable of consistent application. All told, this Court's jurisprudence leaves courts, governments, and believers and nonbelievers alike confused.

Confusion is but the least of our nation's worries when we remove concepts like the Ten Commandments from the public arena. David Myers, one of those sentenced in the World Com scandal, said, "In the single most critical characterizing moment of my life, I failed. It is something I will take with me the rest of my life." To this responded a recent editorial writer, "In this world of relativism and rationalization, where oaths and ethical guidelines are easily disregarded and moral absolutes are ridiculed, the World Com case leaves some warnings other than those for corporate CEOs. Characterizing moment choices have consequences."[40] We pay a price when we abandon absolutes. Where there are no absolutes, unwed and teenage pregnancies increase. Where there are no absolutes, greed takes over and an Enron or a World Com can cost thousands their retirement savings, their college funds, their jobs, and their life savings.

Supreme Court decisions and the culture war have created an environment where pornography and anti-religious messages are much more prevalent on university, college, and school campuses than any expression of religious faith—particularly Christian faith. That is deeply disturbing to people of faith.

While it is true traditionalists have largely lost the battle with most of the media and the academic community, they have not lost the battle for heartland America. The societal debates over abortion, special rights, marriage, and pornography will continue in the courts and in the legislatures as each side wins some and loses some. Paul Weyrich, president of the Free Congress Foundation and longtime conservative activist, spurred outrage and reexamination among social leaders on the right with a letter advocating withdrawal from the culture war.

Weyrich wrote, "politics has failed because of the collapse of the culture . . . . I no longer believe that there is a moral majority . . . . I believe that we probably have lost the culture war." He recommended that traditionalists should "turn off" the media, "tune out" and seek stillness, and "drop out of this culture, and find places, even if it is where we physically are right now, where we can live godly, righteous, and sober lives." He admitted in the letter that it is important to pursue politics and be involved in government, and he encouraged people to retake the cultural institutions captured by the other side. But he lamented, "even when we win in politics, our victories fail to translate into the kind of polices we believe are important."[41]

Charles Colson disagreed with Weyrich in one of his Break Point commentaries, saying, "I certainly respect Weyrich, but in this case, I think he's dead wrong. When great culture wars are raging, Christians have no business fleeing the field of battle. This was a lesson taught to us some 200 years ago by . . . William Wilberforce." Wilberforce's two ambitions were "the abolition of the slave trade and the 'reformation of manners' . . . 50 years after Wilberforce began his twin crusades . . . slavery was abolished in the British Empire. Piety and virtue went from being despised to being fashionable."

Colson says Wilberforce should be an example to us all: "Yes, the prospect of turning around our culture may seem overwhelming. But withdrawal from the fray is inconsistent with loving our neighbor— whether that neighbor is an unborn child or the abortionist who takes his life. We cannot choose between godly, righteous lives or participating in the culture. For our neighbor's sakes, as well as for God's, we're called to do both."[42]

Secularists would purge religion from our society and history just as has been done in France where secularism is enshrined in the Constitution. Author George Orwell, himself a secularist, wrote,

> I thought of a rather cruel trick I once played on a wasp. He was sucking jam on my plate, and I cut him in half. He paid no attention, merely went on with his meal, while a tiny stream of jam trickled out

of his severed esophagus. Only when he tried to fly away did he grasp the dreadful thing that had happened to him. It is the same with modern man. The thing that has been cut away is his soul.[43]

America was founded on Judeo-Christian principles with a rich religious heritage. America never was a religious theocracy. America should never become a religious theocracy. Secularists today try to rewrite history and remove all traces of our historic and religious beginning and establish a "secularocracy." But government should no more favor secularism than it favors religion. Favoring either is wrong.

For the secularists to succeed in stripping away America's soul—the tradition, history, and foundation of religious life—they organize Far Left special-interest groups to promote liberal activist judges and fight strict constructionist jurists. Thus, ideologue generals lead the special-interest group armies into battle to fight for the secular side of the culture war. If the Right wishes to stop this advance, they too must continue to engage in the battle.

CHAPTER FIVE

Culture Warriors

THE GENERALS IN the culture war lead armies of volunteers, command millions of dollars in political contributions, coordinate media campaigns, and use the Internet, phone banks, and direct mail to move their ideology forward.

On the Right are organizations such as Progress for America, the Committee for Justice, the Coalition for a Fair Judiciary, the American Center for Law and Justice, and social conservative groups like the American Family Association, Focus on the Family, and the Family Research Council. This is the side of traditionalists and conservatives.

On the Left is the Coalition for a Fair and Independent Judiciary, an alliance of more than seventy left wing organizations including the People for the American Way, the Alliance for Justice, the National Organization for Women, NARAL Pro Choice America, MoveOn.org, the Sierra Club, the AFL-CIO and big labor, the American Civil Liberties Union, left wing "civil rights" groups, Human Rights Campaign (the gay and lesbian lobby), the Feminist Majority, and the Planned Parenthood Federation of America. This is the side of secularists and liberals.

Today the special-interest groups don't simply mobilize for elections; their pressure can be felt during every step of the governing process. When Republican senators considered using a parliamentary procedure to stop the Democrats from filibustering President George W. Bush's judicial nominees, the People for the American Way spent $5 million in a public opinion campaign to stop the GOP. MoveOn.org generated

110,000 calls to Congress, 60,000 letters to the media, and $1.3 million to pay for ads and other activities.[1]

Each of the Far Left groups has their own mission and fulfills its own role. People for the American Way sets the agenda and provides a lot of heavy lifting. NARAL assembles a vast network of pro-choice lobbies to the cause. NOW speaks with a national voice as the feminist authority. And the Alliance for Justice provides a link specially geared to focus on the courts. These four organizations illustrate the Left's organization in fighting for its agenda during the judicial confirmation process.

People for the American Way (PFAW) led the smear campaign against a number of President Bush's nominees. Founded in 1980 by television producer Norman Lear, PFAW portrays itself as "an energetic advocate for the values and institutions that sustain a diverse democratic society . . . threatened by the influence of the radical right and its allies who have risen to political power."[2] The name "People for the American Way" sounds like an organization dedicated to traditional values, like a hero fighting for "Truth, Justice, and the American Way." But it does not support traditional America. Its first TV ad in 1980 asked for donations in the name of "religious tolerance and diversity,"[3] but the evidence suggests PFAW doesn't tolerate expressions of traditional religious faith.

PFAW stands for flag burning,[4] "art" portraying the Virgin Mary splattered with elephant dung,[5] and "theater" portraying Christ and his apostles as homosexuals. PFAW supports the legalization of drugs and opposes school vouchers for poor parents. It worked to defeat a constitutional amendment to permit prayer in public schools,[6] and their founder Norman Lear called school prayer "a joke."[7] PFAW opposes porn filters on public library computers, fought against the Boy Scouts for excluding homosexuals from being troop leaders, and doesn't want to allow teachers to present intelligent design in addition to evolution in our schools as a theory for the origin of life.[8] That is PFAW's "American way."

PFAW has two wings: a lobbying and advocacy organization that participates in partisan battles like the confirmation of judges; and a nonprofit wing that engages in educational programs that can receive tax-deductible contributions but cannot engage in political activity.

Byron York reported in *National Review* how the two work together. In 2000, the former received $5,140,131 in contributions and the latter received $7,469,722. PFAW's Ralph Neas serves as president of both and derives his salary from both wings (in 2000 $79,556 from the political wing and $119,335 from the educational wing). Essentially those supporting the educational wing are paying the salaries of Neas and his number 2 officer Carol Blum—both generals in the Left's fight in the judicial confirmation battle.

Some of those who support PFAW with monetary contributions include the New York Times Company, CBS, NBC, Disney/ABC, America Online, and *Time Magazine*—though *Time* no longer contributes, saying, "We determined that for news organizations such as ours, it would not be appropriate for us to do that, so we stopped doing it."[9] In addition to these news organizations, PFAW is heavily funded by Hollywood interests like the Screen Actors Guild, the Motion Picture Association of America, Dreamworks, and Playboy Enterprises. PFAW is Hollywood's voice in Washington.

PFAW is not shy about their advocacy work, stating on their website that "we are in frequent, daily contact with Congressional offices," and adding that "forces on the right are well organized and well represented on Capitol Hill . . . . People for the American Way, working with a variety of coalition partners, vigorously opposes . . . the conservative agenda."[10]

PFAW's president Ralph Neas built his career by defeating Robert Bork's nomination to the Supreme Court and furthered his influence during the attack on Clarence Thomas. In 2001, President Bush nominated me and several others for the federal judiciary, and Neas boasted he would "mobilize 1,000 organizations" to oppose us.[11] Those organizations put the necessary pressure on the Senate Democrats with Neas calling the shots.

An editorial in the *Wall Street Journal* profiled Neas, saying his

> official biography describes him as the "101st Senator," from an admiring comment by Teddy Kennedy. Actually, that's selling him short. When it comes to judicial nominations, Mr. Neas might as well be the one and only Senator. The ten Democrats on the Judiciary

Committee salute and follow orders. Mr. Neas has issued new directives from his command center at People for the American Way. The
war plan remains the same: Keep as many Bush nominees as possible
off the bench.[12]

It was clear which general in the culture war was in charge. Again,
an editorial in the *Wall Street Journal* reported,

> By all normal appearances Senate Democrats were in charge of yester-
> day's hearing before the Senate Judiciary Committee. But anyone who
> knows anything about modern legal politics knows that the real chair-
> man was the talkative fellow holding court with the press corps in the
> hallway nearby. That man is Ralph Neas, president of People for the
> American Way and ringleader of what promise to be years of attacks
> on President Bush's judicial nominees. Politically speaking, he's Edgar
> Bergen and Senate liberals are his Charlie McCarthys. He gives them
> their attack themes, and they then repeat them to skewer some hapless
> nominee . . . . Democrats sang Mr. Neas's tune while pounding
> appeals-court nominee Charles Pickering Sr. . . . [Neas] orchestrated
> the original borking, against Robert Bork in the late Reagan era, but
> has also lent his expertise to the trashing of Clarence Thomas and a
> host of other conservative nominees . . . . Neas is back, this time
> giving attack orders to Judiciary Chairman Pat Leahy . . . the Senators
> themselves, all lip-synching lines from Mr. Neas's anti-Pickering
> position paper.[13]

When President Bush announced John Roberts as his first appointment to the United States Supreme Court, the *New York Times* reported
that commanding general Neas was ready for battle once again.

> By 10 a.m., Mr. Neas had his armies in motion. E-mail messages were
> sent to the bulk of the group's 750,000 members and supporters, as
> well as 10,000 reporters. Volunteers streamed into what the organiza-
> tion calls its war room, a 2,500-square-foot space in downtown
> Washington with 40 computers and 75 phone lines. At seven regional
> offices across the country—in California, Florida, Illinois, New York,

and Texas—staff members were rounding up supporters to bombard the Senate and White House with e-mail messages . . . .[14]

PFAW's agenda and structure is the shine and chrome of the opposition's attack on the Bush nominees. But the engine that drives the opposition is the issue of abortion. NARAL (National Abortion and Reproductive Rights Action League) Pro-Choice America was the first special-interest group out of the gate to launch a heavy advertisement against the nomination of John Roberts to the Supreme Court. But it was such a personal and misleading attack that their own allies asked them to pull the advertisement off the air.

According to the nonpartisan Annenberg Political Fact Check (a project of the Annenberg Public Policy Center of the University of Pennsylvania), NARAL ran "an attack ad accusing Supreme Court nominee John Roberts of filing legal papers 'supporting . . . a convicted clinic bomber' and of having an ideology that 'leads him to excuse violence against other Americans' It shows images of a bombed clinic in Birmingham, Alabama. The ad is false."[15]

NARAL's misleading and false attack brought criticism from other liberal groups. Fact Check quotes the president of Catholics for a Free Choice, who said "she was 'deeply upset and offended' by the ad and said it 'does step over the line into the kind of personal character attack we shouldn't be engaging in.' As quoted in the *New York Times*, she said: 'As a pro-choice person, I don't like being placed on the defensive by my leaders. NARAL should pull it and move on.'"[16]

Fact Check then cites the news conference announcing the ad where NARAL president Nancy Keenan comments on the message: "I want to be very clear that we are not suggesting that Mr. Roberts condones or supports clinic violence. I know he said he finds bombing and murder abhorrent." The nonprofit media research concludes, "Yet her ad conveys the opposite, showing pictures of a bombed clinic and a bombing victim while saying that Roberts supported a clinic bomber and violent fringe groups and that he excuses violence . . . . The message contained in the juxtaposition of words and powerful images is that

Roberts condoned the mayhem being shown on screen, which even Ms. Keenan has stated is untrue."[17]

NARAL's actions were those of a powerful special-interest group unused to criticism but familiar with questionable tactics. This is not an isolated incident; this is NARAL's modus operandi. NARAL came into prominence disseminating false information that it created out of thin air. Dr. Bernard Nathanson was co-founder of NARAL, but now as an active member of the pro-life community he opposes the organization and its pro-abortion position. His personal account of the NARAL's beginning reveals a history of outright fabrication of facts regarding abortion in the name of achieving a desired goal—making abortion legal and available:

> We persuaded the media that the cause of permissive abortion was a liberal, enlightened, sophisticated one. Knowing that if a true poll were taken, we would be soundly defeated, we simply fabricated the results of fictional polls. We announced to the media that we had taken polls and that 60 percent of Americans were in favor of permissive abortion . . . . We aroused enough sympathy to sell our program of permissive abortion by fabricating the number of illegal abortions done annually in the U.S. The actual figure was approaching 100,000, but the figure we gave to the media repeatedly was 1,000,000 . . . The number of women dying from illegal abortions was around 200-250 annually. The figure we constantly fed to the media was 10,000. These false figures took root in the consciousness of Americans, convincing many that we needed to crack the abortion law . . . . In two years of work, we at NARAL struck that law down. We lobbied the legislature, we captured the media, we spent money on public relations.[18]

Today the organization bills itself "as the political and grassroots arm of the pro-choice movement . . . mobilizing millions of pro-choice supporters to achieve these goals." NARAL is active at home and abroad both in the culture war and through direct political involvement.

In New York in 1998, NARAL's New York branch "conducted a highly visible and effective campaign to educate voters on the difference between . . . [Republican] Al D'Amato and pro-choice candidate Chuck

Schumer." Schumer is now one of the most loyal spokesmen for the abortion industry and NARAL in Washington D.C. Schumer helped lead the attack on me and other nominees. "I am proud to have served as a partner of NARAL/NY throughout my career in public service," Schumer says on the NARAL/NY website.[19] Hillary Rodham Clinton, the junior United States senator from New York, states that "NARAL-NY is an inspired and effective leader—the organization has influenced battles for choice throughout the country."[20]

NARAL knows the importance to the abortion industry of electing and maintaining senators like these. In 2003, their ally Planned Parenthood received $254.4 million in taxpayer money, with an additional $228.1 million from corporations, foundations, and other donors. "In its 2002–2003 annual report, Planned Parenthood reported a hefty operating gain of $36.6 million. At a time when companies are struggling to remain profitable, Planned Parenthood reported a 200 percent increase over the previous year's $12.2 million gain."[21]

During the 2004 Election Cycle, NARAL Pro-Choice America spent $3,038,145. EMILY's List, another ally in the abortion wing of the Democratic Party, spent $34,175,207 on political action during the 2004 cycle.[22]

While promoting abortion as a major platform, the National Organization for Women (NOW) also makes the issue of special rights for homosexuals a significant plank in their opposition to conservative nominees to the judiciary. It claims to be "the largest organization of feminist activists in the United States. NOW has 500,000 contributing members and 550 chapters in all 50 states and the District of Columbia."[23]

Started in 1966, NOW seeks to "secure abortion, birth control, and reproductive rights for all women" as well as to "eradicate racism, sexism, and homophobia." The NOW website prominently advertises Planned Parenthood, the National Abortion Federation, and Ann Rose's Abortion Clinics Online as good places to "find a list of abortion providers." Although NOW says it is "a non-partisan organization" and that "candidates of all political parties are eligible for endorsement by . . . NOW Political Action Committee," in reality it endorses almost exclusively Far Left Democrats. Any person who supports pro-life measures need not apply for NOW PAC money.

By 1971, NOW was linking the fiftieth anniversary of women's suffrage with the "oppression of lesbians as a legitimate concern of feminism."[24] The NOW website boasts "supporting lesbian and gay rights."[25]

Gandy and NOW also push for special rights for transgender people. "As NOW strengthens its alliance with the transgender community, we encourage all feminists and progressives to take a stand on this important issue," states the NOW website. NOW describes the groups they consider to be "transgender" and worthy of their support and special rights:

> Transsexuals are people who change their gender roles and sometimes their bodies in order to live as members of another sex. This process may include surgery, electrolysis, or synthesized sex hormones. Crossdressers wear the clothing of another sex on occasion, but do not desire to change their bodies. Other groups of people who feel that they do not fit into a rigid gender system may identify as Genderqueers, Androgynes, Gender Blenders, or Gender Benders. These people may feel that they are both male and female or that their gender identity falls outside the system all together.[26]

NOW considers President Bush's judicial nominees extreme and outside the mainstream of America.

NOW and the Alliance for Justice hope activist judges will create special rights for these groups.[27] The Alliance for Justice originated in 1979 from the Council for Public Interest Law (CPIL). The alliance had seven staffers in 1995; it grew to forty-two budgeted workers in 2001 and now occupies a "custom-designed office with 13,000 square feet, which will permit the organization to grow through 2011."[28]

The Alliance for Justice's president, Nan Aron, founded the alliance's Judicial Selection Project in 1985 to counter Ronald Reagan's conservative judicial appointments. They claim their "first big victory came in 1987, with the retirement of Supreme Court Justice Lewis Powell, and Reagan's nomination of ultra-conservative D.C. Circuit

Judge Robert Bork to fill the vacancy. . . . The Alliance for Justice helped coordinate the campaign to defeat Bork, with civil rights, women's rights, and a variety of other liberal groups."[29]

In 1991 the alliance opposed Clarence Thomas and suggests their work has increased the scrutiny nominees receive:

> Since the Thomas confirmation battle, there has been much commentary from senators, professors, and the public interest community about the need to question judicial nominees more rigorously and to insist on clear responses to critical questions. The Judicial Selection Project has continued to work with progressive senators to set standards for federal judges and promote the appointment of judges who will protect our basic rights.[30]

When Bill Clinton was president, the alliance shifted gears, working for what it deemed to be "deserving nominees, including Richard Paez and Marsha Berzon."[31] But today the alliance is again in attack mode. In 2003 alone, it raised $4,920,601 to wage its Far Left attacks.[32] The group states that "with George W. Bush's assumption of the presidency, the Project has turned to working with the Senate to ensure that only fair judges with a record of respect for precedent and a commitment to upholding basic rights are confirmed."[33] The basic rights they talk about protecting are far different than what the majority of Americans consider as basic rights. They are not talking about judges who respect America's historical religious precedents.

Aron has condemned the work of Supreme Court justice Antonin Scalia as "out of the mainstream" for "his views on originalism, abortion, school prayer, and federalism."[34] Scalia takes traditional and long-held positions on those issues. Aron also described judicial nominees Janice Rogers Brown, Priscilla Owens, and William Pryor as "extreme," though they were all eventually confirmed with bipartisan support from the United States Senate. Aron said Brown has a record of "hostility" to civil rights, that Owen is "a hard-right activist," and of Pryor that "the administration may have broken the records for right-wing extremism previously set by some of its nominees. With Pryor's record, there is something to offend virtually every constituency in the county."[35] If these judges had been out of the mainstream they would not have received bipartisan support for confirmation.

Cultural warriors like Ralph Neas of People for the American Way, the abortion lobby, feminists, Nan Aron from the Alliance for Justice, and other left wing organizations forced Democratic senators into obstruction during the judicial confirmation fight. If a senator had a pang of conscience and considered backing away from the extreme wing of the party, these groups kept them in line and made it politically impossible to take an individual stand. Empowered by the support of grassroots secularists and Democratic senators, these special-interest groups were willing to go beyond qualifications and judicial temperament and challenge nominees on something very personal: their faith.

CHAPTER SIX

Attack on Faith

WHEN I WAS growing up in the 1950s, Billy Graham conducted crusades all over America. Tens of thousands of people gathered at football stadiums or other public arenas to hear him preach. In 1952, he held his first integrated crusade in Jackson, Mississippi, at Newell Field, where he personally pulled down the ropes that separated the black and white sections and showed the power the gospel of Jesus Christ possesses to break down racial barriers. From that moment on, all of his crusades in all parts of the country were integrated.

In the 1950s, no one questioned the importance of religion to America and Americans; it was accepted fact. Living in America, I had a difficult time comprehending the passages from the Bible indicating the proclamation of the gospel and teaching of the Bible would be considered "foolishness." I never thought Christians in America would be criticized and condemned for their beliefs, considering how important religion has always been to our nation.

Historically, I knew governments struggled with Christianity since the beginning of the church. The state has persecuted Christians in many parts of the world and still does in unfree lands. Our country's first European settlers came to America to escape religious persecution and to worship as they saw fit. It never occurred to me that during my lifetime, those in America who consider themselves "wise" would boldly declare that the preaching of the gospel is "foolishness." Neither did I anticipate living in a time when Christians would be told they should not express their convictions in the political arena. But that time has arrived.

Far Left secularist groups organize and orchestrate an attempt to remove the mention of God from the public square, from the public arena. According to Emmy-winning news reporter Bernard Goldberg, many in the national media find this perfectly reasonable. Lacking respect for traditional religious views—which they consider outdated—they are frequently accomplices in the secular movement.

In April 2005, Senator Bill Frist of Tennessee agreed to participate in a Sunday night simulcast at a church in Louisville, Kentucky, to promote the confirmation of judges. There was a steady drumbeat from secularist groups and from Democratic senators condemning Frist's participation.

> As the debate heated up in April over ending Democrats' use of the filibuster to block votes on judicial nominees, the secular left worked itself into a frenzy when religious leaders organized a multi-church telecast to focus attention on the fact that the president's blocked appellate court nominees all happened to be "people of faith." Their indignation focused principally on Senate Majority Leader Bill Frist's apparent endorsement of this neuralgic observation. Liberal editorialists, organizations and senators tried to get Mr. Frist to pull out of the event, but he stood his ground.[1]

Is it permissible for Democratic presidential candidates John Kerry, Al Gore, and Bill Clinton to campaign in African-American churches, but not appropriate for conservative Christians to become involved in the political process? It is either wrong for both or right for both. One cannot argue that Christians involved in liberal politics may bring politics to church, but Christians involved in conservative politics may not. That is rank hypocrisy; it is a double standard.

The church as an institution should be careful involving itself in politics; that is not its primary role. I am a member at First Baptist Church of Laurel, which is not political, and I agree with that posture. But such decisions are matters for each church to decide.

The Constitution grants specific protections for religious organizations, and a historic perspective reveals churches have always been understood to be a cornerstone of a community, sometimes including political activism. During our War of Independence, church buildings were used for debates and even military recruitment. Following the Revolution, church buildings housed debates on the nature of the Constitution. As our Constitution was being debated at the Constitutional Convention, the Bible was the source most frequently quoted, accounting for one-third of all quotes.[2] Following ratification of the Constitution, the church continued an active role in politics with many early sermons directed specifically at the actions of elected leaders: praising or condemning both policies and individuals.

Henry Wadsworth Longfellow recounts in his famous poem "The Midnight Ride of Paul Revere":

> If the British march
> By land or sea from the town to-night,
> Hang a lantern aloft in the belfry arch
> Of the North Church tower as a signal light,—
> One if by land, and two if by sea;
> And I on the opposite shore will be,
> Ready to ride and spread the alarm
> Through every Middlesex village and farm,
> For the country folk to be up and to arm.

No one, except perhaps the British of that day, complains of the role this church building had in the birth of our country. And where did Patrick Henry make his immortal quote "Give me liberty or give me death!"? He made this statement at St. John's Church in Richmond, Virginia.[3] Not a word was heard about separation of church and state. No Americans told Patrick Henry that if he chose liberty, he would have to do it somewhere else. Religion was the cornerstone of life during those revolutionary times, to suggest religious liberty was not a motivation of our Founding Fathers is to ignore the reality of that culture, that time, and our history.

Today, some of the issues in the political debate involve the historical teachings of the church and even the church itself. Certainly if the church can play a role in the politics of our nation, it can defend itself and its role and its teaching in the political arena. And why shouldn't it? Certainly, individual Christians should be involved in politics. Political involvement is a civic responsibility of all Americans—including Christians. Christians possess the same constitutional rights to freedom of speech, freedom of association, freedom of religion, and freedom to petition their government as any other citizen.

What about the antithesis to Christianity, secularism? Is it permissible for secularists to participate in government and politics and not Christians? Those who claim that Christians should sit on the sidelines and be quiet, while secularists are heavily involved in political debate, are arguing for Americans to hear only one side of the debate. They want one side of the debate silenced. The American tradition of the vigorous exchange of ideas embraces various viewpoints. Right or wrong, the democratic process allows all sides to make their own case before the American public. To silence one side of the debate, to prevent one perspective from participating, stands against not only the Constitution, but the entire American experience.

I firmly believe in separation of church and state. Every time in history when government became involved in the church—when the two became intertwined—the consequences were disastrous for the church. For the first one hundred and fifty years of the history of our nation, we had separation of church and state as understood by the Founding Fathers. Congress established no church and favored no church. But references to God permeated public and private life, and this was not perceived to violate separation of church and state.

The constitutional prohibition against an "establishment of religion"—separation of church and state—applies only to the government, not to people who are religious and not even to churches. There is no constitutional prohibition or restriction against religious people or organizations, including churches, from being involved in the political process. In fact, through the right to petition, free speech, and the right to free exercise of religion, everyone, including Christians, has a constitutional right to affect government. The constitutional provision requiring a separation of church and state is not a roadblock for the church but a one-way street against the state. Religious people and institutions can participate in the state, but the state cannot establish or favor a particular church or denomination.

The contention that Christians should not be involved in political matters ignores both the Constitution and historical tradition. America's rich heritage of Christian participation in government and politics has been a positive and constructive force not only for the state but also for individuals and humanitarian causes.

In 1984, Democratic New York governor Mario Cuomo gave a speech at the University of Notre Dame in which he discussed the role of religion and politics.

> The same amendment of the Constitution that forbids the establishment of a State Church affirms my legal right to argue that my religious belief would serve well as an article of our universal public morality. I may use the prescribed processes of government—the legislative and executive and judicial processes—to convince my fellow citizens—Jews and Protestants and Buddhists and non-believers—that what I propose is as beneficial for them as I believe it is for me; that it is not just parochial or narrowly sectarian but fulfills a human desire for order, peace, justice, kindness, love, any of the values most of us agree are desirable even apart from their specific religious base or context. And surely, I can, if so inclined, demand some kind of law against abortion not because my Bishops say it is wrong but because I think that the whole community, regardless of its religious beliefs, should agree on the importance of protecting life—including life in the womb, which is at the very least potentially human and should not be extinguished casually. No law prevents us from advocating any of these things: I am free to do so. So are the Bishops. And so is Reverend Falwell.[4]

One editorial writer wrote, "Cuomo's position then seems at odds with the prevailing liberal position today, which is that religiously informed arguments are essentially illegitimate, at least when they lead to conservative conclusions."[5]

William Wilberforce's Christian convictions caused him to lead the movement in England to abolish slavery and the slave trade. It was Christian morality and thought that motivated the abolitionist movement in America. Christian morality and motivation drove the civil rights movement. The Reverend Dr. Martin Luther King Jr., a

Baptist preacher, found inspiration for his campaign for equal rights from his Christian beliefs and launched that movement in African-American churches.

The biblical teaching of compassion and love for one's fellowman motivated William Booth to found the Salvation Army. Christian love and compassion motivated Millard and Linda Fuller to found Habitat for Humanity. Christian love and compassion motivated Chuck Colson to found Prison Fellowship. More recently, when government failed in the aftermath of Hurricane Katrina, it was churches by the hundreds and thousands who expressed their Christian love and compassion by cutting through the red tape and delivering truckload after truckload of aid and assistance to Louisiana, Mississippi, and Alabama.

Let me make it abundantly clear that many of the judges who were confirmed without filibuster were men and women of faith. Not every nominee of faith was opposed. But if a nominee had openly spoken of his or her faith, and if the liberal special-interest groups perceived the personal religious conviction of a nominee differed from their left wing position on abortion, pornography, and other "new rights" issues, then the groups opposed that nominee. If they thought they could get by with it, they filibustered that nominee. Abortion was the primary issue that caused nominees to be opposed and filibustered because of their faith.

In fall 2001, before the special-interest groups announced opposition to my nomination, a fellow judge told me he heard from someone with Washington contacts that my nomination would be resisted. He said, "You know they're going to oppose you, don't you? They think you are too religious." I dismissed this conversation as idle chatter, but his contact was right. Below the radar screen there was talk of opposing my nomination, and it centered on my faith.

On January 24, 2002, one week before Senator Patrick Leahy scheduled a second hearing for my nomination, the special-interest groups opposing my nomination held a press conference setting out their opposition. The groups released separate reports, but the crux of the opposition was contained in a twenty-four-page report released by People for the American Way. The PFAW report was the bible for the Democratic senator's interrogation of me.

The Far Left groups wanted to build a case that I had used my position as a judge to sentence defendants to attend church. They called the National Association of Criminal Defense Lawyers (NACDL) to find the evidence of this charge. But they found none because none existed. I never sentenced any defendant to church, though exposure to teachings of the church might have benefited some of those who came before me. Sentencing criminal defendants to church is neither constitutional nor biblical. Accepting or rejecting a belief in God can only come from a free and voluntary decision by each individual. Salvation cannot be coerced. The NACDL representative called its Mississippi members and found no opposition, only support.

The religious charge the groups hoped to oppose me with did not exist, but they didn't let the facts get in their way. People for the American Way devoted four pages of their report alleging I promoted religion from the bench. But their first criticism had nothing to do with my judicial duties. It involved a statement I made as president of the Mississippi Baptist Convention to Mississippi Baptists in the 1980s. I delivered the address six years before my unanimous confirmation to the federal district court bench.

In that speech, I told Mississippi Baptists that the Bible is "the absolute authority by which all conduct of man is judged." I challenged Mississippi Baptists to live according to the teachings of the Bible. People for the American Way attacked me not for an action or even my words as a judge, but as a private citizen and a lay leader of a religious organization supporting one of the most basic tenants of Christianity: the authority of Scripture.

Roger Clegg, vice president and general counsel of the Center for Equal Opportunity, wrote a law journal article detailing the People for the American Way's attack on my religious views. Clegg wrote,

> PFAW apparently considers [the above quote made to Mississippi Baptists] a damning quote . . . . But there are millions of Americans who believe that; indeed, those who believe the Bible is scripture could hardly believe otherwise. (Would someone begin a sentence by saying, "According to God—and I agree with Him on this . . ."). For Pickering's statement to be troublesome, then, surely it appeared in one

of his judicial opinions, or at least in a speech delivered at a judicial conference, right? Well, no: the quote is from a speech Judge Pickering gave eighteen years ago to the Mississippi Baptist Convention when he was its president. If, as H. L. Mencken declared, Puritanism is the fear that someone, somewhere is happy, then surely the PFAW report betrays its own fear, that someone, somewhere believes in God.[6]

Republican senator Mitch McConnell of Kentucky, speaking at my confirmation hearing, said, "Frankly, as a Southern Baptist myself, I don't know what else you would say at an annual meeting of the Southern Baptist Convention, particularly when you are the president. Given that you were speaking on a purely theological matter, in your personal, private capacity. I thought the only thing disturbing about this was that people would seek to hold it against you."[7]

Next, PFAW criticized me for quoting Scripture in an opinion. It is true that I did quote a passage from Exodus in an opinion, but this seems an absurd criticism. The book of Exodus has been cited fifteen times in Supreme Court decisions.[8] Liberal justices Earl Warren, Thurgood Marshall, and William Brennan quoted passages from the Old Testament.[9] Considering I was a district judge required to follow Supreme Court precedent, it hardly seems a just criticism that I did as the Supreme Court has done on a number of occasions.

The case in which I quoted from Exodus involved a brutal double murder during a 1982 robbery of a convenience store for the sake of $560. An elderly man was killed simply because he made the mistake of driving up right after the robbery took place. Seventeen years later, there was a petition for habeas corpus before me in which the defendant did not allege that coercion, duress, or threat caused his confession, rather he complained that there was a three-day delay between his arrest and initial appearance before a magistrate. He claimed that because of this three-day delay, his confession was involuntary, and he wanted to be released from the penitentiary, or require the state to retry him with his confession excluded. I wrote, "judges and legal scholars throughout the ages have warned against what we are now doing [re-examining legal issues that have no relationship to guilt or innocence fifteen to twenty years later]. One of the oldest recorded codes of laws provides: 'The innocent and the just you shall not put to death, nor shall you acquit the guilty'" (Exodus 23:7).

Clegg wrote,

> The book of Exodus is, indeed, one of the oldest extant legal texts of Western civilization, and is widely cited not only by Mississippi Baptists but by all Christians, Jews, and Moslems. In any event, PFAW may not like the fact that our legal system has deep roots in these Middle Eastern religious beliefs, but it is a fact nonetheless. It is hard to see how Judge Pickering could have made the valid point he wanted to make without citing an ancient text, and an ancient text would almost necessarily be one with religious as well as jurisprudential significance.[10]

There was nothing unusual or unconstitutional in my citing the Exodus passage. I stand by that statement. It is as appropriate today as it was then. (Subsequently, after I decided this case, Congress passed a statute reforming habeas corpus by putting in place a one year statute of limitations and barring many petitions for habeas corpus.)

PFAW criticized me for responding in kind to comments made by a defendant during sentencing. Pete Halat was the former mayor of Biloxi, Mississippi, and a former law partner of state circuit court judge Vincent Sherry. Judge Sherry and his wife Margaret were murdered gangland style in a story so dramatic that Hollywood is preparing to shoot a movie of the story.

Halat was attorney for Kirksey Nix, who masterminded an infamous homosexual scam operated out of Angola State Penitentiary in Louisiana. Evidence indicated Halat traveled to Angola and advised Kirksey Nix that Judge Sherry had left the firm and carried with him a considerable amount of the scam money. For this reason and others, Judge Sherry was murdered. The government inferred Halat, not Sherry, took the money. Pete Halat was convicted for being a member of a conspiracy to conduct the homosexual scam and a number of other crimes including the murder of the Sherrys.

Before any criminal defendant is sentenced, the presiding judge must offer the defendant an opportunity for allocution—the chance for the defendant to speak before sentence is imposed. During his allocution, Halat advised me that Christianity played an important role in his life: he attended mass, he sponsored Latin masses in the conference room of his office, and he abstained from meat on Fridays as a part of his religious practice. He mentioned his wife served as a Eucharistic minister at their church and his children attended parochial schools. Halat invoked God as his "judge" and mentioned the "final judgment" before the "final arbiter" where the truth will finally be accounted. In response, I told him, "It is not too late for you to form a new beginning. For yourself and others, I hope you will do that. You have a lot to offer. You can become involved in Chuck Colson's prison fellowship or some other such ministry, and be a benefit to your fellow inmates and to others and to their families."[11] I did not coerce or force religion on Mr. Halat in any manner. I responded to his statements about his religious convictions and encouraged him to make a positive contribution in the future in a manner that he suggested his own beliefs advocated.

In responding to PFAW's attack on these comments, Senator McConnell observed,

> Given the proven success of Mr. Colson's prison programs, I don't think that was at all inappropriate. In fact, Democrat Joe Califano, writing in the Washington Monthly in his article "A New Prescription," noted that a study of New York inmates participating in Chuck Colson's Prison Fellowship Program showed that they were less likely to commit infractions while incarcerated and had a much lower rate of recidivism upon release from prison—only 14 percent, compared to 41 percent of those who did not participate in this program. . . . Chuck Colson's Prison Fellowship Program works in conjunction with 1,400 prison chaplains across the country. If merely suggesting this program to an inmate out of concern for the inmate is impermissible, then I guess we should no longer have prison chaplains. I don't know. Maybe that is what this organization prefers.[12]

PFAW criticized me for remarks at another sentencing as well—that of Mike Gillich, a co-conspirator with Halat, who cooperated with the government and testified against Halat. The government made a motion for reduction of sentence based on his cooperation to "time served." I rejected the government's request; the evidence demonstrated Gillich had lived a life of crime, running illegal operations from his strip club joint on the Mississippi Gulf Coast. But as he had cooperated and the government requested, I did reduce his sentence significantly, though with personal discomfort.

Gillich brought a nun and priest to court to testify on his behalf. In fact, nuns and priests were frequently in attendance over the six weeks of his trial. I told Gillich when he was released from prison and on supervised release, "You will involve yourself in some type of systematic program whereby you will be involved in the study and consideration of effects and consequences of crime and/or appropriate behavior in a civilized society. This may be a program through your church or some other such agency or organization so long as it is approved in advance by the probation service."[13]

Judges frequently require defendants to take rehabilitative efforts while they are on supervised release. Usually this is done through secular organizations. In this instance, I gave Gillich the freedom to choose his church or some other organization; I did not impose his church on him, and this choice in no way violated the Constitution.

The PFAW report further criticized me for my sentencing colloquy involving a young attorney who pled guilty to possession of child pornography. The young lawyer, son of a prominent attorney, had undertaken considerable rehabilitation efforts in advance of sentencing hoping to avoid the penitentiary.

The guideline range for his conviction was eighteen to twenty-four months, but because of his rehabilitative efforts, the defendant and his family wanted me to depart downward and to sentence the defendant to home confinement on supervised release with no jail time. I sentenced the defendant to eighteen months in prison but acknowledged his effort to rehabilitate himself.

The defendant had enrolled in a twelve-step rehabilitation program for addictive behavior. One purpose of the program was to promote the patient's sense of spiritual values. The defendant's father testified to a "dramatic change" in the defendant's "religious attitude" and his "relationship to God." The defense attorney noted a change in the defendant since his indictment, mentioning he is now a person "who has a spiritual foundation" and suggesting the rehabilitation program had given him a "renewed sense of spirituality." I received many letters on his behalf indicating his "spiritual growth."

In response to defendant's representations of what had been going on in his life, I suggested to him, "There are many areas of service and ministry that you can engage in in the penitentiary." Again, I forced religion on no one. I suggested that if this was a growing area of focus in his life as he claimed, there were ways to continue that growth if he chose them. Can you imagine an organization so hostile to religion that it considers an encouragement "to service and ministry" as an "establishment of religion"? They consider such benign comments are somehow a violation of the Constitution.

PFAW continued their criticisms. In another case, on motion of the government for his cooperation in other cases, I reduced an African-American defendant's sentence from life to ten years—a quantum reduction. During the course of the hearing, his attorney stated, "His heart is filled with religious convictions . . . his . . . greatest concern is that God be involved in his life." On his own behalf, the defendant made numerous professions of his religious faith, quoted Scripture, and related a conversion experience. He told me he wanted to become a role model in the community as someone who had recently been converted. When it came time for me to reduce his sentence, I reflected back on the history of the case and the history of the defendant's life and the comments both he and his attorney had made in open court about him becoming a Christian. He was a young man who had exchanged legitimate opportunities for drug dealing, and I told him I viewed his case as a real "tragedy." I remarked, "What a waste when there is such a great need for role models, for Christian examples." PFAW criticized me for responding to the representations made by defendant and encouraging him in the new life he told me he had chosen.

Clegg summarized the accusations:

The PFAW report concludes from these snippets that Judge Pickering is a dangerous theocrat. This is absurd. Taken in context, it is clear that this judge (who, incidentally, PFAW elsewhere suggests is insensitive and uncaring about prisoners) believes any individual—even a killer, pornographer, or drug trafficker—can reclaim his life. Apparently PFAW would prefer a judge withhold from such an individual any suggestion that this redemption might have a moral or religious element to it. In refusing to do so, Judge Pickering was establishing no religion. Instead, he was showing far greater compassion, and saving far more lives, than the People for the American Way ever will.[14]

Senator McConnell concluded,

> So, Judge Pickering, I find these accusations against you that are based upon your religious activities in your private life, or de minimis religious comments in your public life such as the one just referred to, to be troubling, not because of anything you did, but because they evidence a hostility toward religion by your accusers . . . . but I wanted to address those accusations myself because I found them really quite incredulous and completely inappropriate in the context of what we are considering today.[15]

So much do they stand opposed to faith that People for the American Way would rather criminal defendants never be rehabilitated than to be exposed to religion in any manner, way, form, or fashion—even when they simply exercise their own constitutional right to pursue it. Our Constitution guarantees freedom of religion, not freedom from religion. In none of the instances did I coerce religion, nor does my own faith even permit such action. In order to manufacture criticism, PFAW dishonestly took these incidents out of context and failed to present the facts of each occasion to show my words were in response to what the defendants had said or done. That I was concerned about the lives of the defendants and responsive to them was not the story they wanted to tell—or rather—the fiction they wanted to write.

Shortly after NARAL and PFAW and these other groups announced their opposition, a Mississippi newspaper editorialized: "Are Baptists not Qualified to Serve?" They wrote,

> NARAL seems to suggest that a Southern Baptist—simply by virtue of his or her personal religious faith—is somehow disqualified from serving on the federal bench. That suggestion is nothing short of religious bigotry. . . . Pickering's opposition comes from special inter-est groups who don't know him and who haven't to date produced a single judicial opinion from him that supports their accusations of racism or religious activism. If such decisions exist, where are they? . . . Despite withering attacks on his personal religious beliefs by special interest groups, U. S. District Judge Charles Pickering's record of fairness, compassion and racial equality remains unsullied.[16]

My nomination was far from the only one opposed by PFAW and its allies on the basis of religion. That liberal special-interest groups targeted, and some Democratic senators opposed, selected nominees because of religious convictions is clearly demonstrated and documented in the fights over the nominations of William Pryor to the Eleventh Circuit Court of Appeals and J. Leon Holmes to a district court in Arkansas.

As attorney general of Alabama, William Pryor was one of the most outspoken public officials I have ever followed or read about. He labeled abortion as an abomination, as the murder of thousands of innocent lives. He strongly criticized *Roe v. Wade* and the judges who rendered the decision. Yet Pryor has one of the best records of any public official for putting aside his personal and religious convictions and beliefs and following the rule of law. He instructed Alabama public officials to strictly follow Supreme Court decisions on abortion—decisions with which he strongly disagreed—and he did the same in regard to a Ten Commandments case. William Pryor consistently demonstrated his ability to follow the rule of law regardless of his personal and religious convictions.

Pryor had strong support from Democrats in Alabama. He was praised by a broad range of Alabama African-American leaders for his record of fighting for civil rights and equal treatment under the law for all. He has a record of advocating the creation of laws to protect women from domestic violence, and has helped to create innovative new women's assistance programs. Yet, when Pryor was nominated to the federal bench, he was attacked by left wing special-interest groups as being insensitive to the rights of women and a danger to civil rights including the voting rights of African Americans.

Democratic legislator Alvin Holmes stated,

> I am a black member of the Alabama House of Representatives having served for twenty-eight years. During my time of service in the Alabama House of Representatives I have led most of the fights for civil rights of blacks, women, lesbians and gays and other minorities . . . . [A]s one of the key civil rights leaders in Alabama who has participated in basically every major civil rights demonstration in America, who has been arrested for civil rights causes on many occasions, as one who was a field staff member of Dr. Martin Luther King's SCLC, as one who has been brutally beaten by vicious police officers for participating in civil rights marches and demonstrations, as one who has had crosses burned in his front yard by the KKK and other hate groups . . . I request your swift confirmation of Bill Pryor to the Eleventh Circuit because of his constant efforts to help the cause of blacks in Alabama.[17]

Dr. Joe Reed, chairman of the Alabama Democratic Conference and a member of the Democratic National Committee, called Pryor a "first-class public official" who "will be a credit to the judiciary and will be a guardian for justice." Democrat Don Siegleman, who served as governor of Alabama for much of Pryor's tenure as attorney general, stated, "Bill Pryor is an incredibly talented, intellectually honest attorney general."

The Democrats in Alabama who actually knew William Pryor could not overcome the Washington abortion lobby. Democratic senators followed these national liberal groups and turned a deaf ear to Democrats and African Americans in Alabama. The left wing groups distorted Pryor's record and fought him to the end.

Democratic senator Russ Feingold of Wisconsin questioned Pryor about a couple of positions he had taken in court as attorney general of

Alabama and as an associate attorney general of Alabama; one of these turned out to be diametrically opposite the position Pryor had actually taken. But the exchange attracting the most attention involved not an action Pryor committed as a public servant, but rather the personal decision he and his wife made regarding a family vacation to Disney World. Senator Feingold said, "News accounts also report that you even went so far as to reschedule a family vacation at Disney World in order to avoid Gay Day." He then asked, "In light of this record, can you understand why a gay plaintiff or defendant would feel uncomfortable coming before you as a judge?" Pryor responded, "I think my record as attorney general shows that I will uphold and enforce the law. . . . As far as my family vacation is concerned, my wife and I have two daughters who at the time of that vacation were six and four, and we made a value judgment, and that was our personal decision." Feingold repeated, "But are you saying that you actually made that decision on purpose to be away at the time . . . ." Pryor said clearly, "We made a value judgment and changed our plan and went another weekend."[18]

Feingold implied a Christian who questions homosexuality cannot be a fair judge for a gay person. One would wonder if Feingold would also hold that a homosexual judge would not be fair to a Christian. Here is another example of criticisms against a nominee not for official actions as a public servant, but for private and personal faith choices. Feingold was at best insensitive to and at worst intolerant of Christianity. Whether the nominee is homosexual or a Christian who disagrees with homosexuality should not be at issue; the question should be whether a judge follows the rule of law. Bill Pryor's record clearly proves he has, and he does.

The day before the Senate confirmed William Pryor to the Eleventh Circuit Court of Appeals, the National Organization for Women (NOW) proclaimed, "The elevation of William Pryor, Jr., to the U.S. Court of Appeals is a slap in the face to women, people of color, people with disabilities, the lesbian, gay, bi-sexual, and transgender community and anyone who believes in the separation of church and state."[19]

The Committee for Justice issued a twenty-six page document titled "Bill Pryor: A Public Official Dedicated to Following the Law." That report states, "To suggest that General Pryor is unfit for judicial office because of his religious convictions threatens to violate the Constitution's Religious Test Clause which specifically forbids disqualifying candidates for office on the ground of their religious convictions."

A guest editorial in the *Wall Street Journal* noted,

> Today the Senate Judiciary Committee has become a modern-day lion's den with people of faith being savaged for embracing their beliefs. . . . Alabama Attorney General William Pryor, the most recent Daniel to face the hungry lions, has made the "mistake" of not distancing himself from his faith. In a recent confirmation hearing for Mr. Pryor, a nominee to the Eleventh Circuit Court of Appeals, Senator Charles Schumer (D., N.Y.) said plainly that Mr. Pryor's deeply held personal convictions as a pro-life Catholic simply would not be left at the courthouse door. In other words, being a Catholic is just fine if you are Senator Leahy or Senator Kennedy and selectively follow the doctrines of the faith. But if you actually practice Catholic teaching, you need not apply for a federal judgeship. . . . Believers need not apply.[20]

You don't have to agree with someone's views in order to be a fair judge toward that individual or group. A nominee committed to the rule of law can be fair and treat an individual or group with impartiality and respect even while disagreeing. Such was the case when the Log Cabin Republicans, the nation's largest gay and lesbian Republican organization, supported my nomination. They supported me because I had treated homosexuals who came before me fairly. I had protected their rights just as I protected the rights of all Americans who came before me. Their statement of support said,

> This isn't about fairness, because Judge Pickering's record is clearly on the side of fairness. This is not about civil rights, because Judge Pickering has strong support from the African-American community in Mississippi and has a long record of supporting civil rights. . . . The judge who threw out the anti-camp Sister Spirit case and rebuked homophobia from the bench in the Deep South over ten years ago deserves a promotion, not a rebuke . . . .[21]

The opposition based their rejection of the nomination of J. Leon Holmes to a district court position in Arkansas on his religious convictions. Holmes is an orthodox Catholic who once served as president of Arkansas Right to Life. He and his wife once wrote an article discussing Paul's letter to the Ephesians and the relationship of men and women in marriage. To many Americans, Holmes is a man like themselves who lets his faith influence his private life. But to liberal special-interest groups, Holmes was a threat to their agenda. Opinion-editorial pieces and the debate on the Senate floor tell Holmes's story.

An opinion piece titled "The Constitution Be Damned— Democrats Try to Impose a Religious Test on Judges" poses a question: "Are Senate Judiciary Committee Democrats trying to establish a religious test for federal judges?" It continues,

> In Mr. Holmes's case the attacks are shocking, for the Democrats are openly targeting his religious convictions. Mr. Holmes's professional qualifications are impressive. . . . Mr. Holmes received a "well qualified" rating from the American Bar Association, and both Democratic Arkansas senators—Blanche Lincoln and Mark Pryor—support his nomination. . . . The lightning rod here, of course, is abortion. It's no secret that the pope and the Catholic Church are squarely against abortion on demand. Abortion gives the Democrats some of their most fanatical supporters. So Sens. Schumer, Dianne Feinstein, and Dick Durbin feel safe in demonizing Mr. Holmes. . . . Sens. Schumer, Feinstein, Durbin, and others, in their zeal over abortion, are now attempting to screen out judicial candidates who take their faith seriously. Judiciary Democrats may not like Catholic doctrine, but to hold religious convictions against a nominee is a blatant violation of the Constitution.[22]

Republican senator Rick Santorum of Pennsylvania eloquently addressed the paramount issue in the debate over the confirmation of Judge Holmes:

> . . . an article he wrote with his wife for his diocese, for his church, the Roman Catholic Church in Arkansas. It was an article about a particular passage in one of Paul's letters discussing marriage and the role of

husbands and wives. . . . What he gave was the orthodox Catholic interpretation of those sections of the Bible. . . . It is an interpretation that has been around for a couple of thousand years. If you say . . . you are disqualified for writing an article for your church—you cannot be a Federal judge. I find that to be rather chilling. . . . Because of his Catholic faith, because he holds these beliefs that the Catholic Church teaches, he cannot be a Federal judge. Is that what freedom of religion means in our Constitution? Is that what the term "free exercise of religion" means in our Constitution—that we are going to eliminate anybody who is nominated for a Federal judgeship who actually exercises their religious beliefs and states them for his own church, and that now disqualifies them? . . . We had letters signed by people on both sides of the aisle in large numbers encouraging religious pluralism in Iraq, that we now say religious pluralism doesn't necessarily apply here anymore in the Senate. . . . This is a big vote . . . . This is a vote about religious freedom. This is a vote about the free exercise of religion, and this is a vote about tolerance. . . . Where is the tolerance of people who want to believe what has been taught for 2,000 years as truth? You have a right to disagree with that teaching. You have a right to adapt your contemporary mores to that teaching. But where is the tolerance of people who choose to keep the faith? . . . We will have a vote on Judge Leon Holmes, but it will be a bigger vote than just on that judge. It will be a vote on the soul of the free exercise of religion clause and of tolerance to religion.[23]

Republican senator Orrin Hatch of Utah—a committed Mormon—summed it up this way:

A fair reading of the article would show support for the equality of women. I have read it a number of times. And by the way, if it comes down to a choice between St. Paul and my distinguished friend from Massachusetts, Senator Kennedy, or my distinguished friend from Illinois, Senator Durbin, I think I will take St. Paul every time, and I think most everybody else in the country would, too. He and his wife were quoting St. Paul.[24]

Alabama senator Jeff Sessions, another Republican, correctly pointed out,

> The question is, Will that person follow the law? . . . That is the classical test we have always had. . . . We have Members . . . in this body who say we just ought to consider ideology, we just ought to consider their politics. . . . But I say to you that is a dangerous philosophy because it suggests that judges are politicians, that judges are people who are empowered to make political decisions; therefore, we ought to elect judges who agree with our politics.[25]

Manuel Miranda, who formerly served Majority Leader Bill Frist as chief aide for judiciary matters, summarized the discrimination against people of faith:

> Throughout the controversy last spring, journalists, especially, seemed to disbelieve the charge that Democrats—of all people—could discriminate against, well, against anyone. But the proof, to anyone paying attention these past three years, was overwhelming. First there was the circumstantial evidence; filibustered circuit court nominees included Charles Pickering, a former president of the Mississippi Southern Baptist Convention; Priscilla Owen and Henry Saad, who sang in their church choirs; Carolyn Kuhl, who organized adult baptism classes; and William Pryor, a papal knight. There were also the smoking guns: Opponents mocked Judge Pickering because he was "too pious" and noted that Justice Owen too showed "piety." They noted that Judge Pickering quoted from the Bible and the Code of Jewish Law and rebuked him for advising convicted juveniles to seek out prison ministries (programs with proven success in reducing the number of repeat offenders). Democrats savaged the reputation of Arkansas's Leon Holmes, a devout Catholic nominated as a trial judge. Sens. Diane Feinstein of California, Charles Schumer of New York and Richard Durbin of Illinois showed invidious ignorance in mocking Arkansas's finest appellate lawyer for an article he and his wife had published in a Catholic newspaper, in which the couple explained St. Paul's letter to the Ephesians on Christian marriage. "They don't have a problem with Holmes," Senator Orrin Hatch

observed. "They have a problem with St. Paul." And then came the Judiciary Committee hearing for William Pryor in June 2003. As if they had all received the same memo, senator after senator expressed his concern over Mr. Pryor's "deeply held beliefs." Behind the dais, Democratic staffers circulated a printout on the pro-life advocacy of the Catholic Knights of Columbus, as if it was damning proof of those erstwhile deep convictions. In fact, Judge Pryor is a knight of the Holy Sepulcher. But to Democrats that day, all Catholic knights looked alike. . . . The religious right wins whenever it can get the secular left to utter the word "religion," because it is invariably preceded or followed by something condescending, untruthful or offensive.[26]

Christians throughout American history have been welcome to participate in government and politics. Only after *Roe v. Wade* and following the secularist attempt to rewrite religious history, redefine marriage, and change the Pledge of Allegiance were Christians invited to leave the political arena.

I discounted the impact of the vitriolic press conference held by these liberal special-interest groups when they opposed my nomination and attacked me based on my religious convictions. Their allegations and attacks flew in the face of constitutional and historical facts and tradition. Their complaints lacked substance other than a philosophical disagreement with my personal beliefs that would not impact my role as a judge. I dismissed their press conference with confidence the national media would ignore their rhetoric and choose to instead focus on more germane questions of qualification. My faith in God was not misplaced, but my faith in the media was proven wrong.

An institutional bias in the national media establishment aided these special-interest groups as they argued their secularist position. While those in the press who truly investigated my record found the facts were contrary to the presentations of the special-interest groups, the majority of the national press bought into the Washington mischaracterizations.

CHAPTER SEVEN

Media

VOICE OF THE
CONFIRMATION CONFLICT

FEW AMERICANS PERSONALLY know, or personally know anything about, nominees to the federal bench. The information about any nominee likely comes from the news media. The media establishment informs the public—sometimes accurately and sometimes inaccurately. The media establishment shapes public opinion—sometimes using fair analysis and other times blinded by institutional bias. The media establishment broadens the debate over judicial nominees from political players to all interested Americans—sometimes expanding the civic process and other times manipulating the public for a political agenda. For better and worse, the media plays its own role as the voice of the judicial confirmation conflict.

The media is one of the major battlefields where culture warriors wage the confirmation conflict. The media influences, and is influenced by, those engaged in the struggle. The media cannot be—even if it desired to be—apart from the struggle. And institutional bias in the national media prevents a fair playing field.

Newspapers once were Americans' chief news source. Today, 74 percent of Americans mainly consult TV network and cable news, followed by newspapers (44 percent), the Internet (24 percent), radio (22 percent), and magazines (5 percent). Online consumers of news often visit the web pages of traditional media and view the same news in a different medium. Americans still believe the power of the press is increasing rather than decreasing (49 percent-36 percent), but at a lower rate than just two years ago (55 percent-29 percent). But attitudes concerning the performance of the press in areas of fairness, bias and patriotism are at record low levels.[1] There is an old saying: "Fool me once, shame on you; fool me twice, shame on me." Skepticism of the press has increased based on a number of recent high-profile scandals.

Whether it was Dan Rather's false Bush National Guard documents at CBS, Jack Kelley's *USA Today* war reports containing fabrications, or Jayson Blair's concoctions that rocked the leadership at the *New York Times*, the American public sees that sometimes the media gets it wrong and other times the media makes it up.

A media culture forcing reporters to get the story no one else has, or to write the story in a way no one else does, and to post the story before anyone else can, is driving sloppy and inaccurate news reporting. "The more pressure that is put on journalists to produce more, faster, quicker, cheaper, the more industry encourages cutting corners, which is just another way of saying cheating," says University of South Florida media ethics professor Deni Elliott in the *American Journalism Review*.[2] This isn't lost on the public where "most Americans [79 percent] agree that news organizations, when deciding what stories to report, care more about attracting the biggest audience rather than about keeping the public informed [19 percent]."[3]

Scandals have taken a toll on the media's credibility inside and outside the industry. Half of national journalists themselves believe journalism is going in the wrong direction, and 45 percent believe their "news reports are full of factual errors."[4] The 2005 First Amendment Center/*American Journalism Review* survey finds that 65 percent of Americans agree: "The falsifying or making up of stories in the American news media is a widespread problem."[5] A majority of the general public (53 percent) does not trust what news organizations report.[6]

Unfortunately, the media's mistakes are not merely driven by the greed and prestige of ratings, circulation, and awards. Sometimes the media gets it wrong because of bias, and other times the media gets it wrong because it doesn't know how to get it right.

A recent survey finds 67 percent of Americans disagree that "the news media tries to report the news without bias."[7] That means two-thirds of Americans believe the news media does not even try to avoid bias in reporting. Even among journalists there are concerns about media bias. A study of journalists revealed that 40 percent of news professionals believe the media "too often let their ideological views show in their reporting." Nearly a quarter of journalists don't even believe it is "a bad thing if some news organizations have a 'decidedly ideological point of view' in their news coverage."[8]

This has led to greater mistrust by Americans of the media.

> Six-in-ten see news organizations as politically biased, up from 53 percent two years ago. More than seven-in-ten (72 percent) say news organizations tend to favor one side, rather than treat all sides fairly; that is the largest number ever expressing that view. And by more than three-to-one (73 percent-21 percent), the public feels that news organizations are "often influenced by powerful people and organizations," rather than "pretty independent."[9]

Bias in the media creates at worst manipulative propaganda and at best a misperception of an issue's significance. John Tierney of the *New York Times* explains,

> The problem isn't so much the stories that appear as the ones that no one thinks to do. Journalists naturally tend to pursue questions that interest them. So when you have a press corps that's heavily Democratic . . . they tend to do stories that reflect Democrats' interests. When they see a problem, their instinct is to ask what the government can do to solve it . . . they usually focus on the need for more regulations and bigger budgets, not on whether the government should be doing the job in the first place.[10]

Media types tend to resist this characterization and relish in criticism from both sides of the political spectrum, using those anecdotes as proof they are occupying the middle ground. But research suggests they are not in the middle ground and one side clearly has the advantage on this playing field. Only 7 percent of national journalists describe themselves as conservative; 34 percent admit their liberal ideologies; the remainder claims the "moderate" position. But what is moderate? According to the survey analysis, while 58 percent of Americans believe "it is necessary to believe in God to be a moral person," 91 percent of journalists disagree.[11] The moderate media has a problem with understanding and communicating on issues of faith and religion.

John McCormick, deputy editorial page editor for the *Chicago Tribune,* said, "for many of us in journalism, evangelical America is a parallel and foreign universe."[12] Cal Thomas writes of this disconnect between secularist reporters and a culture of faith during the media confusion over a Baptist, "born-again" president. He said a White House correspondent once claimed "'the only way to understand Carter is to go to Sunday school with him.' . . . I would take the Carter story one step further: the best way to understand at least half of this country's citizens is to go to Sunday school with them. Yet the press has avoided Sunday school like the plague."[13]

Researchers Louis Bolce and Gerald De Maio[14] conducted a statistical analysis of the *New York Times* and the *Washington Post,* revealing a dramatic disparity between religious and secular coverage in politics. Between 1990 and 2000 there were 682 stories and editorials about the Republican Party's "relationship with evangelical and fundamentalist Christians." There were only 43 stories identifying a "secularist outlook with the Democratic party." That is a ratio of 16 to 1. Likewise, while there were just "14 stories that pointed out that the Republican and Democratic parties were split along a traditionalist-secularist divide," there were 392 articles on the gender gap: a ratio of 28 to 1.

Bolce and De Maio found this imbalance extended throughout issues of the culture war from abortion to prayer in schools to gay adoption to judicial nominees to special-interest groups. Christian fundamentalism and a conservative worldview were emphasized on one side, but secularism was not linked to liberalism on the other side. They write,

One explanation involves the difficulties journalists might have in taking notice of an outlook that is so close to their own. Survey research indicates that professionals who work in news organizations, compared to the larger public, are more highly educated and cosmopolitan, much more likely to vote Democratic, appreciably more liberal ideologically and culturally, and less likely to be religious. In their study, the Media Elite, Robert Lichter and his associates found that one of the most distinctive characteristics of the media elite "is its secular outlook." Half of the journalists they surveyed claimed no religion and more than eight of ten never or seldom attended religious services. Taking secularist views for granted, journalists may not see secularism as a distinct ideology or think secularists are definable as a political category.

If most national reporters view secularism as mainstream and religion as extreme, then their news stories will reflect those feelings. This is not malicious, but simply a failure to put themselves, their personal views, and their own reporting into proper context. But it does—whether through intentional bias or lack of perspective—tip the balance of the playing field toward one side of the culture war.

Bolce and De Maio note,

> a majority of television news directors and newspaper editors polled in the survey felt that evangelical and fundamentalist Christians had "too much power and influence" and a third thought both religious groups were a "threat to democracy." In contrast, not one of the media elites sampled in this survey perceived secularists as threats, and only 4 percent thought nonbelievers and secularists had too much influence over public life. From such a perspective, political activism by religious conservatives no doubt appears to endanger the wall of separation between church and state, and therefore warrants intense scrutiny.

This, they continue, is why, "Beginning in 1992, 'Religious Right' became a category for election-night analysis, along with such staples as gender, income, race, region, and age. What viewers do not hear about is the secularist vote, which has gone two to one in the Democratic direction in the past three presidential elections."

Former CBS news correspondent Bernard Goldberg lived and worked nearly thirty years among those he calls the "media elite." He agrees that they simply think secularism is the norm and those with a traditional religious faith are not. According to Goldberg's bestselling 2002 book, *Bias*, this accounts for the major media's "liberal bias . . . how they see the world."[15]

The Emmy-award-winning Goldberg is convinced his former network colleagues—including Dan Rather—truly "think conservatives are out of the mainstream—and therefore must be identified—while at the same time thinking that liberals are the mainstream." The media's worldview affects how they "report on all the big social and cultural issues of our time, everything from feminism and abortion to race and affirmative action, to gay rights, to the homeless." Goldberg adds, "The old argument that the networks and other 'media elites' have a liberal bias is so blatantly true that it's hardly worth discussing anymore. No, we don't sit around in dark corners and plan strategies on how we're going to slant the news. We don't have to. It comes naturally to most reporters."

Fred Barnes, executive editor of *The Weekly Standard* and co-host of *The Beltway Boys* (Fox News Channel), is a respected evangelical Christian and excellent Washington journalist. He believes social conservatives are considered red meat by a national press corps, which is predisposed to oppose them.

> The press corps is poised to pounce on any statement that can be construed as favoring Christianity over other religions or atheism, as critical of homosexuality, as dubious about many claims to women's rights or as leery of calls for "racial justice." Along with the media, liberal interest groups, which are growing in number, are allied against social conservatives. And liberal elected officials are ready to attack as well.[16]

With the confirmation fight over judicial nominees steeped in the culture war, and the reporting of that struggle biased toward one side of the conflict, the impact of the media on the confirmation process is evident. Far Left groups use press releases, fax machines, and websites to distribute spurious attacks to convince the public that conservative nominees are "out of the mainstream." Reporters and producers—in full agreement from their own perspective—become at best willing accomplices and at worst co-conspirators. I remember one article in the *Washington Post* on judicial nominees with an attached information graph with numbers and details of confirmations. I expected the graph key to say something like "*Washington Post* Analysis." No, they were honest in their reporting—the graph key said, "Source: Democratic Judiciary Committee Staff"—straight from the Democratic talking points to your morning newspaper.

In the previous chapter I discussed the organization People for the American Way. Its president, Ralph Neas, characterized me as out of the mainstream while he supports abortion on demand, same-sex marriage, the accessibility of pornography on public library computers, art portraying the Virgin Mary splattered with elephant dung, and a play depicting Christ and his disciples as homosexuals. Either the views of Ralph Neas are mainstream (which they are not), or his attack on me went unchallenged because the major media is sympathetic to his views. Bolce and De Maio note the media's lack of qualifying this organization. While the Christian Coalition is often labeled as "religious right," People for the American Way is not labeled as the "secular left." PFAW "is most often characterized in press accounts as a civil-liberties and civil rights group, rarely as a secularist organization. But a visit to the organization's website shows that its cultural agenda is the mirror opposite of the Christian Coalition's."[17]

When New York senator Charles Schumer—who has a "liberal vote" rating of 82.4 according to the nonpartisan *National Journal*—constantly referred to me and other conservative judges as "extremists," no member of the national media ever asked him to define "extremism." When Massachusetts senator Edward Kennedy—whom *National Journal*[18] rates as one of the five top liberals in the U.S. Senate—called me "out of the mainstream," no one asked Senator Kennedy to enlighten the public regarding what he thinks constitutes the "mainstream." When Nan Aron stated she wanted courts to "create new rights" or that a certain nominee will not protect "basic" and "fundamental" rights, no member of the press questioned what "rights" she was talking about. By allowing this lack of clarity, the national media showed its own preferences; they think Schumer, Kennedy, Neas, and Aron are mainstream. When these questions are not asked, the public is disserved.

Goldberg offers helpful insight on this phenomenon: "This blindness, this failure to see liberals as anything but middle-of-the-road moderates, happens all the time on network television. The Christian Coalition is identified as a conservative organization—so far, so good—but we don't identify the National Organization for Women (NOW) as a liberal organization, which it surely is."

He continues,

> Robert Bork is the "conservative" judge. But Laurence Tribe, who must have been on the CBS *Evening News* ten million times in the 1980s (and who during the contested presidential election in 2000 was a leading member of Team Gore, arguing the vice president's case before the U.S. Supreme Court), is identified simply as a "Harvard law professor." But Tribe is not *simply* a Harvard law professor. He's easily as liberal as Bork is conservative . . . . The reason we don't identify NOW as a liberal group or Laurence Tribe as a liberal professor or Tom Daschle as a liberal Democrat is that, by and large, the media elites don't see them that way. It may be hard to believe, but liberals in the newsroom, pretty much, see NOW and Tribe and even left wing Democrats as middle of the road. Not coincidentally, just as they see themselves. When you get right down to it, liberals in the newsroom see liberal views as just plain . . . *reasonable.*"[19]

Goldberg has demonstrated that the big media often lets personal biases slip into news coverage. This was evident in the national media's treatment of my nomination, but fortunately for me, some of the media did not reflect this bias. Rebecca Carr of Cox Newspapers recently pointed out to the *American Journalism Review,* "Washington reporting has become too much like stenography and not enough about asking tough questions."[20] Many in the Washington media elite simply repeated the talking points from special-interest groups and Democratic staffers opposed to Bush nominees like myself. This led Nat Hentoff to write a series of articles in New York City's *Village Voice* criticizing the media: "I write now to illuminate the laziness of the press—with very few exceptions—in reporting in lockstep the debasing accusations against Pickering . . . ."[21]

As he said, there were a few exceptions; there were some fair reports in the national media. With those who actually took time to come to Mississippi and study my record, I fared quite well. Six different reporters from major out-of-state newspapers came to Mississippi to report on my confirmation battle and do in depth research on me. Additionally, Mike Wallace came to Mississippi and did a *60 Minutes* segment. I was pleased with the Mike Wallace story and felt five of six out-of-state newspaper reporters were fair and mostly positive.

David Firestone, a reporter for the *New York Times*, interviewed a number of Mississippians. On February 17, 2002, the article came out on the front page of "America's paper of record" with the headline "Blacks at Home Support a Judge Liberals Assail," and the jumpline inside the paper read, "In Mississippi Words of Praise from Local Blacks for Judge Liberals Assail." Firestone wrote,

> But here on the streets of his small and largely black hometown, far from the bitterness of partisan agendas and position papers, Charles Pickering is a widely admired figure . . . . The judge's widespread popularity in his hometown has been frustrating to the many civil rights and abortion rights groups that have worked to portray him as an ideological relic of the Old South. Several opponents of his nomination have tried unsuccessfully to get his supporters to change their minds, and their inability to do so reflects the distance between national liberal groups and many Southern blacks in small towns.

I appreciate David Firestone coming to Mississippi to find out the truth about my record. Several weeks after publication I took the initiative and called the *New York Times* and located David Firestone. We had not previously spoken. I thanked him for his fairness.

The second major out-of-state newspaper was the *Commercial Appeal* from Memphis, Tennessee. One of the great Southern newspapers in my region, the *Commercial Appeal* has a reputation of accurate and insightful coverage of Mississippi issues. Reed Branson was the *Commercial Appeal's* bureau chief in Jackson, Mississippi, and his report likewise made the front page of his newspaper. The March 14, 2002, headline: "If Vote Were in Laurel Pickering Would Pass."

Branson also mentioned the disconnect between the Beltway accusations and my lifelong reputation at home: "Otherwise, nearly everyone—Democrats and Republicans—interviewed in Laurel and Jones County, and Mississippi for that matter, expressed frustration with Senate Democrats' characterizations of one of their leading citizens." I appreciated Branson closing his article with an important incident in my life: "As county prosecutor, Pickering testified in neighboring Forrest County about the reputation of Ku Klux Klan leader Sam Bowers, who was accused in the 1966 fire bombing and murder of Vernon Dahmer—a move that was unpopular if not dangerous at the time and that probably cost him re-election."

Unfortunately for me, the vote was not in Laurel; it was in the Democrat-controlled Senate Judiciary Committee that rejected my nomination on a party-line vote the same day Branson's article ran.

Despite these two favorable articles, most of the national media coverage of my nomination in 2001 and 2002 was not positive. The media was getting its information from groups waging the culture war. The editorial writers for liberal newspapers were excoriating me. Despite the onslaught by special-interest groups, Democrats and media bias, the public wasn't buying these attacks on me and the other nominees. Republicans made the Democrats' obstruction an issue during the 2002 mid-term elections and regained control of the Senate.

In January 2003, President Bush exhibited his family's characteristic loyalty and re-nominated me. My son Chip—who was elected to Congress from Mississippi in 1996—and I decided we would be more accessible to the press and make sure my side of the story got out. Conservatives were far behind liberals in organizing and messaging on judicial nominees. We concluded we had to take the initiative and work more closely with the media.

It is customary for individuals not to talk to the press while their nominations are pending, and the White House staff routinely requests that nominees avoid the press. There is a fear a nominee will say the wrong thing or will be misunderstood or mischaracterized or that some senator may be offended. Chip and I decided I didn't have much to lose, and we put together information detailing my record and responding to charges. I made myself available to the press off the record so they could probe me with questions to satisfy themselves on what I believed and how I had acted without actually attributing statements to me. This new approach was tested early in 2003.

One February morning I received a call from Steve Henderson, a reporter for Pennsylvania's *Philadelphia Inquirer*, published by Knight Ridder—a newspaper chain with eighty-four Pulitzer Prizes and an established reputation of credible news reporting from the northeast to Miami to California. In Mississippi, it publishes Biloxi's *Sun Herald*.

When he had introduced himself, I never expected what followed next. He said, "I attended church with you yesterday." I was further surprised when he told me, "I have been to the state capitol in Jackson and I have researched your record in the state Senate. Your legislative record doesn't sound anything like what I have read about you in the newspapers." I thought to myself, "This is a welcomed change. This is encouraging." He wanted to know if I would sit down and talk with him. I agreed with the understanding that it would be for background and not for attribution.

When Steve Henderson arrived, I learned he was African American, an irrelevant matter except that for many it gave greater credibility to his defense of me against charges of racial insensitivity. I would later learn from others that he broke the color barrier as the first minority reporter to cover the Supreme Court for a major newspaper.

For the next two hours, we engaged in intense conversation about my life in the transforming South: personal relationships, community involvement, professional advancement, and public service. I had been under siege for almost two years, it was refreshing and invigorating to sit down and visit with a reporter who had a true interest in the facts and who would listen. For me, our conversation was more than a media interview; it was therapeutic.

When Steve Henderson started to leave, he told me I wouldn't believe how liberal he considered himself to be. Maybe so, but I felt confident his professionalism would trump his liberalism. I was right.

When Steve Henderson's article was distributed to the Knight Ridder's 8.5 million readers in their 32 daily newspapers, I could not have been more pleased. I guess no one ever agrees with every word a reporter writes, but I believe he accurately portrayed my life. The first paragraph of that February 23, 2003, article encapsulated my plight: "The assault was so easy. Take a white, conservative, religious judicial nominee from Mississippi. Pluck a few votes from his career in the state senate, a handful of cases from his time on the federal bench. And then use them to brand him as an enemy of racial progress."

Henderson continued,

> This Mississippi judge—who has been re-nominated and faces new hearings as early as next month—is not the person his opponents have depicted. His political views are more mainstream and his judicial record is more balanced. Even those troubling allegations about his racial insensitivity can be reasonably explained. As a state senator, he fought to help those at the bottom of the economic ladder, pioneered initiatives to preserve the environment, tried in many arenas to reform the penal system's harsh treatment of first-time offenders and expanded government aid to the disabled and the infirm.

His story also defied the typical media misunderstanding of faith. He noted the role my faith has in my life:

> Those who know Pickering say he reaches those moral crossroads all the time—and that his faith pushes him toward kindness, forgiveness and conciliation. They say that's what motivated him in 1967, when he was called to testify against Ku Klux Klan leader Sam Bowers, whose minions were firebombing businesses and shooting into people's houses in Laurel. Most kept quiet, but Pickering's faith compelled him to stand up. They say he reached a similar crossroads in 1973, when a proposed school integration plan had split Laurel along racial lines. Pickering played conciliator, and tried to come up with a plan that would appease both black and white. Even when the

final plan motivated many whites to flee the public schools, Pickering and his children stayed behind.

Steve Henderson gave a fair analysis of my record. Sometime later when my wife Margaret Ann and I were in Washington, we had dinner with him and his wife. I hope I don't hurt his reputation among the liberal establishment by letting folks know that a conservative like me would welcome him in my home any time.

The fourth out-of-state reporter to come to Mississippi and do an in-depth investigative analysis was Janita Poe, an African-American female journalist with the *Atlanta Journal Constitution*. She was assisted in writing by Tom Baxter. Under the leadership of noted editor Ralph McGill, the *Atlanta Constitution* was a leader among the Southern press in supporting the civil rights movement even during segregation, and it maintains that reputation of equality and reconciliation still today.

On March 9, 2003, the headlines for Poe's pieces included "Evidence Doesn't Support Charges of Racism Against Charles Pickering"; and "ALJ Review Shows Fairness, Not Bias at Root of Ruling"; and "Jurist's Record Belies Racism Charge."

Poe noted that her firsthand investigation revealed a discrepancy between my actual Mississippi life and the accusations of my Washington opposition:

> In Mississippi, however, many describe a different man than the one feared and vilified by critics inside the Beltway. Rather their up-close description of Pickering is that he is a relative progressive on race, a man who in the 1960s, when much of Mississippi was still fighting efforts to kill Jim Crow, testified against a murderous Ku Klux Klansman. He is a parent who . . . bucked white flight to send his four children to newly integrated public schools . . . he also sought reduced sentences for many black first offenders. He has pushed to establish a racial reconciliation center at the University of Mississippi, his alma mater. And, both on the bench and off, he has pressed white prison officials to ensure the rights of black inmates.

The fifth out-of-state reporter was Neil Lewis,[22] another *New York Times* reporter. Neil covers judicial matters for the *Times* in Washington D.C. My friends in Washington tell me Neil Lewis is very liberal, and maybe he is, but I am convinced he tried to write a balanced article and he certainly did his research, which included hours of reviewing trial transcripts. While I would take issue with some of what he wrote, I thought he and his colleague David Firestone represented the *New York Times* well and reported fairly. I would be happy to break bread with Neil Lewis anytime.

In contrast to Firestone and Lewis, the editorial writers at the *New York Times* savaged my nomination. They either failed to read the stories written by their own reporters or failed to believe them, either of which is a sad commentary on the once most prestigious newspaper in America. Nat Hentoff wrote that Lewis "reviewed 'the transcripts of the trial and sentencing hearings,' as well as conducted 'interviews with people involved in the case,' and examined Justice Department documents. Lewis's 1,823-word story provides key facts that were entirely absent from the Times editorial wholly condemning Pickering's actions concerning the case."[23] I suppose sometimes seeing is believing, and while their reporters saw me and the issues, the editorial board only saw the Democratic talking points and believed those Beltway mischaracterizations instead of the facts as established in Mississippi.

The *Washington Post* also sent a writer to my hometown. His Beltway cynicism was apparent from the beginning and obvious in the reporting, and I believe it failed the "fairness test." We had picked up information that the special-interest groups were trolling for reporters to write a negative piece on me. As I said, the national reporters including those from the *New York Times* came to Mississippi but produced if not favorable at least fair reports. The special-interest groups had yet to find a reporter to do a "hatchet job" on me.

But then I received a call from a *Washington Post* reporter. He came to Mississippi to interview people firsthand. When he talked with me he had already interviewed the people in Mississippi whom special-interest groups had identified as opposing my nomination. But when I offered him names of witnesses who had been supportive of my nomination, he didn't have time to see them. Some of these folks later told me he did call them after he got back to Washington, but he spent more time trying to convince them that they were wrong in supporting my nomination than seeking facts.

As per the off-the-record agreement I had with all the reporters to whom I spoke, he agreed not to publish anything I told him without my permission. He violated the agreement. When I addressed the agreement, he said I should take it up with his editors. My agreement was not with his editors; my agreement was with him.

He had a tip that I had allegedly mishandled a case in which a white sheriff had been charged with using excessive force on an African American. I made copies of the transcript available and showed him where I had refused to allow the defendant, the white sheriff, to remove an African-American juror—a Batson challenge. He wasn't familiar with the legal term and I explained to him a Batson challenge prohibits the striking of a minority juror unless the party excusing the juror can articulate a non-discriminatory reason for so doing. I also showed the reporter where I reprimanded the prosecution for not being prepared to present its case.

A lawyer who had previously been before me reminded me of a case in which he had represented an African-American plaintiff claiming excessive force by a white police officer. Again in that case, I refused to let the defense strike a black juror. I shared the attorney's phone number with the *Post* reporter, but apparently he was not interested; he never called.

Before the article was published, the reporter told me not to worry about the excessive force case because he had concluded I had handled it appropriately. But he did not report that I handled the case appropriately or that I had done so in a previous and similar case. Neither did he report that someone had made a baseless charge against me that he had found to be untrue. That would have been fair, but that was not the story he was looking to tell. When the article came out, the special-interest groups had their negative story to counteract the positive articles of two African American journalists, Steve Henderson and Janita Poe.

A few months later, Chip approached the *Washington Post* on a number of occasions to meet with the editorial board to discuss my nomination as well as the confirmation process involving other nominees. The *Post* was not interested.

I write about these out-of-state newspaper reports because the in-state newspapers knew the story already. Local and community journalists saw the mischaracterizations coming from the Washington Beltway for what they were and ignored or repudiated them. Every major newspaper in Mississippi—liberal or conservative—editorially endorsed me. But the media elite and the liberal establishment in Washington was not interested in local perceptions or fairness because that didn't fit their stereotype of a conservative, Christian, white male judge. Washington Democrats were not interested in what the people who actually knew me had to say because it did not contribute to blocking my confirmation and the agenda of the special-interest groups opposing my nomination.

Unfortunately for the judiciary, the confirmation hearings and struggles now focus on Washington D.C. attacks and accusations rather than the issues of whether a person is fit for the bench and will follow the rule of law. Controversy, sensationalism, and approval from the liberal establishment drive much of the media coverage and communication instead of whether the nominee has the qualifications and integrity to rule faithfully on matters of the Constitution and federal precedent. But for that to change, the media would have to come to a conclusion on what actually is the constitutional role of judges. For many in the culture war, it isn't just a question of judges interpreting a living Constitution, but lifetime appointees providing for secularists the answers they desire from a mystery Constitution.

CHAPTER EIGHT

Mystery Constitution

WHAT DOES THE term "living Constitution" mean? Generally it means a Constitution that changes meaning as culture and society change. Such a Constitution can change meanings over time without being amended. This evolving Constitution could be called a "mystery Constitution" because you don't know what it means until the majority of the Supreme Court decides what it means. Chief Justice Charles Evans Hughes proclaimed this philosophy, saying, "We are under a Constitution, but the Constitution is what the judges say it is."[1]

Justices who subscribe to the concept of a "living Constitution" exercise their "own judgment"—their "independent judgment"—to determine what offends "civilized standards of decency" or "the evolving standards of decency that mark the progress of a maturing society."[2] Under a living Constitution, Supreme Court justices change the Constitution—"amend" the Constitution, if you will. The Supreme Court justices (not the people nor their duly elected representatives) determine the "standards of decency" for American society. This conflicts with the separation of powers doctrine and evades the carefully crafted checks and balances established by our Founders and essential to the rule of law.

Two books in the 1920s outlined the debate over the concept of a living Constitution. James M. Beck, solicitor general of the United States, penned *The Constitution of the United States*, arguing that if the Constitution changed meaning with time, "America would cease to be a government of laws" and would become a government of men. President Calvin Coolidge's foreword to Beck's work stresses "reverence for the

Constitution is the equivalent to support for 'a government of law.'" In 1803, the Supreme Court declared this adherence to the rule of law over the whims of man to be the law of the land: "The government of the United States has been emphatically termed a government of laws, and not of men." But liberals, ignoring the fact that John Adams used this description to promote adoption of the Constitution, derided Beck's work as "pious devotion to constitutional 'principles,'" which they argued was a "deterrent to enlightened judicial decision making." "Beck's critics asserted that judges, as constitutional interpreters were not simply mouthpieces for pre-existing legal principles."[3]

The argument of the liberals "crystallized in a book appearing in 1927 entitled *The Living Constitution* written by Howard Lee McBain, a Professor of Columbia Law School." McBain argued judges who interpret the law "are men . . . made of human stuff like the rest and sharing with us the common limitations and frailties of human nature," rendering "[t]he distinction between a government of laws and a government of men absurd."[4] We must have a government of men, he says, because only through those men can laws be properly and humanly applied to our fellow man.

In his 2005 book *Men in Black*, Mark R. Levin ironically makes the same argument: "The biggest myth about judges is that they're somehow imbued with greater insight, wisdom, and vision than the rest of us . . . the truth is that judges are men and women with human imperfections and frailties."[5] While McBain uses the argument to say we must rely on men and not laws of stone, Levin suggests liberal judges are unqualified to impose their own imperfect ideologies over the written and agreed compact of the American people—our Constitution.

Chief Justice Charles Evans Hughes and Justice George Sutherland provide the clearest early debate regarding a living Constitution (although they did not refer to it as such) in the Supreme Court's 1934 case *Home Building v. Blaisdell.*[6] Hughes argues the Constitution is "intended to endure for ages to come, and, consequently, to be adapted to the various crisis of human affairs . . . . [W]e must realize that they have called into life a being the development of which could not have been foreseen completely by the most gifted of its begetters . . . . The case before us must be considered in the light of our whole experience and not merely in that of what was said a hundred years ago." He rejects "what the provision of the Constitution meant to the vision of that day it must mean to the vision of our time . . . that what the Constitution meant at the time of its adoption it means today." But Sutherland responds, "The meaning of the Constitution is fixed when it is adopted."

Sutherland continues, "The Constitution . . . does not admit of two distinctly opposite interpretations. It does not mean one thing at one time and an entirely different at another time . . . . The Constitution is a written instrument. As such its meaning does not alter. That which it meant when adopted, it means now." Constitutional provisions

> remain binding as the acts of the people in their sovereign capacity, as the framers of Government, until they are amended . . . . The remedy consists in repeal or amendment, and not in false constructions . . . . Their meaning is changeless; it is only their application which is extensible . . . . A principal share of the benefit expected from written constitutions would be lost if the rules they established were so flexible as to bend to circumstances or be modified by public opinion . . . . What a court is to do, therefore, is to declare the law as written, leaving it to the people themselves to make such changes as new circumstances may require.

Sutherland warns the case before the Court, "though serious enough," is of "trivial significance" compared to the "dangerous inroads" he sees will result by exceeding the "limitations of the Constitution." He argues few questions have been submitted "for judicial inquiry this generation" of greater importance. To Sutherland, the notion the Constitution changes over time means the Constitution will "cease to be the supreme law of the land . . . become a mere collection of political maxims to be adhered to or disregarded . . . . Such a doctrine leads directly to anarchy or despotism."

In another dissent, Sutherland writes about "living words" but not a "living Constitution," arguing that the text of the Constitution can cover situations not foreseen by the Founders without changing meaning. Sutherland writes,

> The Constitution does not change with the ebb and flow of . . .
> events. We frequently are told in more general words that the
> Constitution must be construed in the light of the present. If by that
> it is meant the Constitution is made up of living words that apply to
> every new condition which they include, the statement is quite true.
> But to say, if that be intended, that the words of the Constitution
> mean today what they did not mean when written . . . is to rob that
> instrument of the essential element which continues it in force as the
> people have made it until they, and not their official agents, have
> made it otherwise.[7]

Debate over how the Constitution is to be interpreted was not restricted to the courts. It was also being waged in newspaper editorials. The *New York Times* joined the debate on the side of strict construction, but then lost the debate to itself and changed sides. Seth Lipsky wrote in the *New York Sun*[8] that just over the period of Justice Louis Brandeis's term on the Supreme Court (1916–1939), the *New York Times* acceptance of a philosophy of a living Constitution migrated from opposition to embracement.

On May 25, 1916, the *New York Times* "said that if Brandeis 'is to enter public life,' the 'legislative hall, not the Bench of the Supreme Court, is the proper theater for the exercise of his abilities.' Brandeis, it complained, was 'essentially a contender, a striver for changes and reforms that, under our system of Government, can be properly achieved only through legislation, not through the judgments of the courts.'"

Lipsky continues,

> The *Times* reiterated a view it had expressed earlier in the fight, that
> "the voice of the advocate moved to utterance in behalf of theories of
> social justice should be heard in the legislative hall rather than the
> chamber of the court," which, the *Times* said, "sits not to expound on
> theories or doctrines but to judge of the constitutionality of the enact-

ments which Congress may decree to those or other ends." And then the *Times* issued this magnificent paragraph, which could be chiseled into the wall where judges used to hang the Ten Commandments:

"The Supreme Court, by its very nature, must be a conservative body; it is the conservator of our institutions, it protects the people against the errors of their legislative servants, it is the defender of the Constitution itself. To place upon the Supreme Bench judges who hold a different view of the function of the court, to supplant conservatism by radicalism, would be to undo the work of John Marshall and strip the Constitution of its defenses. It would introduce endless confusion where order has reigned, it would tend to give force and effect to any whim or passion of the hour, to crown with success any transitory agitation engaged in by a part of the people, overriding the matured judgment of all the people as expressed in their fundamental law."

Upon Brandeis's retirement, Lipsky writes, the *Times* changed its position:

It quoted Brandeis as noting that the court "has often overruled its earlier decisions" because it "bows to the lessons of experience and the force of better reasoning, recognizing that the process of trial and error, so fruitful in the physical sciences, is appropriate also in the judicial function." The newspaper which only a generation ago had insisted the Court, by its very nature, must be a conservative body, now praised Brandeis for being aware that the Court "is not an abstraction but a vital force which gives direction to the pace and range of economic forces." At the heart of its editorial was this sentence: 'The Constitution is a living law."

While conservatives oppose a living Constitution as an improper usurpation of legislative powers by the judiciary, Brandeis's willingness to overrule earlier decisions should make a living Constitution troubling to liberals as well. If the Constitution's meaning is enshrined in the ideology of judges and not the document itself, its certainty is only as sure and long as those judges' tenure on the Court.

More recently, in 1963, Charles A. Reich,[9] associate professor of law at Yale, argued Justice Hugo Black espoused a "living Constitution." He acknowledged the characterization was his own and not that of Black, but Reich provides insights into the legal philosophy of the time that would divide the country in the coming decades. He writes, "By using the literal language of a provision as a starting point, and its underlying purpose as a guide, Black can voyage outwards but not lose sight of the framers' lines; that is all that 'absolutes' can hope to promise." Reich continues, "How can a dynamic conception of a Constitution be squared with a literal one? The answer is that in a dynamic society the Bill of Rights must keep changing in its application or lose even its original meaning. There is no such thing as a constitutional provision with a static meaning."[10] Reich observes, "the last twenty-five years have seen a revolution in the role of the Supreme Court . . . it has become a prime mover in influencing the direction of American society."

In 1973, Justice Lewis Powell wrote in a concurring opinion in *White v. Weiser*, "The Constitution—a vital and living charter after nearly two centuries because of the wise flexibility of its key provisions."[11] Powell later declared in a 1980 dissent, "We are construing a living Constitution."[12] The concept of a living Constitution had fully arrived.

By the 1970s and 1980s, the term "living Constitution" took on new significance as the concept came to center stage in the culture war. While the term is not referenced, the seminal case decided under the concept of a changing Constitution is *Roe v. Wade*.[13] In Roe the majority acknowledges the Constitution does not explicitly mention a right of privacy and that under the Fourteenth Amendment "only personal rights that can be deemed 'fundamental' or 'implicit' in the concept of ordered liberty" are recognized. But Justice Harry Blackmun delivers the opinion of the Court, finding a right of privacy, including a women's right to an abortion, in the Fourteenth Amendment's Due Process Clause. Justice Potter Stewart concurs, writing the right to an abortion "is embraced within the personal liberty protected by the Due Process Clause of the Fourteenth Amendment."

Justice William Rehnquist dissented, writing abortion is not "so rooted in the traditions and consciousness of our people as to be ranked as fundamental." The right to privacy found by the majority "was apparently completely unknown to the drafters of the Amendment."

Justice Byron White dissented in *Roe* and its companion case, noting, "At the heart of the controversy in these cases are those recurring pregnancies that pose no danger whatsoever to the life or health of the mother but are, nevertheless, unwanted for any one or more of a variety of reasons—convenience, family planning, economics, dislike of children, the embarrassment of illegitimacy, etc.," He criticized the majority opinion as being "an exercise of raw judicial power" which he found to be "an improvident and extravagant exercise of the power of judicial review . . . . This issue, for the most part, should be left with the people and to the political processes the people have devised to govern their affairs."[14]

The most recent debate over a living Constitution began in July 1985 when Reagan attorney general Ed Meese challenged the idea before the annual meeting of the American Bar Association. His speech reignited the debate over the proper method of interpreting the Constitution. Meese proclaimed, "We Americans . . . pride ourselves on having produced the greatest political wonder of the world—a government of laws and not of men. Thomas Paine was right: 'American has no monarch: Here the law is king.'" He argued, "As the 'faithful guardians of the Constitution,' judges [are] expected to resist any political effort to depart from the literal provisions of the Constitution." He cited Madison for the proposition that "the Constitution enabled the government to control the governed, but also obliged it to control itself."

He referenced Chief Justice John Marshall's decisions that proclaimed "[t]he Constitution said what it meant and meant what it said"[15] and "the Constitution is a limitation on judicial power as well as executive and legislative."[16] "The Constitution is the fundamental will of the people," Meese continued.

> To allow the courts to govern simply by what it views at the time as fair and decent [means] [t]he permanence of the Constitution has been weakened. A constitution that is viewed as only what the judges say it is, is no longer a constitution in the true sense. Those who framed the Constitution chose their words carefully; they debated at great length

the most minute points. The language they chose meant something. It is incumbent upon the Court to determine what that meaning was. That is not a shockingly new theory; nor is it arcane or archaic.

Meese felt the Court in its 1984 "term continued to roam at large in a veritable constitutional forest." He advocated resurrecting "[t]he original meaning of constitutional provisions and statutes as the only reliable guide for judgment . . . . Any other standard suffers the defect of pouring new meaning into old words, thus creating new powers and new rights totally at odds with the logic of our Constitution and its commitment to the rule of law."[17]

Then in October 1985, Justice William Brennan Jr., a liberal member of the Supreme Court, chose to respond to Meese's advocacy of originalism:

> [W]e are an aspiring people, a people with faith in progress. Our amended Constitution is the lodestar for our aspirations. Like every text worth reading, it is not crystalline. The phrasing is broad and the limitations of its provisions are not clearly marked. Its majestic gener- alities and ennobling pronouncements are both luminous and obscure. This ambiguity of course calls forth interpretation, the inter- action of reader and text.

Brennan said, "important aspects of the most fundamental issues confronting our democracy . . . arrive in the Supreme Court for judicial determination. Not infrequently, these are the issues upon which contemporary society is most deeply divided. They arouse our deepest emotions." He acknowledged the "source of legitimacy is, of course, a well spring of controversy in legal and political circles." America's commitment "to self-governance in a representative democracy must be reconciled with vesting in electorally unaccountable Justices the power to invalidate the expressed desires of representative bodies on the ground of inconsistency with higher law."

Where does the "higher law" referred to by Justice Brennan come from? Does it come from the words of the Constitution? Or does it

MYSTERY CONSTITUTION | 123

come from the labyrinths of the mind of the particular judge hearing the case?

Brennan vigorously attacked the argument for originalism, charging,

> in truth it is little more than arrogance cloaked as humility. It is arrogant to pretend that from our vantage we can gauge accurately the intent of the Framers on application of principle to specific, contemporary questions . . . . Faith in democracy is one thing, blind faith quite another . . . . While the Constitution may be amended, such amendments require an immense effort by the People as a whole.

Sounding like Chief Justice Hughes, he expounded,

> the genius of the Constitution rests not in any static meaning it might have had in a world that is dead and gone, but in the adaptability of its great principles to cope with current problems and current needs. What the constitutional fundamentals meant to the wisdom of other times cannot be their measure to the vision of our time.[18]

Ten days later in a speech before the Federal Bar Association in Chicago, Justice John Paul Stevens sided with Justice Brennan in attacking Attorney General Meese's speech on originalism. But Meese was not through, and on November 15, 1985, before the D.C. Chapter of the Federalist Society Lawyers Division, he argued,

> A large part of American history has been the history of constitutional debate . . . as we approach the bicentennial of the framing of the Constitution, we are witnessing another debate concerning our fundamental law. It is not simply a ceremonial debate, but one that promises to have a profound impact on the future of our Republic.[19]

Again relying on Chief Justice Marshall, Meese touted "a written, as opposed to an unwritten document" and contended that "John Marshall rested his rationale for judicial review on the fact that we have a written constitution with meaning that is binding upon judges." He quoted Thomas Jefferson: "Our peculiar security is in the possession of a written

Constitution. Let us not make it a blank paper by construction." He pointed out that "Jefferson was even more explicit in his personal correspondence: 'On every question of construction [we should] carry ourselves back to the time, when the Constitution was adopted; recollect the spirit manifested in the debates; and instead of trying [to find], what meaning may be squeezed out of the text, or invented against it, conform to the probable one, in which it was passed.'"

Meese lamented the view of the Constitution

> as a charter for judicial activism on behalf of various constituencies. Those who hold this view often have lacked demonstrable textual or historical support for their conclusions. Instead they have "grounded" their rulings in appeals to social theories, to moral philosophies or personal notions of human dignity, or to "penumbras," somehow emanating ghostlike from various provisions—identified and not identified—in the Bill of Rights. The problem with this approach . . . is not that it is bad constitutional law, but that it is not constitutional law in any meaningful sense, at all.

He quoted Judge Robert Bork: "The truth is that the judge who looks outside the Constitution always looks inside himself and nowhere else." And in citing a brief of the United States before the Supreme Court, he said, "The further afield interpretation travels from its point of departure in the text, the greater the danger that constitutional adjudication will be like a picnic to which the framers bring words and the judges the meaning."

Judge Robert Bork entered the debate three days later, noting interpretation by original intent "has been a topic of fierce debate in the law schools for the past thirty years. The controversy shows no sign of subsiding . . . . Any intelligible view of constitutional adjudication starts from the proposition that the Constitution is law . . . . Freedom of speech covers speech, not sexual conduct . . . the judge's authority has limits and outside the designated areas democratic institutions govern."

Bork decried that

professors at very prestigious institutions . . . deny that the Constitution is law . . . . If the Constitution is not law . . . what authorizes judges to set at naught the majority judgment of the representatives of the American people? . . . [T]here is no reason for the rest of us, who have our own moral visions, to be governed by the judge's moral predilections . . . . The only way in which the Constitution can constrain judges is if the judges interpret the document's words according to the intentions of those who drafted, proposed, and ratified its provisions and its various amendments . . . . The conclusion, I think, must be that only by limiting themselves to the historic intentions underlying each clause of the Constitution can judges avoid becoming legislators, avoid enforcing their own moral predilections, and ensure that the Constitution is law.[20]

President Ronald Reagan used the occasion of the investiture of Chief Justice William Rehnquist and Associate Justice Antonin Scalia on September 26, 1986, to join the discussion. He noted that it was "a good time to reflect on the inspired wisdom we call our Constitution, a time to remember that the Founding Fathers gave careful thought to the role of the Supreme Court."

Reagan said,

In a small room in Philadelphia in the summer of 1787 . . . . They settled on a judiciary that would be independent and strong, but one whose power would . . . be confined within the boundaries of a written Constitution . . . . The framers of our Constitution believed, however, that the judiciary they envisioned would be "the least dangerous" branch of the government, because, as Alexander Hamilton wrote in the Federalist Papers, it had "neither force nor will, but merely judgment." The Judicial Branch interprets the laws, while the power to make and execute those laws is balanced in the two elected branches. And this was one thing that Americans of all persuasions supported . . . in the words of James Madison, if "the sense in which the Constitution was accepted and ratified by the nation is not the guide to expounding it, there can be no security for a faithful exercise of its powers" . . . . The question was and is, will we have a government by the people?

He cited the argument of Justice Felix Frankfurter, "who once said, 'The highest exercise of judicial duty is to subordinate one's personal will and one's private views to the law.'"

President Reagan concluded with a quote attributed to Daniel Webster, "'Miracles do not cluster,' he said. 'Hold on to the Constitution of the United States of America and to the Republic for which it stands—what has happened once in 6,000 years may never happen again. Hold on to your Constitution, for if the American Constitution shall fall there will be anarchy throughout the world.'"[21]

It is fallacious to argue that originalism allows the dead hand of the past to rule the present because originalism empowers the people at any time to initiate an amendment process to change the Constitution. If there is no choice and no popular will to make such a change, that democratic acceptance is a continuing endorsement of the Constitution, providing a vitality to the document as sure as the moment after its ratification. Originalism allows the people of the present to determine when and how to amend the Constitution. Originalism shows proper respect for the participation of the people. Originalism properly recognizes the Constitution for what it is: a fundamental law, a social compact, a contract between the people and their government.

Five individuals on the Court changing the agreement between a people and their country does not respect the right of the people for self-governance. A living Constitution turns the concept of "We the people" on its head.

If the Constitution changes meaning over time, just how frequently does the meaning change? In a 2005 case, the Supreme Court held that the meaning of the Constitution can change within fifteen years.[22] In the future, no one knows how long it will take for the Constitution to change meaning again, nor what it will say when the meaning changes. That is the essence of the mystery Constitution; only five judges know for sure.

[C H A P T E R   N I N E]

Solving the Mystery

HOW A LIVING CONSTITUTION AFFECTS YOUR LIFE

HOW DOES INTERPRETING the Constitution as a living document, rather than a document meaning what it says and saying what it means, affect individual citizens and society? How does the concept of a living Constitution touch your life? Four cases illustrate the impact this concept of interpretation has on all Americans.

CASE 1: KELO AND PRIVATE PROPERTY

The right to ownership of private property is a hallmark of our American heritage. It stands alongside "life" and "liberty"—"no person shall . . . be deprived of life, liberty, or property without due process of law." Dreams of owning one's own home is an aspiration of most Americans. The phrase "a man's home is his castle" recognizes that the home of an individual, lowly or humble though his cottage may be, is as important to that individual as the castle to a king. From our earliest jurisprudence, it was held that private property cannot be taken from one person to be given to another person. Private property can be taken from an individual only in one instance—public use: "Nor shall private property be taken for public use without just compensation."[1]

In 1997, Susette Kelo moved to the Fort Trumbull neighborhood in New London, Connecticut. New London "sits at the junction of the Thames River and the Long Island Sound in Southeastern

Connecticut."[2] Kelo made extensive improvements to her home and prized her view over the water.

Wilhelmina Dery was born in her Fort Trumbull home in 1918 and lived there her entire life. Her home had been in her family for more than a century. Her husband Charles had lived in the home since they married some sixty years ago. Their son and his family lived next door in a home given to him as a wedding present.

In 1998, Pfizer Pharmaceuticals announced plans to build a global research facility near the Fort Trumbull neighborhood. Two months later, the New London City Council authorized a private non-profit development corporation to develop an economic plan to "complement the facility that Pfizer was planning to build, create jobs, increase tax and other revenues."

This private development corporation—whose members and directors were not elected by popular vote—sought to condemn land in the neighborhood, forcing the property owners, including Kelo and the Derys, to give up their land and homes. Their property was not to be used by the public; it was to be used by other private parties.

Kelo, the Derys, and six other landowners in the neighborhood sought to block this action under the Fifth Amendment of the Constitution. But the majority of the United States Supreme Court concluded that in our enlightened society, taking property for economic development reasons—even though it was to be turned over to a private person or business—is "public use."

Justice Sandra Day O'Connor wrote in a stinging dissent, "The specter of condemnation hangs over all property. Nothing is to prevent the State from replacing . . . any home with a shopping mall, or any farm with a factory." She further noted any "Motel 6" can be replaced with a "Ritz Carlton." O'Connor continued,

> Any property may now be taken for the benefit of another private party, but the fallout from this decision will not be random. The beneficiaries are likely to be those citizens with disproportionate influence and power in the political process, including large corporations and development firms. As for the victims, the government now has

license to transfer property from those with fewer resources to those with more. The Founders cannot have intended this perverse result.

Justices William Rehnquist, Antonin Scalia, and Clarence Thomas joined O'Connor in her dissent. Thomas wrote separately that the decision was "against all common sense" and "if such 'economic development' takings are for a 'public use,' any taking is, and the Court, has erased the Public Use Clause from our Constitution."

Walter E. Williams, professor of economics at George Mason University and syndicated columnist, connects the significance of this opinion to the filibuster of President Bush's judicial nominees. He says the "Court's decision helps explain the vicious attacks on any judicial nominees who might use framer intent to interpret the U.S. Constitution. America's socialists want more control over our lives, property, and our pocket books."[3]

CASE 2: NEWDOW AND THE PLEDGE OF ALLEGIANCE

California law requires schools to begin each day with some type of patriotic program. The Elk Grove Unified School District decided to comply with this requirement by having students voluntarily recite the Pledge of Allegiance: "I pledge allegiance to the Flag of the United States of America, and to the Republic for which it stands, one Nation under God, indivisible, with liberty and justice for all." Any student can choose not to recite the Pledge of Allegiance.

In March 2000, Michael Newdow filed suit in federal district court against the Elk Grove School seeking a declaration that the phrase "one Nation under God" is unconstitutional—that it violates the establishment and free exercise clauses of the Constitution. He requested the court prohibit the school district from continuing its patriotic program. Newdow is an atheist "ordained more than twenty years ago in a ministry that espouses the religious philosophy that the true and eternal bonds of righteousness and virtue stem from reason rather than mythology."[4]

The district court dismissed Newdow's complaint, finding no constitutional violation. Newdow appealed to the U.S. Ninth Circuit Court of Appeals. The Ninth Circuit rendered three separate opinions, all declaring the phrase "One Nation under God" in the Pledge of Allegiance unconstitutional.

Following the first Ninth Circuit opinion, Sandra Banning, the mother of Newdow's daughter, filed a motion to intervene, alleging under a California State Court decree she had the sole right to represent the daughter's legal interest and make all decisions about her education and welfare. She maintained her daughter is a Christian who believes in God and would be harmed if the litigation were permitted to proceed. She claimed being a party to Newdow's lawsuit was not in the child's best interest. The California Superior Court entered an order prohibiting Newdow from using his daughter as a vehicle for his lawsuit.

Despite the mother's custody and the California court's ruling, the Ninth Circuit claimed standing to consider the issue. The Ninth Circuit decided it could better determine California state law than the state court in California. The Ninth Circuit decided it could better determine the welfare of a daughter than the mother with custody.

The majority of the court acknowledged the Supreme Court has commented that the Pledge of Allegiance is constitutional and that the Seventh Circuit Court of Appeals has specifically declared the pledge and the phrase "one Nation under God" constitutional. Still, the Ninth Circuit decided the Pledge of Allegiance violated the establishment clause.

Circuit Judge Alfred Goodwin, speaking for the majority of a three-judge panel in Newdow I, wrote,

> The text of the official Pledge, codified in federal law, impermissibly takes a position with respect to the purely religious question of the existence and identity of God . . . . The Pledge, as currently codified, is impermissible government endorsement of religion because it sends a message to unbelievers that they are outsiders, not full members of the political community, and an accompanying message to adherents that they are insiders, favored members of the political community . . . . To be sure, no one is obligated to recite this phrase . . . but it

borders on sophistry to suggest that the reasonable atheist would not feel less than a full member of the political community every time his fellow Americans recited, as part of their expression of patriotism and love for country, a phrase he believed to be false.[5]

Goodwin's subsequent comments regarding the people's elected officials reflect his view of the Constitution as a changing document and the court's role in determining the proper course of the country. Regarding the outrage of representatives and senators over the Ninth Circuit decision, he said, "I never had much confidence in the attention span of elected officials for any kind of deep thinking about important issues . . . . When they pop off after what I call a bumper strip headline, they almost always give a superficial response." And when President George W. Bush called the decision to rule the Pledge of Allegiance unconstitutional "ridiculous," Goodwin said, "I'm a little disappointed in our chief executive—who nobody ever accused of being a deep thinker—for popping off."[6] Goodwin believes the role of the court is to determine public policy and protect the people from the leaders they choose. He does not respect the right of the people to elect whom they will, or to determine public policy.

In a subsequent opinion (Newdow III), Judge Stephen Reinhardt concurred with Goodwin and seemed to jump at the chance to hold the pledge unconstitutional: "It is the highest calling of federal judges to invoke the Constitution to repudiate unlawful majoritarian actions and, when necessary, to strike down statutes that would infringe on fundamental rights, whether such statutes are adopted by legislatures or by popular vote."[7] If such majoritarian actions conflict with the Constitution as written, this would indeed be consistent with the finest traditions of American jurisprudence. But Reinhardt advocates striking down majoritarian actions not contrary to the Constitution as written, but contrary to the meaning of the Constitution as determined, changed, altered, and "amended" by the very judges who are striking down the statute—a flagrant violation of the principle of checks and balances.

Justice Ferdinand Fernandez dissented,

We are asked to hold that inclusion of the phrase 'under God' in this nation's Pledge of Allegiance violates the religion clauses of the Constitution of the United States. We should do no such thing. We should, instead, recognize that those clauses were not designed to drive religious expression out of public thought; they were written to avoid discrimination. Such phrases as "In God We Trust," or "under God" have no tendency to establish a religion in this country or to suppress anyone's exercise, or non-exercise, of religion, except in the fevered eye of persons who most fervently would like to drive all tincture of religion out of the public life of our polity. Those expressions have not caused any real harm of that sort over the years since 1791, and are not likely to do so in the future. . . . [W]e will soon find ourselves prohibited from using our album of patriotic songs in many public settings. "God Bless America" and "America the Beautiful" will be gone for sure, and while use of the first three stanzas of "The Star Spangled Banner" will still be permissible, we will be precluded from straying into the fourth.[8]

Justice Diarmuid Fionntain O'Scannlain also dissented:

if reciting the Pledge is truly "a religious act" in violation of the Establishment Clause, then so is the recitation of the Constitution itself, the Declaration of Independence, the Gettysburg Address, the National Motto, or the singing of the National Anthem. Such an assertion would make hypocrites out of the Founders, and would have the effect of driving any and all references to our religious heritage out of our schools, and eventually out of our public life.[9]

O'Scannlain explained,

Newdow II . . . confers a favored status on atheism in our public life. In society with a pervasive public sector, our public schools are a most important means for transmitting ideas and values to future generations. The silence the majority commands is not neutral—it itself conveys a powerful message and creates a distorted impression about the place of religion in our national life. The absolute prohibition on any mention of God in our schools creates a bias against religion. The panel majority cannot credibly advance the notion that Newdow II is neutral with respect to belief versus non-belief; it affirmatively favors the latter to the former. One wonders, then, does atheism become the default religion protected by the Establishment Clause?

By a 5 to 3 vote, the U.S. Supreme Court averted deciding the case on its merits and reversed the Ninth Circuit on a jurisdictional basis, agreeing with the California State Court that Newdow could not file suit on behalf of his daughter without the mother's consent. The majority—absent justices Rehnquist, O'Connor, Scalia, and Thomas—chose not to address the merits of the case.

Newdow is trying anew and filed suit again. On September 15, 2005, a California Federal District Court judge ruled—citing the Ninth Circuit precedent—teachers in public schools may not lead students in the Pledge of Allegiance. The matter is again on appeal to the Ninth Circuit.[10] This time the Supreme Court will in all likelihood have to address the issue on its merits. Will the Supreme Court decide the issue, so important to many Americans, according to the Constitution as written and understood at the time the First Amendment was adopted? Or will the Supreme Court decide the case based upon what a majority of the justices find to be consistent with their view of "standards of decency"?

In one of the Ten Commandments cases, Justice Scalia comments on why the Court decisions have been inconsistent and why the Court may have been reluctant to prohibit certain religious practices or symbols:

> I suggest it is the instinct for self preservation, and the recognition that the Court . . . cannot go too far down the road of enforced neutrality that contradicts both historical fact and current practice without losing all that sustains it: the willingness of the people to accept its interpretation of the Constitution as definitive, in preference to the contrary interpretation of the democratically elected branches.[11]

Scalia's observation may explain why liberal members of the Supreme Court did not take up the Pledge of Allegiance case on its merits. Even members of the Supreme Court were aware the U.S. Senate voted 99-0 to condemn the Ninth Circuit decision. Such unanimity in the Senate clearly indicates overwhelming public support for a traditional interpretation of the Constitution in the Pledge of Allegiance case. But according to Judge Goodwin that should be ignored—after all, public officials "almost always give a superficial response."

CASE 3: MARRIAGE IN MASSACHUSETTS

In November 2003, the Massachusetts Supreme Court rejected the state attorney general's arguments that a union of one man and one woman should be the standard of marriage. The court invalidated Massachusetts state law and rejected 383 years of Massachusetts history and tradition by ruling same-sex couples could legally marry each other.

The comments in the decision make clear the debate extended beyond the issue of "same-sex marriage" to the question of the role of the court. The majority proclaims the court knows better than the people's elected legislature the right policy for Massachusetts. Some of the minority concede that perhaps there should be same-sex marriages but argue the creation of such right is the role of the legislature and the people, not the court. Chief Judge Margaret Marshall, writing for the majority, declares the law-defining marriage as between one man and one woman has no "rational basis."[12] She writes that other than this issue, the court "leaves intact the Legislature's broad discretion to regulate marriage." At least, that is, until the court decides to act again.

Justice John Greaney concurs, believing the court had to act to allow same-sex marriage: "Simple principles of decency dictate that we extend to the plaintiffs, and to their new status, full acceptance, tolerance, and respect. We should do so because it is the right thing to do." Greaney is perfectly comfortable with judges deciding what is right or wrong. Acting on behalf of the state, by judicial fiat, he is willing to order not only "tolerance" but "full acceptance" and "respect."

Justice Francis Spina argues for the traditional role of the court against the activism of the majority: "What is at stake in this case is . . . the power of the Legislature to effectuate social change without interference from the courts . . . . The power to regulate marriage lies with the

Legislature, not with the judiciary . . . . Today, the court has transformed its role as protector of individual rights into the role of creator of rights." He continues,

> In this Commonwealth and in this country, the roots of the institution of marriage are deeply set in history as a civil union between a single man and a single woman. There is no basis for the court to recognize same-sex marriage as a constitutionally protected right . . . . Such a dramatic change in social institutions must remain at the behest of the people through the democratic process . . . . [T]he power to create novel rights is reserved for the people through the democratic and legislative processes . . . . By extending constitutional protection to an asserted right or liberty interest, we, to a great extent, place the matter outside the arena of public debate and legislative action.

Justice Martha Sosman writes in her dissent that such correction is the role of the legislature to determine:

> In considering whether the Legislature has a rational reason for postponing a dramatic change to the definition of marriage, it is surely pertinent to the inquiry to recognize that this proffered change affects not just a load-bearing wall of our social structure but the very cornerstone of that structure . . . . Before making a fundamental alteration to that cornerstone, it is eminently rational for the Legislature to require a high degree of certainty as to the precise consequences of that alteration, to make sure that it can be done safely, without either temporary or lasting damage to the structural integrity of the entire edifice. The court today blithely assumes that there are no such dangers and that it is safe to proceed, an assumption that is not supported by anything more than the court's blind faith that it is so.

She continues,

> Through the political process, the people may decide when the benefits of extending civil marriages to same sex couples have been shown to outweigh whatever risk—be they palpable or ephemeral— are involved . . . . However minimal the risks of that redefinition of

marriage may seem to us from our vantage point, it is not up to us to decide what risks society must run, and it is inappropriate for us to arrogate that power to ourselves merely because we are confident that "it is the right thing to do."

Judge Robert Cordy in his dissent argues against interpreting the Constitution as a living document.

That decision must be made by the Legislature, not the court . . . . Insofar as the right to marry someone of the same sex is neither found in the unique historical context of our Constitution nor compelled by the meaning ascribed by this court to the liberty and due process protections contained within it, should the court nevertheless recognize it as a "fundamental right?" The consequences of deeming a right to be "fundamental" are profound, and this Court, as well as the Supreme Court, has been very cautious in recognizing them. Such caution is required by separation of powers principles. If a right is found to be "fundamental," it is, to a great extent, removed from "the arena of public debate and legislative action"; utmost care must be taken when breaking new ground in this field "lest the liberty protected by the Due Process Clause be subtly transformed into the policy preferences of [judges]."

Cordy continues, "to enforce its own views regarding better social policies" is a role "our Constitution forbids" and for which the Court is "particularly ill suited." He says, "it is eminently rational for the Legislature to postpone making fundamental changes to [marriage] until such time as there is unanimous scientific evidence, or popular consensus, or both, that such changes can safely be made . . . . The Legislature is the appropriate branch, both constitutionally and practically, to consider and respond to it."

CASE 4: TEN COMMANDMENTS, TWO DECISIONS, TWO RESULTS

On June 27, 2005, the United States Supreme Court handed down two 5-4 decisions involving displays of the Ten Commandments. In one decision, the majority ruled that a display of the Ten Commandments in two Kentucky courthouses is an unconstitutional violation of the Establishment Clause. In a simultaneous decision, the majority ruled that a display of the Ten Commandments on the lawn of the Texas State Capitol is not unconstitutional and does not violate the Establishment Clause. We must indeed have a mystery Constitution. These two decisions, in effect, proclaim that not only does the Constitution mean different things at different times, but the Constitution means different things at the same time.

Justice Thomas writes in his Texas concurring opinion, "the very 'flexibility' of this Court's Establishment Clause precedent leaves it incapable of consistent application . . . . The inconsistency between the decisions the Court reaches today . . . only compounds the confusion."

Justice Scalia points to the confusion between the two authorities as a threat to America's rule of law: "What distinguishes the rule of law from the dictatorship of a shifting Supreme Court majority is the absolutely indispensable requirement that judicial opinions be grounded in consistently applied principle. That is what prevents judges from ruling now this way, now that—thumbs up or thumbs down—as their personal preferences dictate."[13]

Thomas suggests the decisions, rather than speaking for and interpreting the Constitution, only add confusion to the legal debates and focuses attention not on the law, but the preferences of judges: "The unintelligibility of this Court's precedents raise the further concern that . . . adjudication of Establishment Clause challenges turns on judicial predilections . . . . Line drawing in this area will be erratic and heavily influenced by the personal views of the judges."[14]

Justice Thomas further writes, "a park ranger has claimed that a cross erected to honor World War I veterans on a rock in the Mojave Desert Preserve violated the Establishment Clause, and won . . . . If a cross in the middle of a desert establishes a religion, then no religious observance is safe from challenge."[15] Thomas claims, "this Court's precedent permits even the slightest public recognition of religion to constitute an establishment of religion."[16]

Justice Stephen Breyer defends his decision in support of the display in Texas and in opposition to the display in Kentucky by arguing such determinations do not reside in the plain language of the Constitution but rather in the discretion of judges: "If the relation between government and religion is one of separation, but not of mutual hostility and suspicion, one will inevitably find difficult borderline cases. And in such cases, I see no test-related substitute for the exercise of legal judgment."[17]

Justice Stevens strenuously defends the idealism of a living Constitution; a Constitution in which a judge, unconcerned with the language of the law, makes his decision based on his understanding of society rather than the words of the Constitution:

> It is our duty, therefore, to interpret the First Amendment's command that "Congress shall make no law respecting an establishment of religion" not by merely asking what those words meant to observers at the time of the founding, but instead by deriving from the Clause's text and history the broad principles that remain valid today. . . . We serve our constitutional mandate by expounding the meaning of constitutional provisions with one eye towards our Nation's history and the other fixed on its democratic aspirations. . . . Fortunately, we are not bound by the Framer's expectations . . . as religious pluralism has expanded, so has our acceptance of what constitutes valid belief systems.[18]

When judges assume the power to determine "valid belief systems," we travel down a dangerous road.

Thomas encourages that "we return to the original meaning of the word 'establishment.'"[19] He says "coercion" through financial support or force of law is a "hallmark of historical establishments of religion." Thomas says the plaintiff "need not stop to read [the Ten Commandments monument] or even to look at it, let alone to express support for it or adopt the Commandments as guides for his life. The mere presence of the monument along his path involves no coercion and thus does not violate the Establishment Clause." He laments, "This Court's precedent elevates the trivial to the proverbial 'federal case' by making benign signs and postings subject to challenge."

In the Texas case, Thomas notes the court adopts

an unhappy compromise that fails fully to account for either the adherent's or the non adherent's beliefs, and provides no principled way to choose between them. Even worse, the incoherence of the Court's decisions in this area renders the Establishment Clause impenetrable and incapable of consistent application. All told, this Court's jurisprudence leaves courts, governments, and believers and nonbelievers alike confused.[20]

CONCLUSION

In the May 9, 2001, press conference announcing his first slate of judicial nominees, President George W. Bush said,

When a President chooses a judge, he is placing in human hands the authority and majesty of the law. He owes it to the Constitution and to the country to choose with care. A judge, by the most basic measure, has an obligation shared by the President and members of Congress. All of us are constitutional officers, sworn to serve within the limits of our Constitution and laws. When we observe those limits, we exercise our rightful power. When we exceed those limits, we abuse our powers. . . . Every judge I appoint will be a person who clearly understands the role of a judge is to interpret the law, not to legislate from the bench. To paraphrase the third occupant of this house, James Madison, the courts exist to exercise not the will of men, but the judgment of law. My judicial nominees will know the difference. Understanding this will make them more effective in the defense of rights guaranteed under the Constitution, the enforcement of our laws, and more effective in assuming that justice is done to the guilty and for the innocent.

This is what proponents of a living Constitution fear, because judges who do not take the law into their own hands return the culture war battles to elections and legislative bodies—and of late those battles have been won not by the liberal fringe but by traditional values.

The concept of a changing, evolving Constitution undermines confidence in the rule of law, bringing the Court's approval rating to a record low of 41 percent.[21] That should be of concern for all Americans.

Many voters and activists in the culture war were motivated by the abortion issue in the battle over the selection of judges. But other Americans who may have disapproved of abortion yet reluctantly accepted it as a matter of fact were shaken when the Ninth Circuit ruled "one Nation under God" in the Constitution to be unconstitutional and when the Massachusetts Supreme Court redefined marriage. Suddenly a lot more voters connected the dots and understood what the battle over confirming judges is all about. They went to the polls and registered their dissent. Their numbers were particularly noteworthy in Ohio, which played a decisive role in the 2004 presidential election. Rather than deciding and ending the culture war, these activist decisions stirred reinforcements. A sleeping giant awoke.

The battle over the confirmation of judges will continue as long as we permit court rulings based on interpretation of a living Constitution. Those with a philosophy of a living Constitution, by definition, desire activist judges. They need someone willing to legislate from the bench in order to adjust the Constitution to their perceived cultural and societal desires. Thus they will seek to defeat any nominee who differs from them ideologically, or who will seek to interpret the Constitution according to original meaning.

How does the concept of a living Constitution—a mystery Constitution—affect the average American? The effect on Susette Kelo and Wilhelmina Dery's family was that they lost their homes. The impact on 10.6 million students in the public schools of nine western states was that they were prohibited from voluntarily reciting the Pledge of Allegiance.

The effect for the citizens of Massachusetts was that the definition of marriage in their state was changed by judicial decision. It means the citizens of McCreary County and Pulaski County, Kentucky, cannot display the Ten Commandments in their courthouses despite thousands of such displays across the United States, including one specifically protected in Texas.

How will it affect you and me in the future? We do not know. That is a mystery we cannot solve until five members of the Supreme Court make a decision. There will be no public debate. You and I will have no say. Nine judges will meet in secret and then tell us what the Constitution means and how it will affect all Americans.

Proponents of this living, mystery Constitution are so determined to have their way and block non-activist judges, they believe the ends justify the means and will do whatever is necessary to accomplish their objectives. Just as they choose not to take the culture war fight through the democratic process, so they choose not to take the confirmation battle to the court of public opinion. Instead, they employ the unprecedented tactic of judicial filibuster.

CHAPTER TEN

Filibuster

THE HISTORIC AND CONSTITUTIONAL CASE FOR CONFIRMATION BY MAJORITY VOTE

MY PERSONAL FOOTNOTE in judicial confirmation history will list me among President Bush's nominees blocked from confirmation without precedent by a minority of the U.S. Senate. Democrats didn't use the parliamentary procedure known as the filibuster to preserve the nature of the Senate, or pay tribute to the wishes of our Founders, or even to protect debate on legislative matters. They employed the filibuster to prevent confirmation, thus stopping the Senate from fulfilling its "Advice and Consent" responsibility.

While in years past, the full Senate approved or rejected controversial nominees by majority vote, a number of Bush's nominees were for years denied that opportunity. The left wing views the battle for America's courts too valuable to trust democracy, or they would allow a majority of the people's elected senators to vote on judicial confirmations. The Far Left special-interest groups are determined to have their way, regardless of what means are necessary.

An examination of the filibuster, past confirmation battles, and most importantly the U.S. Constitution builds a historic and constitutional case for confirmation by majority vote. Temporary agreements may enable the Senate to move judicial confirmations efficiently for a time. But ultimately, a parliamentary ruling, a comprehensive rules change or a corrective legislative measure may be necessary to ensure fairness not only to the current nominees, but also to future nominees, presidents, political parties, the courts, and more importantly, the American people.[1]

Neither the Framers of the Constitution nor the Senate "created" the filibuster. The filibuster may be "considered Congress's most famous procedural tool," but it is one with a disgraceful heritage as the means employed for nearly a century to defend Jim Crow laws and prevent the enactment of civil rights legislation.[2]

The term "filibuster" originated in the Dutch word *vrijbuiter*, which means "looters and robbers," The English anglicized *vrijbuiter* into "freebooter," a term for "pirate." The Spanish translated it into *filibusteros* to describe pirates who looted the Spanish West Indies.[3] Americans adopted the word in the mid-1800s as "a synonym for pro-Slavery mercenary pirates who would attack Latin American governments to try to spread the Slave system."[4] Opponents of the procedure in Congress applied the term to "legislative minorities who used what the majority deemed piratical, disorderly, [and] lawless methods of obstructing business in the Senate."[5]

When the Senate organized in 1789, it adopted a rule for a motion of the "previous question," which when agreed to by a simple majority moved any proceeding to final consideration of the question at hand without further debate or delay. The Senate used this motion only once between 1789 and 1806 and dropped it from the 1806 rules—perhaps inadvertently—creating an opportunity for a filibuster by omitting a means to end debate.[6]

No senator engaged the procedural option for filibuster until the 1840s and then only against legislation. In 1841, Senator John C. Calhoun of South Carolina originated the filibuster to defeat legislation he viewed as a threat to the rights of the minority, the rights of individual states, and the institution of slavery.[7] Henry Clay of Kentucky, who saw a major banking bill he proposed blocked by Calhoun's concoction, threatened to change Senate rules to allow the majority to close debate, but this would not happen until the nation faced a world at war.[8]

From 1841 until 1917, the Senate operated under a tradition of endless debate. Senators routinely blocked legislation because the rules gave no process to end discussion as long as one member continued to object. But an approaching war and an angry president forced action.

By 1915, the Senate had become a breeding ground for filibusters. In the final weeks of the Congress that ended on March 4, one administration measure related to the war in Europe tied the Senate up for thirty-three days and blocked passage of three major appropriations bills. Two years later, as pressure increased for American entry into that war, a twenty-three-day, end-of-session filibuster against the president's proposal to arm merchant ships also failed, taking with it much other essential legislation.[9]

On March 4, 1917, President Woodrow Wilson—exasperated by the filibuster's use to prevent Congress from doing the work of the country—declared, the "Senate of the United States is the only legislative body in the world which cannot act when its majority is ready for action. A little group of willful men, representing no opinion but their own, have rendered the great government of the United States helpless and contemptible."[10]

President Wilson demanded the Senate adopt a cloture rule, and four days later it agreed to a rule, but essentially preserved the tradition of unlimited debate. "The rule required a two-thirds majority to end debate and permitted each member to speak for an additional hour after that before voting on final passage. Over the next forty-six years, the Senate managed to invoke cloture on only five occasions."[11] A two-thirds majority (sixty-seven votes) to end debate continued until 1975 when it was changed to three-fifths (sixty votes) by Senator Robert Byrd, a West Virginia Democrat by then very familiar with the filibuster.

The filibuster has a colorful history in the Senate—sometimes humorous and sometimes disgraceful.

Louisiana senator Huey Long began a fifteen-and-one-half-hour filibuster on June 12, 1935, to retain Senate confirmation for the National Recovery Administration's senior employees. Senator Long wanted to block his political enemies from Louisiana allied with

President Franklin Roosevelt from obtaining these jobs without his consent. After reading and expounding on every section of the Constitution, he noticed many of the other senators were napping. He asked the presiding officer, Vice President John Nance Garner, to compel the senators to listen. The response from Vice President Garner: "That would be unusual cruelty under the Bill of Rights." As he continued speaking, Senator Long needed more material and offered to "accommodate any senator on any point on which he needs advice." No senator responded, though he did receive several notes from the press gallery on potential subjects. After discussing life, politics, and cooking recipes, he retired to the rest room. His measure was defeated, but senators from across the county learned how Senator Long preferred his cornbread, oysters, and turnip greens.[12]

Americans are most familiar with the filibuster portrayed by Jimmy Stewart's character Jefferson Smith in *Mr. Smith Goes to Washington*. In this film, a virtuous young man uses the filibuster to hold the Senate floor in an attempt to vindicate himself and expose corruption.[13] But history records a more sinister use of the filibuster: a tool of obstructionists seeking to defeat anti-lynching and civil rights laws during Jim Crow and segregation. The Senate recently passed a resolution apologizing for the previous failure to enact anti-lynching laws—three of which passed the House of Representatives only to meet defeat on the floor of the Senate at the hands of the filibuster.[14] "Since its inception in 1841, the filibuster of legislation has been used to block legislation protecting black voters in the South, in 1870 and 1890-91; to block anti-lynching legislation in 1922, 1935, and 1938; to block anti-poll tax legislation in 1942, 1944, and 1946; and to block anti-race discrimination statutes on 11 occasions between 1946 and 1975."[15]

In 1957, as the Senate considered significant civil rights legislation, the filibuster appeared again. Senator Strom Thurmond, then a Democrat from South Carolina, spoke for twenty-four hours and eighteen minutes—the record for a one-man filibuster remaining today. His goal was to defeat the Republican-backed Civil Rights Act of 1957. Southern Democrats and Senate Majority Leader Lyndon B. Johnson of Texas had succeeded in watering down the bill, but it was still too much for Senator Thurmond. But without the support of even his like-minded colleagues (who felt passing the weak bill was better than defeating a strong bill), the measure passed shortly after Senator Thurmond completed his speech.[16]

In 1964, Senator Robert Byrd, a Democrat from West Virginia, spoke for fourteen hours and thirteen minutes against the Civil Rights Act of 1964. His speech was part of a fifty-seven-day debate (including six Saturdays). Proponents of the bill were able to invoke cloture and pass the bill over the filibuster.[17]

For more than two hundred years of American history, the filibuster was used—for good or for ill—only to block legislation. Never was it used to block the confirmation of judicial nominees. This historical practice took a radical turn during George W. Bush's tenure as president of the United States. Democrats filibustered ten of President Bush's nominees to the U.S. Courts of Appeals and threatened filibusters of six more.[18]

As described by Professor Steven Calabresi, "for the first time in 214 years of American history a minority of Senators is seeking to extend the tradition of filibustering from legislation to judicial nominees who [the minority of senators] know enjoy the support of a majority of the Senate. This is a change of constitutional dimensions and amounts to a kind of coup d'etat."[19] The legislative filibuster, right or wrong, has no place in preventing the Senate from completing its Constitutional duty of "Advice and Consent."

I have heard Democrats argue with a straight face that should Republicans be successful in eliminating the use of the filibuster to block judicial nominees, they would destroy a safeguard given to us by our Founders, and they would violate the principle of checks and balances between the parties. They suggest such a move would change the very nature of the Senate and trample the rights of the minority. These claims move rhetoric to hyperbole.

As we have already seen, the Founders did not give us the filibuster. Democratic senator Ted Kennedy affirmed this on the floor of the U.S. Senate in 1975: "The filibuster rule is not enshrined in the Constitution."[20] Furthermore, the system of checks and balances so firmly ingrained in both our system and concept of government applies not to political parties but to the three independent branches of government—the executive, the legislative, and the judicial—holding each within its constitutional scope and moderating power among the other two. Checks and balances does not apply to political parties. It has always been understood that way, and there has never been a suggestion that this concept protects the minority party from the majority party—until now.

Only two presidents in the last fifty years have served with a filibuster-proof Senate of their own party,[21] but every Democratic president during that time has served some time with their party in majority control of the Senate.[22] Yet never during these times did the Republicans filibuster judicial nominees to protect their minority rights.[23]

The U.S. Constitution empowers action by a minority in only one instance. One-fifth of either house of Congress may order a recording of any vote.[24] But in no case does the Constitution mention or give protection to a minority political party. The Framers left that up to the American people: voting is the check and balance between parties, not the filibuster.

The Democrats further suggest the filibuster is essential to the nature of the Senate. They argue that without the filibuster, the Senate would not serve as the deliberative body it was designed to be and would instead function under majority rule like the House of Representatives. Stopping the filibuster of judicial nominees will do nothing of the sort. The Senate will maintain its function as the "higher" house of Congress due to its makeup (100 rather than 435 members) and its longevity and stability (six-year terms rather than two-year terms). Additionally, the legislative filibuster and the practice of acting on unanimous consent (giving great power to each senator) would remain unchanged even when judicial nominees are approved by a simple-majority vote. Considering the Senate has confirmed judicial nominees for more than two centuries without filibustering, but by majority vote, continuing that practice today would not deter the deliberative nature of the Senate.

It has been Democrats who have sought to end even the legislative filibuster, not Republicans. Democrats tried to end all filibusters in 1995 on a motion by Senators Joseph Lieberman and Tom Harkin. The

Senate defeated their motion 76-19. The only senators voting to end the legislative filibuster were Democrats, including Senators Jeff Bingaman, Barbara Boxer, Russ Feingold, Tom Harkin, Ted Kennedy, John Kerry, Frank Lautenberg, Joseph Lieberman, and Paul Sarbanes.[25] No Republican then or now sought to end the legislative filibuster. On May 9, 2003, Senators Bill Frist, the majority leader from Tennessee; and Zell Miller, a conservative Democrat from Georgia, introduced the Frist-Miller Proposal. This proposal to the Senate rules would specifically protect extended debate on legislative matters, while guaranteeing majority-supported nominees would receive an up-or-down vote on the Senate floor.[26]

Democrats seem to suggest the filibuster of ten of President Bush's nominees is not such a big deal because they have approved so many of his other nominees. They contend 95 percent (204 out of 214) of President Bush's judicial nominees were confirmed during his first term in office. That argument is not only grossly misleading, it is factually incorrect. During his first term, President Bush made 177 nominations to the district courts, 51 nominations to the appellate courts, and one nomination to the Court of International Trade: 229 nominees, not 214. And 204 confirmations out of 229 nominees produces only 89 percent, not 95 percent. Of the appellate court nominees, where the fight was taking place, only 35 of President Bush's 51 nominees were confirmed: an overall rate of only 69 percent for the full 4 years.[27] The old phrase appropriated by Mark Twain comes to mind: "There are three kinds of lies: lies, damned lies, and statistics." While both sides can twist numbers to make a point, the Democrats are disingenuous to suggest they confirmed 95 percent of President Bush's nominees to the federal courts.

Attempting to minimize their obstructionism, Democrats claim they confirmed all but ten of President Bush's nominees. Should they be proud they didn't follow the Constitution ten times? They did the proper thing in giving President Bush's other nominees an up-or-down vote, but doing the right thing sometimes does not allow you to do the wrong thing other times. I do not suggest the Senate is required to confirm every nominee a president submits. I do believe nominees who

accept the assignment to public service deserve the courtesy of a vote—
and not just some of them some of the time.

In reality, the filibuster is a means to continue debate on legislation.
It should not be applied to judicial nominees, but if it were, it should be
employed properly: for the purposes of extending debate. Senator Byrd
likes to defend his side's filibuster of the 1964 Civil Rights Act by
contrasting it to previous legislative battles, saying it "differed from other
lengthy filibusters of the past, in that there was serious and informed
'extended debate' over the entire period during which it was before the
Senate. The discussion avoided the time-consuming dilatory tactics that
had been the trademark of many earlier filibusters, and neither side
resorted to parliamentary gamesmanship."[28]

Senator Byrd seems to make the point that there are good and bad
filibusters: the former being constructive discussions to continue
examining an issue, the latter simply a means to delay, obstruct, or block
legislation or to conduct political grandstanding. But Democrats did not
wish to use the filibuster as a means of extending debate or construc-
tively considering a nominee. They used the filibuster as a means of
blocking Senate consideration of these nominees and preventing the
Senate from fulfilling its Constitutional duty of "Advice and Consent."

In April 2003, Republican senator Robert Bennett sought to bring
forward six additional hours of debate to consider the nomination of
Judge Priscilla Owen to the Fifth Circuit Court of Appeals before a final
vote. Senate Minority Whip Harry Reid objected and suggested they
instead consider other nominees. Senator Bennett revised his motion
and asked for unanimous consent for ten additional hours to debate
Judge Owen's nomination before voting. Again, Senator Reid objected,
saying there were more constructive matters for the Senate to consider
than her nomination. Senator Bennett then said, "I ask what number of
hours would be sufficient" for Senator Reid. Senator Reid responded,
"there is not a number in the universe that would be sufficient."[29]
Senator Reid's response revealed the truth: their purpose was obstruction
not discussion.

The impropriety of filibustering judicial nominees was well-stated
in 1968 by a non-partisan coalition called the "Lawyers' Committee on

Supreme Court Nominations," which comprised the deans of most major law schools and the past presidents of the American Bar Associations. The committee wrote, "If . . . nominations do not win the support of a majority of the Senate, they will fail. If they do win such support, they deserve the Senate's consent. Nothing would more poorly serve our constitutional system than for the nominations to have earned the approval of the Senate majority but to be thwarted because the majority is denied a chance to vote."[30]

The Framers saw the Senate's role of "Advice and Consent" as limited to the prevention of "the appointment of unfit characters from State prejudice, from family connection, from personal attachment, or from a view to popularity."[31]

During the Clinton administration, Attorney General Janet Reno made the same point: "The Senate, of course, has a constitutional duty to advice and consent, but surely the Framers did not intend Congress to obstruct the appointment of much-needed judges, but rather simply to ensure that well-qualified individuals were appointed to the federal bench."[32]

The limited role of the Senate in the confirmation process was noted by historian Joseph Harris, who wrote, "the debates of the Convention indicate that 'advice and consent' was regarded simply as a vote of approval or rejection. The phrase was used as synonymous with 'approbation,' 'concurrence,' and 'approval,' and the power of the Senate was spoken of as a negative on the appointment by the President."[33]

It is not just Republicans who believe nominees should receive an up-or-down vote or that a majority should confirm judges to the bench. Democrats also recognize our courts need judges. They know obstructing confirmation delays the administration of justice. Consider these statements by Democratic leaders who faced frustrations during the Clinton administration:

• Senator Joe Biden: "I also respectfully suggest that everyone who is nominated is entitled to have a shot, to a hearing and to have a shot to be heard on the floor and have a vote on the floor."[34]

- Senator Carl Levin: "Mr. President, the Senate today will vote on the confirmation of a number of judicial nominees. I not only have no problem with that, I very much favor it. These nominees deserve a vote. The districts in which they will serve surely deserve to have their nominations acted upon. I believe the nation, as a whole, deserves to have these nominees, and other nominees awaiting hearings and votes acted on by this Senate as well."[35]

- Senator Patrick Leahy, ranking member of the Senate Judiciary Committee: "I have stated over and over again on this floor that I would . . . object and fight against any filibuster on a judge, whether it is somebody I opposed or supported; that I felt the Senate should do its duty."[36] "Those who delay or prevent the filling of these vacancies must understand that they are delaying or preventing the administration of justice."[37] "A President should be given a great deal of latitude on who he nominates to the Federal court. If we disagree with a nomination, then we can vote against it. But, frankly, Mr. President, not only does it damage the integrity and the independence of the Federal judiciary by just holding judicial nominations hostage where nobody ever even votes on them, but I think it damages the integrity of the U.S. Senate."[38] "Every Senator can vote against any nominee. Every Senator has that right . . . . They can vote against them in this committee and on the floor. But it's the responsibility of the U.S. Senate to at least bring them to a vote."[39]

- Senator Tom Daschle: "The nation cannot afford to continue to see cases delayed and backlogs grow to judicial vacancies that could be filled if [the Senate] would stop seeking to delay or block well-qualified and capable judges."[40]

- Senator Barbara Boxer: "I don't think it does any good to have these judgeships vacant. Justice needs to be done, and it is hard to serve it when you don't have the judgeships filled."[41]

- Senator Ted Kennedy: "We owe it to Americans across the country to give these nominees a vote. If our Republican colleagues don't like them, vote against them. But give them a vote."[42]

Unfortunately, these Democrats changed their stories following the election of George W. Bush as president. While they believed in the necessity of giving judges the opportunity of a vote—some like Senator Leahy specifically said even judges he opposed should have an up-or-down vote—they all chose to filibuster President Bush's nominees. They gave no justification, no apology; they simply said one thing and did something else.

What prevents the Senate majority from acting and ending this obstruction? The Senate rules give each individual member of the body great power to determine the course of legislation and debate; nearly every matter of business is conducted by unanimous consent (meaning everyone either agrees or agrees not to object). However, if even one senator objects, the proper procedures to counter the objection must be followed.

There are three ways to change the procedure: (1) by a rules change, (2) by a statute, or (3) by a parliamentary interpretation setting a new precedent. Any rules change must be passed by Senate resolution requiring a two-thirds majority (sixty-seven votes), unless the change is made at the beginning of a new Congress. A statute must be passed by the Senate, passed by the House, and then signed by the president. A statute needs only a simple majority to pass; however it is subject to the endless debate of a legislative filibuster which can only be cut-off by a three-fifths majority (sixty votes).

A new parliamentary precedent involves a complicated but conventional procedure. A Republican senator would make the point of order that the filibuster of judicial nominees is unconstitutional. The presiding officer would submit that point of order to the Senate for a decision, but would rule the point is not debatable (otherwise, a filibuster on the point of order could occur). At this point, a Democratic senator may appeal the ruling that the motion is not debatable. A Republican would move to table or indefinitely suspend the Democratic appeal. By approving the motion to table (under Senate rules only a simple majority is necessary to table and it is not debatable), the Senate would sustain the ruling that the original Republican point of order is not debatable. Then a simple majority of the Senate could decide that the filibuster against judicial nominees is unconstitutional.[43]

This procedure has been termed by some "the constitutional option" and by others "the nuclear option." Senator Trent Lott noted in the epilogue of his recent book *Herding Cats* that the phrase "nuclear option"

> first came from my lips—at least according to some reporters and pundits. What happened, as I recall, is that a reporter told me the Democrats would go nuclear if we tried this ploy. Well, fine, I responded, let 'em go nuclear. In any event, political journalists embraced the term, predicting that the Democrats would pull down the Senate walls and bring the body to a standstill rather than submit to what we were doing. I prefer to call it the 'constitutional plan,' since it's inspired by prose about appointing judges found in both the Constitution and the Federalist Papers.[44]

Following the Constitution should not be controversial; it shouldn't be explosive. Many Republicans now refer to it as "the Byrd option" because Senator Byrd has employed this procedure on a number of occasions.

Senator Robert Byrd of West Virginia is the U.S. Senate's most senior member. When he takes to the Senate floor, one is as likely to hear a speech about the history of the Roman Senate as a discussion on pending legislation. He has fought Senate procedural battles for decades, and the media delights in referencing his arcane knowledge of Senate rules and precedent. Senator Byrd's actions demonstrate how the constitutional option is neither unprecedented nor destructive to the nature of the Senate.

Four times when he served as Senate majority leader, Senator Byrd used a simple majority to change Senate procedures apart from altering the standing rules: (1) ending post-cloture filibusters (1977); (2) limiting amendments to appropriations bills (1979); (3) governing consideration of nominations (1980); and (4) governing voting procedures (1987). Two of these overturned standing precedents and two reinterpreted the language of an existing standing rule.

Democrats dispute these occasions serve as precedent for the constitutional option, but each of these changes was made by a point of order and sustained with a simple majority vote. This is the exact process that would be followed under the constitutional option.

Senator Byrd expressed the concept of majority rule well in the 1979 incident:

> This Congress is not obliged to be bound by the dead hand of the past. . . . The first Senate, which met in 1789, approved 19 rules by a majority vote. Those rules have been changed from time to time. . . . So the Members of the Senate who met in 1789 and approved that first body of rules did not for one moment think, or believe, or pretend, that all succeeding Senates would be bound by that Senate . . . . It would be just as reasonable to say that one Congress can pass a law providing that all future laws have to be passed by two-thirds vote. Any Member of this body knows that the next Congress would not heed that law and would proceed to change it and would vote repeal of it by majority vote.[45]

In 1975, Democrat Senator Ted Kennedy also argued the case for majority rule in the Senate: "[The filibuster] is a rule that was made by the Senate, and it is a rule that can be unmade by the Senate. . . . Mr. President, the immediate issue is whether a simple majority of the Senate is entitled to change the Senate rules. Although the procedural rules are complex, it is clear that this question should be settled by a majority vote."[46]

The description "nuclear" is not applied because of the ruling, but due to the anticipated response by the Democratic minority. The rules change will not "blow up" the Senate; instead the Democrats' retaliation to the rules change could grind the Senate to a halt. Democratic Minority Leader Harry Reid wrote to Majority Leader Bill Frist warning Republicans if they changed the rules, "the Majority should not expect to receive cooperation from the Minority in the conduct of Senate business."[47]

Senator Reid made it clear he would shut down the Senate if Republicans removed the filibuster on judicial nominations. No funding bills; no education bills; no healthcare bills; no energy bills; no homeland security bills; no military support bills: the Democrats claimed they were prepared to stop business to maintain endless debate on judicial nominees. But they were not interested in debate, only in preventing an up-or-down vote. Senator Reid said, "If they, for whatever reason, decide to do this, it's not only wrong, they will rue the day they did it, because we will do whatever we can do to strike back. I know procedures around here. And I know that there will still be Senate business conducted. But I will, for lack of a better word, screw things up."[48]

Filibustering judicial nominees had already accomplished Reid's goal to "screw things up." Any measures the Republicans took in response to the unprecedented filibusters would simply be trying to restore the Senate's historical tradition of confirmation by majority vote, though Democrats would view it as part of the ongoing escalation.

Some conservatives caution Republicans not to invoke the constitutional solution. They say in the future, conservatives might want to filibuster a judge. David Broder recounts a conversation with Republican senator Robert Bennett of Utah who said that "whatever the outcome of this vote, he fears that a sword has been unsheathed that will forever change the way the Senate operates. 'Once we [Republicans] try to change the rules with 51 votes, the precedent is on the table,' he said. 'If Hillary Clinton becomes president with a Democratic Senate and wants to appoint Lani Guinier to the Supreme Court, Harry Reid could make that happen with 51 votes.' That is a thought for Republicans to ponder."[49]

Still it is wrong for conservatives to advocate following the Constitution when it serves their purposes but disregard the Constitution when it conflicts with their goals. Considering Republicans have never used the judicial filibuster in the past, it seems unlikely they would need to in the future, unless this escalation by the Democrats is permanent and Republicans retaliate in like manner.

In essence, these filibusters were not about the appellate nominees, but a future Supreme Court nominee. Former Nixon White House counsel John Dean said, "It is clear that both the White House and the Democratic leadership of the Senate have been preparing for vacancies on the Supreme Court. That's what the current Senate filibuster of lower-court judges is really all about."[50] But history shows us contentious Supreme Court nominees can be discussed, vetted, and even defeated without need of a filibuster. In fact, the Senate has defeated twelve Supreme Court nominees by majority vote without filibuster. This warm-up with appellate nominees was unnecessary.

From 1960 until 2003, there were contentious and high-profile fights over several Supreme Court nominees and even a couple of Court of Appeals nominees. But no nominee to the federal courts with majority support during this period, or at any time in history, was denied confirmation by filibuster. In the past, whenever the escalation reached the point of filibuster, senators backed off to maintain the tradition and comity of the Senate. When it came to President Bush's nominees, history changed and the Senate changed with it.

Some Democrats cite President Lyndon B. Johnson's 1968 nomination of Supreme Court justice Abe Fortas to the position of chief justice as precedent for their use of the filibuster to block President Bush's judicial nominees. However, the historical record does not support the claim that Justice Fortas was filibustered. The nomination of Justice Fortas failed because it could not "obtain the support of fifty-one Senators . . . due to allegations of ethical improprieties and the bipartisan opposition of twenty-four Republicans and nineteen Democrats."[51]

When a cloture vote was sought on the Fortas nomination, he had the support of only forty-five senators. The opposition to Fortas did not seek to block his confirmation; they wanted additional time to investigate why he should not be confirmed. The vote against cloture was bipartisan and it was clear to everyone involved he did not enjoy the support of a majority of senators; a contrast to all of the blocked Bush nominees. Senator Robert Griffin led the opposition against Justice Fortas and made it clear there was never an intention to filibuster Justice Fortas.[52] This was merely an effort to obtain more time and more information.[53] This cloture failure would not have occurred except President Johnson was convinced Fortas would be rejected unless the Senate acted quickly; he knew each day Fortas was losing more support. He attempted to rush the Senate into a vote. The Senate responded to his haste with a move to continue consideration.[54] President Johnson withdrew the nomination within a few days, not because there was a filibuster, but because Fortas did not have majority support.

Soon after the election of President Richard M. Nixon, Justice Fortas resigned from the Supreme Court under threat of impeachment. President Nixon chose federal Appeals Court judge Clement Haynesworth of South Carolina to sit on the High Court. Some Democrats were embittered over Fortas's resignation, although other Democrats opposed Fortas. There was retaliation. Democrats charged Haynesworth improperly ruled on a case involving a firm to which he had ties before coming to the bench. On November 21, 1969, the Senate rejected Haynesworth on an up-or-down vote: 45 for his confirmation and 55 against it. There was no filibuster. There simply was no majority support.

Next, President Nixon selected G. Harold Carswell, a federal appeals court judge from Florida. But in 1948 Carswell had delivered a speech where he espoused his "vigorous belief in the principles of white supremacy." The Senate defeated this nomination as well: 45 for Carswell and 51 against him. Again no filibuster and no majority support.

In 1971, President Nixon was prepared to select Richard H. Poff, a conservative Republican congressman from Virginia, to serve on the Supreme Court. As opposition and personal attacks mounted, he withdrew before his name was formally submitted, not wishing to subject his ill wife to the battle. *Time* magazine discusses the matter:

> Besieged from many sources on the type of nominees he should select to fill two vacancies on the Supreme Court—including persistent pressure to name a woman—Nixon quietly pursued his own course. He asked the American Bar Association to give its opinion of the fitness of Virginia Representative Richard H. Poff, despite rising complaints from civil rights groups and the threat of another Senate nomination fight by Democratic Senator Birch Bayh, who led the successful opposition to Nominees Clement Haynesworth and G.

Harold Carswell. But just as the A.B.A. was about to make its private recommendation to the President, Poff telephoned a Nixon aide and said that he did not wish to have his name considered for the nomination. He noted the charges of "racist" already raised against him and the probability of a Senate battle over confirmation. Poff, whose wife is ill, told House Republican Leader Gerald Ford: "Jerry, I'm just not going to let my family and my name be subjected to that kind of abuse." Actually, Poff was supported by some liberals in the Congress for renouncing any segregationist views, and a White House count revealed that at least 55 Senators would have approved his nomination. Presidential Press Secretary Ronald Ziegler said that Nixon still felt that Poff is "highly qualified" but that he "respects the decision which the Congressman has made."[55]

President Nixon next chose William Rehnquist who, even after a failed cloture vote, was given an up-or-down vote and approved 68-26 by the full Senate. In 1986, President Ronald Reagan elevated Rehnquist to chief justice of the United States. Again Rehnquist faced extended debate. After successfully invoking cloture, the Senate confirmed Rehnquist's elevation on a vote of 65-33.[56]

But President Reagan's nomination of Judge Robert Bork to the Supreme Court in 1987 was the "turning point in the nomination process and a triumph for unrestrained politicization of the judicial confirmation process."[57] Bork's confirmation fight was so vicious it resulted in the coining of a new verb: "bork"—to conduct a coordinated political, personal, and public attack on the beliefs, history, and character of a nominee. Another authority defined the verb: "Bork, v. tr.: An ideological orchestrated assault upon the character, motivation, and abilities of an individual with the aim of preventing his election or appointment to public office."[58] The rhetoric of a new media age produced the most contentious Supreme Court fight ever. Yet through all the fight there was no effort to filibuster him. While maligned and assaulted by the left, he was still given an up-or-down vote. Judge Bork was defeated 42-58.

Many Republicans felt then and now that Robert Bork was treated inappropriately and unfairly. But whether or not Bork should have been rejected, his opponents employed the proper process—an up-or-down vote. The Senate rejected him by majority vote, not obstruction by filibuster.

The 1991 confirmation battle over Justice Clarence Thomas brought unprecedented allegations of sexual harassment into the Senate Judiciary Committee, attacks Thomas denied and described as a political "lynching." Thomas fought the charges and was confirmed by a 52-48 majority vote. While he possessed majority support, he would not have had the necessary support to break a filibuster. But despite the controversy, no filibuster was launched.

During 2000, near the end of the Clinton administration, two nominees to the Ninth Circuit Court of Appeals long held in committee were finally about to face their opportunity for a vote by the full Senate. A small group of Republican senators sought but failed to filibuster Richard Paez and Marsha Berzon.

Republicans criticized Paez's ethics for speaking publicly as a sitting federal judge against California voter initiative Proposition 209. He called it an "anti-civil rights initiative" while the measure was yet before the voters. Judicial ethics prohibit a judge from speaking out on political issues unless they affect the judiciary. Conservatives also criticized his decision to invalidate a Los Angeles law forbidding "aggressive panhandling" on grounds the measure violated the First Amendment's guarantee of freedom of speech. The opposition to Berzon was based on liberal issues she promoted on behalf of the American Civil Liberties Union. Berzon was extremely liberal.

Regardless, Republican senator and majority leader Trent Lott told the Associated Press, "My feeling is that we should not start filibustering these nominations." He joined Democratic Minority Leader Tom Daschle and filed for cloture before the filibuster attempt could get off the ground. More than twenty Republicans who opposed these individuals and on final passage voted against both nominees, joined with Senator Lott and Senator Daschle to vote for cloture, preventing a filibuster.[59] There was no filibuster because Republicans did not support the attempt.[60]

Abe Fortas did not have majority support of the Senate; both parties opposed him for reasons that led to his resignation from the Supreme

Court. Additionally, President Johnson withdrew his nomination before the Senate could fully consider him. Haynesworth, Carswell, and Bork were controversial but received up-or-down votes that failed. Rehnquist, Paez, and Berzon were opposed for ideological reasons but were given a vote and confirmed. Thomas had support from a majority of the Senate but not a filibuster-proof majority; still, he was given a vote and confirmed.

Everything changed in 2003. More than two hundred years of Senate tradition fell victim to continuing escalation of the battle over judicial nominees as Democrats began what would be the actual or threatened filibuster of sixteen of President Bush's nominees to the Courts of Appeal. Each of these nominees had support of a majority of the U.S. Senate, but a willful minority prevented the opportunity for a vote.

No judicial nominee with majority support in the entire history of the United States Senate was ever prevented from an up-or-down vote by filibuster. The Senate has no history and no tradition of such obstruction. But what about the Constitution? Is the filibuster of judicial nominees constitutional? The answer is categorically "no." The Constitution clearly provides federal judges shall be confirmed by majority vote.

Our Founding Fathers were the most able group of people ever assembled to draft a governing document for any nation at any time in history. Article II, Section 2 of the Constitution provides the president shall have the power "by and with the Advice and Consent of the Senate to make Treaties, provided two-thirds of the Senators present concur; and shall nominate, and by and with the Advice and Consent of the Senate shall appoint...Judges to the supreme Court, and all other Officers of the United States, whose Appointments are not herein otherwise provided for . . . ." The Constitution spells out treaties must be ratified by a two-thirds vote of the Senate. The very next clause in the Constitution provides judges of the Supreme Court shall be nominated by the president and appointed by the president with the "Advice and Consent" of the Senate. There is no requirement of a super-majority vote for judges. Our Founders knew what they were doing. They knew how to require a super-majority vote and they did in several instances.

The Constitution specifically requires a super-majority vote for: impeachment conviction (Article I, Section 3), expulsion of a member (Article I, Section 5), overriding a veto (Article I, Section 7), approving treaties (Article II, Section 2), proposing a constitutional amendment (Article V), and removing certain disqualifications to public service (Amendment XIV, Section 3), but not for judges.

In the "Advice and Consent" clause regarding judicial nominations, the language is identical to the immediately preceding treaty approval clause, except for the two-thirds requirement that the Framers clearly omitted from being a requirement for confirmation. It is perfectly clear the Framers of the Constitution intended judges to be confirmed by majority vote and that is what the Constitution provides.

Filibustering judicial nominees is completely contrary to the tradition and heritage of the United States Senate. For two centuries the United States Senate has confirmed judges who had majority support, even when extraordinarily controversial. The attack on President Bush's nominees was the first time the constitutional provision for the confirmation of judges by majority vote was totally ignored. If judicial nominees are filibustered in the future, the constitutional option should be implemented. But unless we permanently protect majority confirmation in Senate Rules (requiring two-thirds of the Senate—67 votes, unless done at the beginning of a new Congress), or pass legislation securing this custom for the future (requiring House and presidential agreement), any simple parliamentary ruling or agreement of understanding can be reversed or terminated when someone else's ox is being gored.

The judicial confirmation process is in chaos with political battles being fought from the halls of Congress to our neighborhoods, with the media and special-interest groups stirring up the mix. Secularists and elitists push against traditional values and advocate a living Constitution to move their agenda forward. In 2005, an agreement of understanding for a time diminished the fight in the Senate. A group of Senators later deemed "The Gang of 14" by the Washington press corps put together a temporary agreement that put to pause the filibustering of nominees, just a few months before two Supreme Court seats opened up.

CHAPTER ELEVEN

Overreach and Compromise

THE GANG OF 14

WHILE DEMOCRATIC SENATORS under direction of the liberal special-interest groups held President Bush's judicial nominations in filibuster limbo, Republicans explored methods to force the Senate to give each nominee an up-or-down vote. Some sought compromise from moderate Democrats who would reject their party's leadership and the interest groups and allow the votes. Others considered filing a lawsuit before the United States Supreme Court seeking a directive that the Senate carry out its constitutional responsibility of "Advice and Consent." But the maneuver with the most Republican support, and that of the conservative base, was a parliamentary procedure known as the "constitutional option."

Senate Republicans openly discussed with the press the constitutional option as early as spring 2003. But it was not until April 2005 when the movement really began to pick up speed, and May when Republican majority leader Bill Frist announced it would be implemented. Still, it appeared Democrats would hold firm; they stated unequivocally they would filibuster President Bush's nominees: Priscilla Owens, Janice Rogers Brown, and William Pryor. Minority Leader Harry Reid threatened to bring Senate business to a halt.

On Friday, May 20, Frist's office filed cloture on the nomination of Priscilla Owen and announced a roll call vote to proceed to consideration of her nomination on Tuesday, May 24:

> If the Senate invokes cloture on the nomination, the Senate will be required under its rules to give the Owen nomination a fair up or

down vote. In the event the Senate fails to invoke cloture on the Owen nomination and no reasonable arrangement for fair up or down votes is agreed to, the Majority Leader will begin the constitutional option by making a point of order to the Presiding Officer regarding the appropriate amount of time to be used by the Senate to debate Circuit and Supreme Court nominations. To ensure that all 100 Senators have the opportunity to decide on the precedent, the Majority Leader remains hopeful that parliamentary tactics will not be employed to prevent all 100 Senators from deciding the question. If the motion to table is successful and completed, the precedent regarding judicial nominations will then take effect.[1]

Frist was poised to raise a point of order that the filibuster of nominees was unconstitutional (based on Senator Byrd's precedents discussed in the previous chapter).[2] The presiding officer (presumably Vice President Dick Cheney) would have then ruled the point of order not debatable and submitted it to the Senate. Following an anticipated objection by Democrats, a Republican would have moved to lay the Democratic point of order on the table. By a simple majority, the Senate would have laid the Democratic objection on the table and then sustained the original point of order. The precedent would have been established—filibustering judicial nominees is unconstitutional—judges would be confirmed by majority vote.

Senator Trent Lott, who has the distinction of being the only person ever to serve as party whip—chief vote seeker and counter—both in the house of Representatives and in the Senate, carried around a list of senators and their leanings and seemed to feel secure that the constitutional option would prevail. But Lott said, "You never have the votes until you have the votes. You've got your clear voters, you've got your nervous nellies, and you've got those who will never tell you until the vote is taken. . . . In the end I think they'll be there."[3]

The stakes were high. If the constitutional option prevailed, Democrats would have no certain means to block Bush nominees—no opportunity to filibuster. If the constitutional option failed, Democrats would be assured the power to block any Bush nominee as long as they could take the political heat.

Senator Lott and Senator Ben Nelson, a moderate Democrat from Nebraska, had been meeting for some months to discuss the confirmation impasse and to work out some type of agreement. Both experienced negotiators, they came to the table with all options and sought two outcomes. Lott's politics of pragmatism wanted nominees confirmed: an end to the filibuster of those nominees currently languishing in the Senate, quick passage, and then a commitment for verifiable reasonableness in the future. Nelson wanted to preserve the Democrat's power to filibuster: maintain that threat hopefully to shape the president's choices of nominees, remove the obstructionist label from his party, and ensure the Senate continued to move forward on important legislation by avoiding a nuclear meltdown.

As their discussions progressed, they brought in additional Republican and Democratic senators and the shape and nature of proposed deals began to leak out. But no one had a clear picture of the deal's framework and the early rumors differed from the final result. Regardless, activists—liberals and conservatives alike—opposed the deal. Moveon.org's PAC director Ben Brandzel "said he does not believe Democratic leaders will compromise on preserving filibuster rights—but that it would not be well received by the online liberal group if they did."[4] Conservative organizations, assured the constitutional option would prevail and facing an opportunity to confirm essentially all of President Bush's current and future nominees, felt any deal was unnecessary and any concession too great.

Mississippians had followed the judicial confirmation controversy closely over several years. I am constantly humbled and honored by the support I received for my nomination back home in Mississippi, from both blacks and whites, Democrats and Republicans. My confirmation was part of a greater national struggle, but one that often made the newspapers and television in Mississippi. In 2002, my son Chip ran for (and won) his fourth term as a congressman from Mississippi. Due to redistricting, the campaign was against another incumbent congressman, a Democrat. With the national Democrat's aggressive rhetoric against me and slander against our state, Chip's opponent could not claim support from or effectiveness with his national party. In 2003, the

incumbent Democratic governor of Mississippi—Ronnie Musgrove—
was running for reelection against former Republican National
Committee chairman Haley Barbour. Musgrove and the other statewide
elected Democrats all supported my nomination. But Barbour's
campaign claimed no conservative Mississippi Democrat could influence
their Washington colleagues on issues like my nomination, a critique of
Musgrove's effectiveness, or the effectiveness of any conservative
Democrat. Mississippi Democrats are simply no match against the
liberal special-interest groups in the Democratic Party, said the Barbour
campaign.

In 2004, President Bush's reelection campaign in Mississippi
reminded folks about the national Democrats' attack on me—especially
that of North Carolina senator John Edwards, their nominee for vice
president. Since my nomination in 2001, my fight for confirmation, and
three campaigns continuously discussing this issue in Mississippi, folks
at home—generally a conservative group of people anyway—knew what
was going on with judicial nominations and followed it closely.

Thus when Dr. James Dobson, head of Focus on the Family, and
Reverend Don Wildmon, head of the American Family Association
(AFA), discussed the proposed deal on AFA's statewide Mississippi radio
network, things got tough for Trent.

"I don't remember being so disgusted and alarmed by what I just
heard confirmed in the Senate as I am now. . . . Senator Trent Lott is
about to sabotage Majority Leader Frist and cut a separate deal with the
Democrats to preserve the filibuster of judges," said Dobson. Wildmon
called the deal "exactly the kind of compromise the liberals have been
looking for. . . . Senator Lott's proposal will do nothing but allow the
liberals to still be in control."[5] They gave out Trent's office phone
numbers and Mississippians lit up his phone lines.

Dobson and Wildmon were correct in their concern about the
"deal" but had been given wrong information. In fact, Trent had worked
closely with Senator Frist on the matter and took the deal—the person-
alities, the demands, the compromises—to Frist to allow him to make
the decision on where to give, what to concede, and what not to concede
to bring the Senate as a body back together. Frist had his own dilemmas,

presidential aspirations, and plans and had to respond to the base and the majority of his Senate colleagues. He did not make a decision.

Trent understood Frist's position—he had been there himself. He had negotiated in good faith with opposing senators of good faith, but he personally could not accept the compromise they demanded; it was not strong enough for him. So Trent removed himself as the informal leader of the negotiations. Senator John McCain took over the Republican lead and with Ben Nelson of the Democrats fashioned a deal.

For three days preceding the anticipated execution of the constitutional option, news commentators kept up a barrage of coverage on the impending "crisis." Despite Senator Lott's seeming optimism, no one was really sure of the outcome. Over that weekend, some senators still believed a compromise agreement could be reached preserving traditional Senate comity and collegiality and averting what they felt would be a catastrophic vote.

On May 23, 2005, on the eve of the action, seven Democratic senators signed an agreement—a "memorandum of understanding"—specifically stating they would not oppose appeals court nominees Priscilla Owen, Janice Rogers Brown, and William Pryor, and they would not filibuster any other judicial nominees absent "extraordinary circumstances." Seven Republican senators agreed they would not vote for the constitutional option. These senators were dubbed the "Gang of 14" by the media. But the agreement only applies to the 109th Congress (expires at the end of 2006) or until any of the fourteen members back away from the nonbinding memo of understanding. The text of the memorandum is below:

MEMORANDUM OF UNDERSTANDING ON JUDICIAL NOMINATIONS

We respect the diligent, conscientious efforts, to date, rendered to the Senate by Majority Leader Frist and Democratic Leader Reid. This memorandum confirms an understanding among the signatories, based upon mutual trust and confidence, related to pending and future judicial nominations in the 109th Congress.

This memorandum is in two parts. Part I relates to the currently pending judicial nominees; Part II relates to subsequent individual nominations to be made by the President and to be acted upon by the Senate's Judiciary Committee.

We have agreed to the following:

Part I: <u>Commitments on Pending Judicial Nominations</u>

Votes for Certain Nominees. We will vote to invoke cloture on the following judicial nominees: Janice Rogers Brown (D.C. Circuit), William Pryor (11th Circuit), and Priscilla Owen (5th Circuit).

Status of Other Nominations. Signatories make no commitment to vote for or against cloture on the following judicial nominees: William Myers (9th Circuit) and Henry Saad (6th Circuit).

Part II: <u>Commitments for Future Nominations</u>

Future Nominations. Signatories will exercise their responsibilities under the Advice and Consent Clause of the United State Constitution in good faith. Nominees should only be filibustered under extraordinary circumstances, and each signatory must use his or her own discretion and judgment in determining whether such circumstances exist.

Rules Changes. In light of the spirit and continuing commitments made in this agreement, we commit to oppose the rules changes in the 109th Congress, which we understand to be any amendment to or interpretation of the Rules of the Senate that would force a vote on a judicial nomination by means other than unanimous consent or Rule XXII.

We believe that, under Article II, Section 2, of the United States Constitution, the word "Advice" speaks to consultation between the Senate and the President with regard to the use of the President's power to make nominations. We encourage the Executive branch of government to consult with members of the Senate, both Democratic and Republican, prior to submitting a judicial nomination to the Senate for consideration.

Such a return to the early practices of our government may well serve to reduce the rancor that unfortunately accompanies the advice and consent process in the Senate.

We firmly believe this agreement is consistent with the traditions of the United States Senate that we as Senators seek to uphold.

The memorandum was signed by fourteen members of the Senate, equally divided between Democrat and Republican:

THE GANG OF 14

DEMOCRATS	REPUBLICANS
Robert Byrd (West Virginia)	Lincoln Chafee (Rhode Island)
Daniel Inouye (Hawaii)	Susan Collins (Maine)
Mary Landrieu (Louisiana)	Mike DeWine (Ohio)
Joseph Lieberman (Connecticut)	Lindsey Graham (South Carolina)
Ben Nelson (Nebraska)	John McCain (Arizona)
Mark Pryor (Arkansas)	Olympia Snowe (Maine)
Ken Salazar (Colorado)	John Warner (Virginia)

The *Clarion Ledger*, a Jackson, Mississippi, newspaper, reported how the compromise materialized:

Republican Sen. John McCain of Arizona got much of the credit this week for a deal that ended a bitter partisan debate in the Senate. But the outlines of the deal were really Sen. Trent Lott's idea, according to a spokesman for another senator who helped sell the deal. . . . David DiMartino, press secretary for Sen. Ben Nelson, D-Neb., a key member of the group of 14 Democratic and Republican moderates that drew up the agreement, said Lott and Nelson had worked for about six months to end the dispute over judges. The senators first considered two options that would have largely barred Democrats from filibustering the president's judicial nominees. But they realized that neither bill would garner enough support in the Senate, DiMartino said. They were inspired to come up with a third option after Sen. Lamar Alexander, R-Tenn., made an impassioned plea in March for warring Democrats and Republicans to come together on the judges issue, DiMartino said. . . . The result: something very similar to the plan ultimately adopted by the group of moderates headed by McCain. However, Lott felt he couldn't embrace the plan because it was impossible to define "extraordinary" circumstances and it would be unfair to allow confirmation votes on some nominees and not others. . . . So Lott instead opted to back the nuclear option, the same approach supported by Sen. Bill Frist of Tennessee, who replaced Lott as Senate Republican leader. . . . "Had Senator Lott been able to stay with the deal, he would have been the head of the negotiators," DiMartino said.[6]

There is no way you can look at that agreement as a Democratic victory. Two days after the deal was announced, Owen was confirmed by the Senate. Two weeks later, Brown was confirmed, and the next day, the Senate confirmed Pryor. These confirmations were exactly what President Bush and the Republicans had tried to accomplish for five long years and the Democrats had blocked. The deal showed these nominees were not outside the mainstream. In the words of Senator John Cornyn,

> The agreement is thus an effective admission of guilt—an admission that these fine nominees should never have been filibustered in the first place. Moreover, by forbidding future filibusters of judicial nominations except under "extraordinary circumstances," the agreement establishes a new benchmark for future conduct in the United States Senate—namely, that other qualified judges who are firmly committed to the law, like Owen, Brown, and Pryor, deserve an up-or-down vote, too.[7]

In a sense, the seven Republicans made an empty gesture in the agreement. If the Democrats did not filibuster, there would be no reason or occasion for the Republicans to vote for the constitutional option. In essence, the Republicans ceded nothing.

But the agreement fails on several points. It does not guarantee an up-or-down vote on all judicial nominees. It does not restore the Senate's 214-year tradition of majority vote on judicial nominees. It attempts to give the Senate an advice and consent role in the nomination as well as the confirmation of judges. It is neither permanent nor objective. However, it did lead to the confirmation of some nominees and created a temporary reprieve in the judicial confirmation battle.

The Gang of 14 agreement was a temporary fix based only on specific senators at a certain time. It was not a permanent or institutional remedy, again another example of different people doing it different ways at different times. Ultimately, this agreement may only be an interlude in the escalation, but it shows that there is still room for senate collegiality and reason when the special-interest groups are excluded from being the decision makers.

After the deal was announced, Senators Lindsey Graham and Mike DeWine, both Republican members of the Gang of 14, expressly announced that were the Democrats to attempt a filibuster on nominees not in "extraordinary" circumstances, they would both vote for the constitutional option. Senator Frist agreed, "Let me be very clear. The constitutional option remains on the table. It remains an option. I will not hesitate to use it if necessary." Democratic Senate Minority Leader Harry Reid disagreed, "The nuclear option is gone for our lifetime. We don't have to talk about it anymore."[8]

Liberal activists were split. The National Organization for Women called it a "carefully scripted backroom deal" in which the Senate "shirked its constitutional role to meaningfully advise and consent."[9] "[Ralph] Neas hailed it as defeat of the 'radical Republican' agenda, while [Nan] Aron said it was 'very disappointing.'"[10]

The fight over the constitutional option was a fight over the Supreme Court with no nominee for the Democrats to attack. All they could attack was a democratic process that seemed reasonable to the American people—majority rule. It was hard to make the case that majority rule is un-American.

Some of the Democratic senators, without doubt, reached the compromise agreement for reasons of principle. They wanted to de-escalate the fight and restore a working relationship between Democrats and Republicans in the Senate. But as a whole, the deal allowed the confirmation of Republican nominees and raised the filibuster threshold for the future.

Why did the Democrats blink? First, the obstruction charges resonated with the public and the Democrats had lost all the Senate seats they could afford. Second, moderate Democratic senators had their own political concerns apart from the special-interest groups focus, which was only on the courts. Finance bills, energy bills, funding bills—Democratic moderates were concerned with other priorities, the success of which impacted their own reelections. A "nuclear summer" in the Senate was inhospitable to that agenda. Third, the fight over the constitutional option was a fight over the future of the Supreme Court and if the Democrats lost that battle, all their previous opposition to nominees would have been in vain. A constitutional option would allow the majority Republicans to confirm any judicial nominee without concession from the Democratic minority. The Left would have lost the anticipated battle for the Supreme Court before it ever started.

To some extent, the Gang of 14 decision had that effect anyway, which became clear just months later when President Bush had two seats open on the Supreme Court of the United States. During a time of increased political pressure on the White House from many directions, with Bush's approval ratings low, at a time when his nominees should have been the weakest, the special-interest groups discovered they had overreached during the lead-up to the "big fight" and had lost some of their effectiveness before the real battle began. The American people and the Senate had grown tired of the special-interest groups fighting every day for five years to keep Bush's nominees off the Courts. And with the new Gang of 14 threshold in place, the climate of debate had changed.

The special-interest groups had not given up as three nominees were about to learn. The Gang of 14 had crafted a ceasefire, but the war would continue over John Roberts, Harriet Miers, and Sam Alito.

CHAPTER TWELVE

Roberts, Miers, and Alito

FOR NEARLY FIVE years, left wing special-interest groups pushed, prodded, and cajoled Democrats into blocking President George W. Bush's courts of appeal nominees. They saw each filibuster and each withdrawal as an immediate victory to keep a conservative judge off a circuit court. But each fight carried with it a political victory as well: these groups raised their profile, raised campaign and political action funds, and forced Democratic senators into an ever escalating fight over judicial confirmations. They trained their staffs, perfected their talking points and fired warning shots at the Bush administration that a Supreme Court battle would be much worse than any lower court battles.

But the political buildup was not without cost for these left wing groups. In 2002 and 2004, three Senate Democrats—including the Democratic leader Tom Daschle—lost reelection as Republicans won those and most other open senate seats, in large part because of the obstruction of judicial nominees issue. Furthermore, Republicans created their own organizations, hired staff, and took up the public debate to fight back and challenge the liberal special interests. The White House revamped their nominee strategy and employed the political tactics from two successful presidential campaigns for governing and nominations. And by pushing the Republican leadership to the brink of using the constitutional option, special-interest groups allowed the Gang of 14 to come in and create a temporary filibuster disarmament—but one which raised the benchmark of who Democrats could "legitimately" filibuster.

Through all their battles and character attacks, the left wing groups had overreached and were unable to sustain their effectiveness. They were still strong and they still attacked, but they failed in their first shot at a Bush Supreme Court nominee.

As the Supreme Court's 2005 spring term closed out in June, Supreme Court pundits expected an announcement from Chief Justice William Rehnquist that he would retire due to his failing health from thyroid cancer. The final day of the term came and went with no announcement.

Then on July 1, less than six weeks after the Gang of 14 announced their decision, Supreme Court Justice Sandra Day O'Connor surprised Washington and the national media when she announced her retirement effective upon the confirmation of her successor. Only Bill Kristol at the *Weekly Standard* made the right prediction: "There will be a Supreme Court resignation within the next week. But it will be Justice O'Connor, not Chief Justice Rehnquist."[1]

An O'Connor replacement allowed for more imaginative speculation than a Rehnquist vacancy. O'Connor was viewed as a chief swing vote on the Court, and she was the first woman on the Supreme Court. Conventional wisdom held that Bush should choose a moderate and seek a woman or a minority to fill O'Connor's seat, whereas a Rehnquist nominee could more easily be conservative.

Speculation increased as a renewed rumor circulated that Rehnquist was going to step down and provide the White House with a two-seat vacancy strategy. But Rehnquist silenced that rumor. On July 15 he released a statement saying, "I want to put to rest the speculation and unfounded rumors of my imminent retirement. I am not about to announce my retirement. I will continue to perform my duties as chief justice as long as my health permits."

Pundits and speculators predicted President Bush was going to select Judge Edith Clement or Judge Edith Jones—both on the Fifth Circuit Court of Appeals—to fill O'Connor's seat. This was not Jones's first time to be on a Supreme Court short list. In 1990, President George H. W. Bush had an opportunity to fill the seat of Justice William J. Brennan. He had narrowed the choice to two individuals and both were in the

White House as he prepared to make his announcement. In one room was Edith H. Jones, a strong conservative. In the other room was David H. Souter who would become to conservatives a reference for evermore of a "stealth nominee," an unknown quantity who would be sold as a conservative but once on the court, not rule as expected. President Bush walked out with Souter instead of Jones. It is amazing how different the court would have been had a different choice been made that July day in 1990.

But for the O'Connor seat, pundits soon settled that it would be the "other Edith"—Judge Clement—who would be chosen this time. The media focused on Clement, but the President made a different choice and surprised the press corps.

On Tuesday, July 19, President George W. Bush made his decision, and called D.C. Circuit Court of Appeals judge John G. Roberts Jr. a little after noon to offer him the appointment. Roberts had been interviewed by the president the Friday prior and accepted the opportunity.[2] The prime time television announcement later that day featured Bush, Roberts, and the judge's family: his wife, Jane, and two children, Josie and Jack. The four-year-old Jack charmed the press corps as he danced around in youthful excitement during the event.[3]

Bush called Roberts "one of the best legal minds of his generation," and he certainly had the résumé to confirm that praise. Roberts edited the *Harvard Law Review* at Harvard University, where after three years of law school he was graduated summa cum laude. He clerked for Judge Henry Friendly on the Second Circuit Court of Appeals and later for Justice William Rehnquist at the Supreme Court. After a stint at the Department of Justice, he served as associate counsel to President Ronald Reagan. Following three years in private practice, Roberts returned to the Department of Justice as principal deputy solicitor general. Roberts had argued thirty-nine cases before the Supreme Court, a record few can match.

President George H. W. Bush nominated Roberts to the D.C. Circuit in 1992, but the Democrat-controlled Senate stalled his nomination until President Bill Clinton could take office. Roberts's name was not resubmitted. President George W. Bush again nominated Roberts to serve on the District of Columbia Court of Appeals in May 2001. This court is sometimes called the "Second Highest Court in the Land" because of its capital jurisdiction and because of the reputation as a feeder court to the Supreme Court. After two years of delay, Roberts was confirmed.

The left wing special-interest groups wasted no time in their attacks. Ralph Neas and People for the American Way sent out 400,000 e-mails in opposition to Roberts immediately following the announcement.[4] Nan Aron with the Alliance for Justice, as well as the Leadership Conference on Civil Rights, both issued statements in opposition to Roberts. But again, for the special-interest groups, this wasn't at all about Roberts.

Sid Salter, perspective editor for the *Clarion Ledger* in Mississippi, had seen this all occur before and he nailed the liberal attacks on Roberts in a July 24 column:

> For groups like the dubiously-named People for the American Way, the Alliance for Justice and the National Abortion and Reproductive Rights Action League, it wouldn't have mattered who President Bush nominated to the Supreme Court. It could have been Snow White, Rin Tin Tin or your Aunt Sudie from Itta Bena, and the result would have been the same—pro-abortion groups and the Democratic U.S. senators in their pockets would be opposed to anyone Bush nominated to the high court.

Salter said he and news organizations around the country were bombarded with e-mails from the liberal groups attacking Judge Clement, who was the presumptive nominee. When Roberts was announced, they sent out "essentially the same attack e-mails" but changed "Clement" to "Roberts." The groups already had their attack pieces prepared. All they had to do was fill in the name of the nominee. They were going to attack regardless of who the nominee might be.

He continued,

> The Alliance for Justice's take on the Roberts nomination is the most succinct statement of opposition: "John Roberts's legal career and

professional writings reveal that he is out of the mainstream in his legal views in a number of areas, most prominently civil rights and the right to choose." Sound familiar? It ought to. That's the very same criticism from the Alliance for Justice and other key players in the nation's pro-abortion movement aimed at Mississippi's Judge Charles Pickering when Bush attempted to appoint him to the 5th Circuit bench in 2002.

There's that phrase again, "out of the mainstream," with no definition of "mainstream." Salter writes,

That's become the formula for Democrats attempting to block a Republican judicial nomination—demonizing the nominee as a racist, a religious zealot and one unable to set aside personal beliefs in interpreting the law. Hidden behind all this talk of justice, right and the American way is the plain old politics of the partisan smear. Mississippi's Pickering was no racist, no zealot and was a capable judge. But even when Senate Democrats were told that by leading Mississippi Democrats like Mike Moore and Ronnie Musgrove, they turned a deaf ear and pilloried Pickering simply because they disagreed with his politics.

Sid got it right. This wasn't about Roberts, just like it wasn't about me earlier. This was about the liberal special-interest groups doing everything they could to keep conservative judges off the court for fear that they would reject the liberals' mystery Constitution.

This attack was just another culture war battle. Kate Kendell, executive director of the National Center for Lesbian Rights, made it clear: "There is nothing in Roberts's history as a lawyer, policymaker or judge to indicate that he would be anything other than hostile to . . . the emerging protections expressed in *Romer v. Evans* and *Lawrence v. Texas* . . . in the lives of lesbian, gay, bisexual and transgender Americans."[5]

A weekly e-mail report from NARAL made it clear their concern was also the mystery Constitution:

There's a reason, you know, that the men who drafted our Constitution used words like "liberty," "freedom," "rights." These words have fluid meanings. They don't mean the same thing to all people at all times. As our society ages, and we're faced with new challenges and new situations, ideas of "liberty" and "freedom" are able to evolve alongside. To lock them in a box and refuse any further discussion on how they apply in today's world would be . . . well, downright un-American.[6]

The left wing used television campaign style commercials to attack Roberts and posted videos and attack web pages on the Internet, and NARAL even offered "all-expenses paid trip" to Washington D.C. for whoever gathered the most signatures for its National Stop Roberts Petition Drive. NARAL also sponsored anti-Roberts house parties.[7]

But the attacks failed to gain traction with the American people. Even his opposition agreed Roberts was a very personable and likable man and his credentials were without challenge. In every public appearance, and as he met personally with United States senators, the press reported his total grasp of constitutional principles and sharp intellect. His attackers were reduced to saying, "He is a nice guy and very smart, but . . . ."

July became August and the Senate Judiciary Committee scheduled hearings for September 6. I was watching this play out in Mississippi until another event of immediate emergency occurred.

On Monday, August 29, a category 5 hurricane named Katrina struck the Mississippi Gulf Coast. I was working on this book in Jones County, Mississippi, more than ninety miles from the Gulf of Mexico, but when the eye moved over our farm, we were still feeling the damage of 125-mile-per-hour winds. I doubt a day has gone by since the storm when I have not uttered the name "Katrina."

It would take too long to describe the devastation and damage of that storm. Mississippi was in great need: water, food, power, fuel, shelter, medicine, and more. We needed help from the private sector as well as from the government. We did not need those in Washington D.C. using the disaster of Hurricane Katrina as an excuse to attack Roberts or slow down his confirmation hearings. But they did. What Katrina had to do with Roberts I still don't know. But sure enough,

It took less than an hour before Senators considering federal Judge John G. Roberts Jr.'s nomination to the Supreme Court fell into disagreement over Hurricane Katrina. In their opening remarks, the two top Democrats on the Senate Judiciary Committee invoked the tragedy as a reminder of the gap between the rich and poor and the need for a Supreme Court that wants to close that gap.

Democrat Senators Patrick Leahy and Ted Kennedy invoked Katrina in their fight against Judge Roberts. Senator John Cornyn (R-Texas) responded,

> We ought not to appropriate a national tragedy in a misguided effort to further a political interest of any sort. . . . Others likely will make similar attempts in a bizarre effort to link Judge Roberts to the tragedies in the Gulf of Mexico. But Katrina victims should not be used to score political points.[8]

But Kennedy suggested Hurricane Katrina was reason to reschedule the hearings: "In the midst of a national disaster of biblical proportions, it is difficult for the American people to participate fully in the selection of the next chief justice, one of the most important positions in our government and the chief protector of our Constitution." The release from Kennedy "also raised questions about Roberts's commitment to voting rights and women's rights."[9]

The real reason Democrats wanted to slow down the confirmation process had nothing to do with Hurricane Katrina. People for the American Way's Ralph Neas said on the Friday following Katrina,

> Momentum has shifted dramatically. Premature predictions that John Roberts would be confirmed with little debate and no real opposition are giving way. The near-daily revelations about his record and judicial philosophy have led to increasing opposition to his confirmation, and the report we are releasing today shows why. John Roberts is out of step with most Americans when it comes to some of the most fundamental questions a Supreme Court justice could face. He should not be confirmed.

Neas wanted the delay to keep opposition momentum. He would get his postponement, but the delay came not to assist Neas's goal of defeating Roberts, but to honor the passing of a chief justice of the United States.

On Saturday, September 3, Chief Justice William Rehnquist passed away at his Virginia home surrounded by his children. President Bush asked Justice O'Connor to stay on a little longer and on September 5 promoted the Roberts nomination to that of chief justice. The Judiciary Committee postponed the hearings a week until September 12, and the nation mourned the loss of the head of America's judiciary.

The stakes had risen for the special-interest groups. Not only did Bush still have an opportunity to replace O'Connor on the Court, but now he had nominated who would be the youngest chief justice since John Marshall in 1801. The chief justice sets the mood of the Court, leads private deliberations, influences coalitions, and when in the majority chooses to write or assign the writing of the ruling opinion. He also serves as chairman of the U.S. Judicial Conference—the arm of the judiciary that oversees the budget appropriations to the Judiciary, interacts with Congress, and establishes ethical and procedural guidelines for the courts.

The last hearings for Supreme Court nominees were those of President Bill Clinton's nominees Ruth Bader Ginsburg and Stephen G. Breyer in 1993 and 1994. As the hearings approached, conservatives began reminding senators, the public, and the media of the "Ginsburg Standard." This unofficial rule refers to the responses given to questions by Ginsburg during her confirmation hearing as established by the Democrat controlled Senate Judiciary Committee.

Before her hearing began, then Senate Judiciary Committee chairman Joe Biden urged,

> the public is best served by questions that initiate a dialog with the nominee, not about how she will decide any specific case that may come before her, but about the spirit and the method she will bring to the task of judging. There is a real difference . . . between questions that focus on specific results or outcomes, the answers to which would risk compromising a nominee's independence and impartiality, and questions on judicial methods and philosophy. The former can under-

mine the dispassionate and unprejudiced judgment we expect the nominee to exercise as a Justice. But the latter are essential and contribute critically to our public dialog.[10]

Former attorney general Ed Meese and Todd Gaziano explain why Biden took this position:

> Ginsburg, while a smart lawyer, had been a radical activist. Her record as an ACLU litigator placed her far outside the mainstream of American law. She had argued for legalizing prostitution, against separate prisons for men and women, and had speculated that there could be a constitutional right to polygamy. Some Republican senators wanted to know whether she still held such extreme views.[11]

But Ginsburg did not answer those questions, and she gave several reasons why it was inappropriate to respond. Robert Novak lists seven types of questions that Ginsburg refused to answer: ". . . no hypotheticals; no requirement for universal legal expertise; no questions outside the nominee's case experience; no cases likely to come before the Supreme Court; nothing regarding management of the U.S. Judiciary; nothing about evolving areas of the law; no discussion of the nominee's personal feelings."[12] Despite Ginsburg's refusal to answer the questions, she was confirmed on a vote of 96-3.

Whether or not the Ginsburg Standard was a political ploy, it certainly is good policy. Meese and Gaziano write that the refusal to answer certain questions is not just an option, but a requirement of judges wishing to remain ethical.

> Canon 5 of the Model Code, among others, forbids judges or judicial candidates from indicating how they will rule on issues likely to come before the courts or making any statement that would create the appearance they are not impartial. This rule is critical to an independent judiciary. Justices must remain open-minded when an actual case comes before them. They must not even hint how they would rule.

Then for what reason would a nominee need to even appear before the Senate Judiciary Committee if their questions are not answered? There is no reason. Novak reminds us, "No Supreme Court nominee was even interrogated by the Senate until 1925, and committee questioning was sporadic until it became standard confirmation practice in 1955. In 1949, former Sen. Sherman Minton refused to appear as his erstwhile colleagues requested and was confirmed anyway."

Today it is politically impractical to suggest a nominee not appear before the committee. And Judge Roberts appeared happy to engage the senators. In his opening statement before the committee, Roberts said, "I come before this committee with no agenda, no platform. I will approach every case with an open mind. . . . My job is to call balls and strikes, not pitch or bat."[13]

Roberts said in answering questions of a legal nature before the committee,

> I tend to take a more practical and pragmatic approach to things, rather than a theoretical or ideological approach. But I do think when it gets into an area where the correctness or incorrectness or my agreement or disagreement with a particular precedent is in an area that is likely to come before the court or could well come before the court, I do have to draw the line there. . . . My views on the cases that I think are not likely to come before the court, I'm perfectly willing to discuss.[14]

Roberts's proper response to questions keeping consistent with the Ginsburg Rule and judicial ethics left Democrats complaining that their questions were not being answered. In fact, Roberts was unflappable under questioning. He answered every question without prejudicing any potential future court decision, to the infuriation of the Senate Democrats. At one point, Senator Schumer said,

> It's as if I asked you what kind of movies you like and you say, "I like movies with good acting, I like movies with good directing, I like movies with good cinematography." And I ask you, "No, give me an example of a good movie" and you don't name one. I say, "Give me an

example of a bad movie," you won't name one. Then I ask you if you like *Casablanca*, and you respond by saying, "Lots of people like *Casablanca*." You tell me it's widely settled that *Casablanca* is one of the great movies.[15]

Chairman Arlen Specter informed Schumer his time was up and called for a recess, but as everyone began to stand Roberts spoke into the microphone that he wanted to respond. "*Doctor Zhivago* and *North by Northwest.*" The audience and Senators alike laughed. Again, they didn't like his politics, but his wit and good nature were winning over even his opponents.

The Democrats had requested certain papers and memos from Roberts during his time as deputy solicitor general in the first Bush administration. But claiming executive privilege and attorney-client privilege, the White House followed the precedent of every administration before them and did not turn over these documents. This also infuriated the Democrats. But these were road bumps not roadblocks and after the hearings, Roberts continued on track toward confirmation. The special-interest groups were annoyed at the easygoing nature of Roberts's confirmation process. They began to pressure Senate Democrats harder.

Minority Leader Harry Reid came out in opposition to Roberts, "surprising both the White House and fellow Democrats still conflicted about how to vote." The *New York Times* reported that Reid was

"very swayed" by the civil rights and women's rights leaders who testified Thursday in opposition to the nomination—and with whom Mr. Reid met privately that same day. Liberal advocacy groups, who raise millions of dollars to support Democratic candidates and who have been putting intense pressure on Democrats to oppose the nomination, were elated. . . . Last Thursday, as Mr. Reid was weighing his decision, representatives of about 40 advocacy groups met with him in the Capitol; the reason, they said, was to underscore the threat they believe Judge Roberts poses to Democrats' core causes, racial and gender equality. Hovering in the background was a political argument, that if Democrats vote in favor of Judge Roberts, they will be held liable by voters for the decisions he makes on the court. "He got the message loud and clear, didn't he?" Kim Gandy, president of the National Organization for Women, said of Mr. Reid on Tuesday.[16]

But the Gang of 14 recognized this was not an "extraordinary" circumstance and so despite Reid's opposition, there was no filibuster of Roberts. The Senate confirmed John Roberts as chief justice of the United States on a vote of 78-22 on September 29. He was sworn in later that day by John Paul Stevens, the senior associate justice on the Court, at a ceremony in the East Room of the White House. The Roberts Era of the Supreme Court had formally begun with Sandra Day O'Connor still in place and a fight for her replacement about to begin.

On Monday, October 3, the same day Chief Justice John Roberts opened his first session of the Supreme Court, President Bush nominated Harriet Ellan Miers, his White House counsel and former personal attorney, to fill O'Connor's seat.

President Bush discussed her qualifications:

Harriet was born and raised in Dallas, Texas. She attended public schools. . . . She went on to receive a bachelor's degree in mathematics and a law degree from Southern Methodist University. . . . She has a record of achievement in the law, as well as experience as an elected member of the Dallas City Council. She served at high levels of both state and federal government. Before state and federal courts, she has tried cases, and argued appeals that covered a broad range of matters. She's been a leader in the American Bar Association, and has been recognized by the National Law Journal as one of the most powerful attorneys in America. . . . Harriet was the first woman to be hired at one of Dallas's top law firms, the first woman to become President of that firm, the first woman to lead a large law firm in the state of Texas. Harriet also became the first woman president of the Dallas Bar Association, and the first woman elected president of the State Bar of Texas. In recognition of her achievements paving the way for women lawyers, Harriet's colleagues in Texas have honored her with numerous awards, most recently the Sandra Day O'Connor award for professional excellence. . . . Harriet Miers will strictly interpret our Constitution and laws. She will not legislation from the bench. . . .

I've known Harriet for more than a decade. I know her heart, I know her character.

Over the years, George W. Bush has developed a reputation of making unconventional choices that surprise the press and pundits alike. This decision was reminiscent of his running mate choice during the 2000 presidential campaign. He chose Dick Cheney to interview and vet potential running mates, and in the end, he chose Cheney. Here again, Miers's role as White House counsel charged her with interviewing and vetting nominees, and Bush chose her as the nominee.

This time Bush's surprise complicated the process. Conservatives remembered the first President Bush sent David Souter to the Supreme Court. He was an unknown quantity who turned out to be different from what conservatives expected. Many feared this surprise was setting the stage for another Souter. The day after her nomination, the *Washington Times*, the *Washington Post*, the *Los Angeles Times*, the *New York Times*, and *USA Today* all ran stories discussing the same issue: conservatives were not happy with the announcement.

Jan Larue at the conservative group Concerned Women for America needed convincing: "it isn't someone who I can come right out of the box saying, 'Great, let's go.'"[17] Bill Kristol at the *Weekly Standard* said on his web page that he was "disappointed, depressed, and demoralized."[18] Rush Limbaugh said, "This is a pick that was made from weakness. There was an opportunity here to show strength and confidence and I don't think this is it. There are plenty of known quantities out there who would be superb for the court."[19] The founder of the Cato Institute's Center for Constitutional Studies, Roger Pilon, said, "I know of nothing in Harriet Miers's background that would qualify her for an appointment to the Supreme Court." Tony Perkins at the Family Research Council said, "our lack of knowledge about Harriet Miers, and the absence of a record on the bench, give us insufficient information from which to assess whether or not she is indeed in that mold [of Scalia and Thomas]." Gary Bauer, president of American Values, echoed this doubt: "The future of the Supreme Court is too important to leave to chance."[20] Manuel Miranda, former staff leader for Majority Leader Bill

Frist's judicial confirmation work and now director of the Third Branch Conference, said Miers has "no judicial record" and "possibly the most unqualified choice" in almost forty years.[21]

Earlier in this chapter I mentioned how Bill Kristol was the only commentator to correctly predict that O'Connor and not Rehnquist would soon be retiring from the Court. More remarkable than that prediction is how Kristol almost got the rest of his prediction correct. In the same column he suggested President Bush would pick Attorney General Alberto Gonzales to replace O'Connor. But Kristol lamented in the column, "A Gonzales nomination would, in my view, virtually forfeit any chance in the near term for a fundamental reversal in the downward drift of American constitutional jurisprudence. But I now think it is more likely than not to happen." Kristol made the point that Bush could not replace a staunch conservative like Rehnquist with a moderate conservative like Gonzales, but he could replace O'Connor with Gonzales. In a rapid turn of events, Bush did not choose his former White House counsel Gonzales, but his current White House counsel Miers. Kristol commented that conservatives like himself would not be too excited about Gonzales; they were less excited about Miers.

She got no support or only lukewarm attention from conservative Republican senators including Rick Santorum, Orrin Hatch, John Thune, George Allen, Trent Lott, Sam Brownback, and Tom Coburn, and she was opposed by many on the Republican Senate staff. This was not necessarily on her own merit; the surprise was such that Republicans were fearful of a Souter repeat.

It didn't help matters that Minority Leader Harry Reid had recommended her to the president and applauded her pick: "I like Harriet Miers. The Supreme Court would benefit from the addition of a justice who has real experience as a practicing lawyer."[22] It could be Bush's strategy echoed that of Clinton who received assurances on Ginsburg before nominating her. But the deal with Reid did not secure approval among the president's own party.

There were items of concern for conservatives in her past. She had made political contributions to Al Gore's presidential campaign in 1988, and to Texas Democratic senator Lloyd Bentsen, as well as to the

Democratic National Committee. During her campaign for Dallas City Council, she made statements that seemed to indicate she supported issues in the gay rights movement.

The White House attempted to counter these concerns to the conservative base by emphasizing her religious experience since those times and her active involvement in evangelical Christianity. While that and reassurances of her pro-life positions placated some, to others it showed a nominee with changing political ideas over time. Conservatives felt they had been stung before by conservative nominees who became more liberal the longer they were on the Court and wanted more consistency in this pick. By the time the Bush administration convinced its allies that Miers was what they wanted, too much momentum had built up and her nomination seemed destined to be withdrawn.

I believe the president truly wanted Miers on the Court. But the judicial confirmation struggles of the past had in some minds reduced the desirability of a Supreme Court nomination. White House spokesman Scott McClellan told Washington reporters "Harriet Miers was the first and only choice in the president's mind," but he did acknowledge, "There were some individuals that withdrew their name because they didn't want to deal with the ordeal of going through the confirmation process."[23]

When qualified individuals decline nominations to the Supreme Court, the battle has truly become rancorous. But sitting justices see this trend as well. Justice Clarence Thomas recently advocated "a briefer, less intrusive confirmation process." He said former clerks and other lawyers often tell him they're not interested in Federal judgeships because of the potential of bruising confirmation battles. "I think that's a problem when the stars are beginning to say, 'Thank you, but no thanks.'"[24] The cost of public service should not be so high.

And during the Miers nomination, Justice Antonin Scalia was interviewed by NBC's Maria Bartiromo. She asked, "You were confirmed by the Senate 98-to-0. Are you concerned that the Supreme Court nomination process has become too politicized? Could you be confirmed today?" He responded,

I don't know. I wouldn't want to go through it today, I'll say that much. It has become politicized, but the reason it has become politicized is that for, oh, maybe 35 years—40 years—the Supreme Court has been making more and more political decisions that are not really resolved by the Constitution at all. And it took a while for the public to figure out what was going on, and I think what has happened is that everybody now understands that courts can make tremendously significant social decisions. You know, whether there should be same-sex marriage, whether, you know, whether there should be a right to die, whether there should be a right to abortion. All of those things. None of which, you know, to tell the truth is at all covered by the Constitution. But the court can say it is and that gives the court a good deal of political power.[25]

The choice of a nominee without a large paper trail was a natural result of the escalating confirmation process. The *Atlanta Journal Constitution* opined,

We have Roberts and Miers because we had the example of Mississippi District Court Judge Charles Pickering, whose reputation was butchered by the left, mostly with media acquiescence, on the basis of one opinion grotesquely and shamelessly distorted. Though given a recess appointment to the 5th U.S. Circuit Court of Appeals, he withdrew from confirmation consideration after Bush was reelected. We therefore have now stealth nominees, as much of a mystery to the right as to the left. There's something very unsatisfying about it.[26]

I publicly supported Harriet Miers. She has the experience and qualifications necessary to be a solid Supreme Court justice. When discussing qualifications, a president weighs intangible characteristics as well as a résumé. Miers's life experiences differed greatly from those already on the Court and she would have expanded the vision and understanding of the body. She is a highly competent lawyer; her resume verifies this. The Court needs members with real life experience, and Miers has that. But nominees also need a clear vision and understanding of issues that come before the Court.

Miers, like Rehnquist before her and more than thirty-five other justices, had no previous experience as a judge. But because Miers was not a conventional choice, because she was not graduated from the traditional East Coast schools, because she had not clerked for the appropriate influential judges, because she was not part of the Supreme Court track fraternity, she had to excel and do better to overcome these realities of the judicial ladder—it is not enough to be as good as your competitors; you must be better. Miers needed superb performances in her private meetings with Senators, but this she did not achieve. Her strengths of diversity were liabilities in this political atmosphere.

I think Miers would have been a reliable vote for the conservative side of the Court. She would have voted with Roberts and Scalia and Thomas. She would have interpreted law and not legislated from the bench. But whether she would have been a leader on the court that forged consensus is another matter—one we will never know.

It was a tough week for the Bush White House. The American death toll in Iraq had reached 2000, and Special Prosecutor Patrick Fitzgerald was preparing to announce what would turn out to be a five-count indictment of Lewis "Scooter" Libby, the vice president's chief of staff. Miers looked no closer to confirmation, and the administration was straining even to get its own party in consistent support. On Thursday night, October 27, President Bush accepted Miers's withdrawal.

A few hours later, White House Chief of Staff Andy Card was on the phone with who would be the next nominee. After a weekend at Camp David, the president returned to Washington D.C. to announce his selection. On Monday, October 31, President Bush presented Samuel Anthony Alito Jr. as now his third nominee to fill the seat of Sandra Day O'Connor.[27]

Alito had long been mentioned as a potential name for the Supreme Court. With a degree from Princeton University and a law degree from Yale Law School (where he served as editor of the *Yale Law Journal*), he had been on the track for federal judiciary service. He clerked for Judge Leonard Garth of the Third Circuit, served as assistant United States attorney for New Jersey, assistant solicitor general during the Reagan administration, deputy assistant to Attorney General Edwin Meese, and United States attorney for New Jersey. The Senate confirmed him in 1990 as a judge on the Third Circuit Court of Appeals, and he has served as an adjunct professor of law at Seton Hall University School of Law. He argued twelve cases before the Supreme Court for the federal government and prosecuted organized crime and drug kingpins.

Because of his similarity in judicial philosophy and common Italian heritage, Alito has often been compared to Justice Antonin Scalia: a badge of honor among conservatives and a mark of disdain among liberals.

The Alito nomination appeared to be the fight everyone was waiting for. The fight was deflected during the Roberts nomination. The fight was aborted during the Miers nomination. But now the conservatives had a true believer they felt secure in going to war over, and the liberals had their opponent with a record to mine for creative opposition.

Michael Gerhardt, a professor at the University of North Carolina School of Law, told *USA Today*, "Interest groups are going to come out strong on [Alito's] nomination. I don't think that's necessarily good. The word I would use is regrettable. It will be all about catch phrases and code words, not an elevated debate about the law."[28]

The Left was ready; Nan Aron said the Alliance for Justice was ready to do whatever it takes to defeat Alito: "You name it, we'll do it."[29] People for the American Way, the Alliance for Justice, and the Leadership Conference on Civil Rights, along with their traditional allies, launched a national media campaign "portraying Alito as the choice of 'extremists' and blasting him for past writings on abortion, racial discrimination, and the use of search warrants."[30]

Just as the nominees before him, Alito's position on abortion drove the opposition. In the words of Judiciary chairman Arlen Specter, abortion "is the dominant question that captures the attention of the American public."[31]

So Democrats seized on Alito's words from a 1985 application for a position in the Reagan Justice Department in which he cites "the greatest influences on my views" as that of William F. Buckley's *National Review* and Barry Goldwater's 1964 presidential campaign. The portion of the application agitating liberals the most was when he wrote,

It has been an honor and a source of personal satisfaction for me to serve in the office of the Solicitor General during President Reagan's administration and to help advance legal positions in which I personally believe very strongly. I am particularly proud of my contributions in recent cases in which the government has argued in the Supreme Court that racial and ethnic quotas should not be allowed and that the Constitution does not protect a right to an abortion.[32]

To liberals, this is the smoking gun, but for supporters of Alito, this provides and example of what the man believes personally in contrast to how the judge has ruled on the bench.

Alito further wrote, "In college, I developed a deep interest in constitutional law, motivated in large part by disagreement with Warren Court decisions, particularly in the areas of criminal procedure, the Establishment Clause and reapportionment." This sentiment on reapportionment has Senator Joe Biden talking filibuster.[33]

Biden told Alito following their private meeting, "you probably don't need my vote to get on the bench but if you are disingenuous in the hearings, you may need my vote relating to a filibuster."[34]

While Minority Leader Harry Reid has suggested the filibuster option may be on the table, with the Gang of 14 in agreement, Democrats face a tough sell on that front.

On Thursday, November 3, the Gang of 14 met to discuss Alito and decided to try to maintain their coalition and to reserve final judgment on the nomination until after the committee hearings.[35] However, two of the Republicans in the group—Lindsey Graham of South Carolina and Mike DeWine of Ohio—had already gone public with their support of Alito and had said they would be willing to vote on the constitutional option to avert a filibuster of the nomination. Republicans only need two of the Republicans in the Gang of 14 to join the rest of the majority in order to successfully execute the constitutional option, and they now have those two. This puts Democrats in a weakened position to threaten filibuster.[36]

Due to the Senate's schedule, the hearings could not be conducted in December of 2005 and were scheduled for January 2006. While this provides the liberal special-interest groups more time to plan their tactics and strategy, few Americans will be interested in hearing attack ads and partisan rhetoric over their Thanksgiving and Christmas holidays. The weeks of delay also disarm the criticism that the liberal interests did not have time to build their case.

But a quiet holiday season was no sign that liberal special-interest groups had given up. "I think right now what you're looking at is not whether or not the opposition will build or exist, but rather when that opposition will be announced with sufficient critical mass to indicate the battle has been joined," Wade Henderson, executive director of the Leadership Conference on Civil Rights, told the *Washington Post*. The story continues, "Given that confirmation hearings are two months away, Ralph G. Neas, president of People for the American Way, said his plan is to slowly marshal opposition to Alito. He pointed out that the opposition that derailed Bork and nearly did the same to Clarence Thomas coalesced just before their respective hearings."[37]

But heading into the confirmation, those on the Right like *National Review* took some comfort in Alito's prospects: "Lots of work remains to be done, and no one should underestimate how nasty the Left will get— or how many Democrats will end up voting against Alito. But those of us who fully expect Alito to be an outstanding justice should be heartened by the fact that his is a battle we are well positioned to win."[38]

As this book went to press, Alito's confirmation fate had yet to be determined, though I expect the left wing special-interest groups to try their best to defeat him by any means necessary. With his impeccable credentials, it is hard to view Alito's nomination as an "extraordinary circumstance," especially in view of the confirmation of Ginsburg and Breyer. The Senate Democrats who signed the Gang of 14 memo are persons of integrity; I predict it will hold.

After Alito, who is next? During the 2000 campaign, pundits claimed the next president could appoint as many as three justices to the Supreme Court. Bush won and appointed zero. In 2004, pundits again claimed that the future of the Court was in the next president's hands. Bush won again and has the opportunity to fill two seats: replacing one conservative with another and one swing vote with a conservative.

If Bush has no more opportunities to shape the Supreme Court, then it will be up to the next president who takes office in January 2009. Then the remaining justices (absent Roberts and presumably Alito) will all be more than seventy years of age, except Clarence Thomas, who will be sixty-one. David Souter will be seventy, Stephen Breyer will be seventy-one, Anthony Kennedy and Antonin Scalia will both be seventy-three, Ruther Bader Ginsburg will be seventy-six, and John Paul Stevens will be eighty-nine. It is conceivable that with good health and sound minds, all these justices could remain on the court another two terms. But eventually another seat will open up, and the fight for the Constitution and the culture war will continue.

Epilogue

MIGUEL ESTRADA CAME to the United States from Honduras when he was seventeen and barely able to speak English. He graduated magna cum laude from both Columbia College and Harvard Law School, where he was editor of the *Law Journal*. He served as a law clerk to a highly respected Democratic appointee to the Second Circuit Court of Appeals and also clerked for Supreme Court justice Anthony Kennedy. His experience includes service as an assistant United States attorney and as assistant solicitor general in the Justice Department.

Estrada joined a major law firm and became a partner. He argued fifteen cases before the U.S. Supreme Court and won ten. When he was thirty-nine, Estrada received a nomination from President George W. Bush for the D.C. Circuit Court of Appeals. The American Bar Association gave him its highest rating of "well qualified": the "gold standard" recommendation for Democrats. He enjoyed the support of prominent Democrats, "including President Clinton's solicitor general and Vice President Gore's counselor and chief of staff."[1]

His was a great success story for anyone, but more so for an immigrant who came to the United States as a teenager. His was the story of America and could have been an inspiration and encouragement to minority youth and immigrants across the nation. But Democrats blocked Estrada's nomination because he was a pro-life Latino.

Leaked Democratic strategy memos reveal that the Far Left special-interest groups did not want Estrada confirmed. They didn't want a Republican president nominating a Hispanic to the Supreme Court, and they saw Estrada's appeals court nomination as a stepping stone to that position. Furthermore, they knew a secret. In 1994, Miguel Estrada told Patricia Ireland, president of the National Organization for Women, that he considered abortion to be the killing of a human being.[2] Estrada was not pro-choice. He did not believe in abortion.

However, Estrada did believe in the rule of law and successfully argued a case prohibiting pro-life groups from blocking abortion clinics. While he himself was pro-life, his constitutional fidelity committed him to following and arguing on behalf of the law. During his nomination he promised to continue this reputation of dedication to the rule of law and Supreme Court precedents, but that was not enough for liberal special-interest groups who only want judges who believe as they believe and feel as they feel.

How could the Democrats oppose an immigrant minority nominee with such an outstanding record dedicated to the rule of law? It wasn't easy, but they were following directives from the special-interest groups. One of the leaked Democratic Judiciary Committee strategy memos made it clear who was calling the shots against Miguel Estrada. Senator Dick Durbin's staff notified the Judiciary Committee member that "The groups . . . also identified Miguel Estrada (D.C. Circuit) as especially dangerous, because he has a minimal paper trail, he is Latino, and the White House seems to be grooming him for a Supreme Court appointment. They want to hold Estrada off as long as possible."[3] They did postpone Estrada. He did not receive a committee vote until twenty months after he was nominated, and only after Republicans regained control of the Judiciary Committee.

What was the basis given for Democratic obstruction of Estrada? They could not appear in public as they did in private and admit to opposing him because he was "Latino." They could not base their opposition solely on the abortion passions of their political base. They could not oppose him simply because he might one day be nominated to the Supreme Court.

So the Democrats claimed they didn't know enough about Miguel Estrada and demanded the memorandums Estrada wrote as an assistant to the solicitor general in the Justice Department. But "every living former Solicitor General—including Democrats Archibald Cox, Seth Waxman and Walter Dellinger—signed a letter to the Judiciary Committee stating that sharing these confidential memos would damage the Justice Department's ability to represent the interest of the United States."[4] There was no precedent for the release of these memorandums, but that fact did not deter the Democrats, nor did it penetrate the media.

Next the Democrats charged Estrada had no judicial experience. But Senator Patrick Leahy and the Democrats during the Clinton administration confirmed nominees with no judicial experience "to the U.S. Court of Appeals for the First, Second, Third, Fourth, Sixth, Seventh, Eighth, Ninth, Tenth, D.C., and Federal Circuits."[5] Besides, "Five of the eight judges [then] on the D.C. Circuit had no previous judicial experience—including Chief Judge, Harry Edwards," appointed by President Carter in 1979 when he was younger than Estrada.[6] The charge that Estrada had no experience was a diversion without the least bit of merit, which should have been articulated by the media.

The left wing groups and Democrats determined to keep Miguel Estrada off the appellate court should have had the integrity, candor, and courage to admit they opposed him for being pro-life. The filibuster of Miguel Estrada was a blatant example of raw partisan politics. The Democrats feared a Republican president would appoint a pro-life Hispanic to the Supreme Court. Any sensitive and thinking American should be offended by what Far Left special-interest groups did to Miguel Estrada. The national news media reported these bogus criticisms of Estrada as if they were of equal value to his credentials. If the media had done its job, the Democrats could not have succeeded with their meritless charges, and Miguel Estrada would have been confirmed.

Had Estrada been pro-choice, or even if he had been Anglo, chances are the left wing would not have blocked him. And had they treated him with the respect he deserved—not as an immigrant, not as an American, but simply as a person—the rancor would have been less abusive on him personally and on his family.

Virginia Thomas, wife of Justice Clarence Thomas, wrote an editorial for the *Wall Street Journal* just after the Democrats on the Judiciary Committee killed my nomination on a straight party-line vote in March 2003. She claimed the groups orchestrating the attack on my nomination did not view me as "human."

I think she was right. These groups don't view nominees as people with families; they treat us like inanimate legislation. A stack of paper is not human; it doesn't deserve respect; it feels no emotion. It is one thing to attack a resolution by any means necessary. But to do so to a person devalues what it is to be human. This is the natural philosophical conclusion of these Far Left organizations. For them, ideology is more important than personhood; so enshrining that ideology certainly would be more important than the treatment of a nominee.

Recently on a work trip to Memphis I attended the annual Freedom Award banquet of the National Civil Rights Museum. I met a young lady who told me she helped one of the groups opposing the Bush judicial nominees monitor the confirmation proceedings, including Judge William Pryor's nomination (but not my nomination). We discussed her work and my nomination and had an interesting and pleasant conversation. One of the anecdotes I shared with her involved my oldest daughter, Paige Dunkerton. Paige had to stop her children from watching the news during my confirmation fight because her five-year-old daughter Emily woke up several times crying from bad dreams. She told her mother she was dreaming that the woman who shouted at her "Uncle Chip" and said bad things about her "Papa" was coming to get her.

My new friend seemed horrified that my five-year-old granddaughter had heard or watched news programs about my confirmation. She seemed shocked that my daughter would let her child watch the news about me. Her shock should have been that the discussion of whether I was qualified to serve as a judge on the Circuit Court of Appeals—something that ought to be fairly boring to non-lawyers—was in fact so uncivil and shrill that it gave children nightmares.

But civility, resolution, and consensus require people of good faith to work together to find common ground. This is not done with character assassinations or radical rhetoric. And when such unity is forged, the lasting affect on the American people is one of acceptance and approval rather than challenge and division.

When Congress passed the Civil Rights Act of 1964, many Americans opposed the measure. But it had been reached, over time, through compromise with the broad consensus necessary for the democratic political process. Within three decades of its passage (in the 1990s), we lived in a different America where the vast majority viewed the denial of equal rights to anyone based on race as wrong and intolerable.

When the Supreme Court decided *Roe v. Wade* in 1973, many Americans opposed the decision. The public did not participate in the decision. The public had no input. Judges debated the decision in private and reached the decision in secret. Now three decades later, abortion divides our nation as much—or more—than in 1973. As one writer says "The debate has not only continued, but intensified."[7]

Why is the Civil Rights Act viewed differently than *Roe v. Wade*? The reason is simple, and speaks to the strength and wisdom of our Constitution. The Civil Rights Act of 1964 went through the legislative process; it was produced using democratic principles. *Roe v. Wade* was imposed by judicial decision; where there is no consensus, there is no resolution. Where there is no resolution, there will always be controversy.

One of real ironies of the confirmation battle of the past six years is that Far Left special-interest groups set out to defeat Supreme Court nominees, and in the end their early efforts positioned them to be powerless to do so. The leaked Democratic memos revealed the real objective was not the filibustered appellate nominees, but the Supreme Court. Their fight was so bitter, so unprecedented, and so unprincipled they lost credibility. They cried wolf too many times. They could not block Roberts.

What did these special-interest groups accomplish by their bitter fight? They succeeded in very little; most of the opposed appellate nominees have been confirmed. And what about the Democrats? They had a net loss of two senators in 2002, a net loss of four more senators in 2004, and George Bush was re-elected president. The Democrats will continue to lose as long as they let these Far Left special-interest groups dictate their policies.

The culture war continues as does the judicial confirmation conflict. After my own journey through the confirmation process and in light of events since, I have come to a few conclusions that I believe will be fair to all sides involved, will deescalate the political battle over judges, and return civility to this aspect of the political process. The story of my personal journey, insights on the continuing culture war and confirmation struggle, and fair solutions available for those of good faith who truly seek to advance a strong, independent, and constitutionally faithful judiciary will be presented in the upcoming sequel to this book. But in order to continue their public debate, I will share them briefly here.

First, when unprecedented attacks are made on judicial nominees because they are committed to the rule of law and personally opposed to abortion, the voters should hold the obstructionists accountable at the ballot box, as they did in 2002 and 2004. Those engaged in the opposition to judicial nominees by filibuster paid a tremendous price at the ballot box. If they don't abandon the filibuster, they should continue to be held accountable at the polls. Enough senators defeated and a filibuster will be unsustainable.

Second, if Democrats filibuster another nominee the "constitutional option" should be implemented. The more than two-century tradition of confirming judges by majority vote should be restored.

The third solution is to pass a statute that could be designated as the "Judicial Confirmation Improvements Act." In such an act, Congress could spell out in detail the process for confirming judicial nominees. Such a bill should specify a time line following the reception of a judicial nomination by the Senate in which a hearing is held, a vote with or without a favorable recommendation is held, and an up-or-down vote before the full Senate is given. Certainly proper time for opponents to research and build a case should be included, but at the end of the day, future presidents under such a bill would know their nominees would be treated fairly. Nominees will know that within a reasonable period of time they will either be confirmed or rejected, and they can get on with life. To be fair to both parties, the effective date of such a statute would need to be applicable for a following administration, say January 2009.

Passage of a statute clearly establishing the procedure and timetable for confirming judges will greatly improve the process; nevertheless, the confirmation process will continue to be a battlefield so long as members of the Supreme Court are committed to a philosophy of interpreting the Constitution according to their "independent judgment" as to society's "evolving standards of decency." This philosophy puts the court in the posture of determining public policy on social issues that should best be left to the people or to legislative bodies. So the fourth and ultimate solution to eliminating the controversy over confirming federal judges should be to adopt a constitutional amendment providing that in the future (I'm not talking about the past), the sole method for changing the meaning of the Constitution will be by the amendment process. That worked for 150 years and it can work again.

In other words, future judges will have a clear prohibition against ruling according to their personal preferences and legislating from the bench. In the future the court will interpret the Constitution as it is written and as it was understood at the time of adoption, confine itself to a judicial role and not intrude on the rights of the people or the responsibility of the legislative branch.

This proposal surely will be controversial. If it should be seriously considered, those of a liberal bent will want to make sure that none of the "rights" added during the last fifty years are taken away. Those of a conservative bent will want to make sure that those rights are not locked in or written in stone. If an attempt is made to amend the Constitution in this manner, there will be rigorous debate and that will benefit America. But in the end, such an amendment would eliminate the root cause of the present controversy over confirming judges. It would remove the judiciary from the culture war.

Some say a constitutional amendment cannot be passed, but from 1933 to 1971 it was done on average once every five to six years. But there have been no constitutional amendments initiated and passed since then because special-interest groups found they could change the Constitution more easily by judicial decision than the method provided by our Founders.

I said earlier that had I known in advance what was going to happen I might have declined the honor. Having lived through the confirmation war, I am glad I did not decline the nomination. I am glad I did not give in to the groups who opposed my confirmation. My hope is that by going through the process, speaking out on the issues, I can in some small way help to improve the process for future nominees and help strengthen the judiciary and restore and strengthen the rule of law.

In the book to follow this one, I discuss my personal odyssey through the political jungle of confirmation and elaborate on the solutions I recommend. I hope you found this book both interesting and informative and will want to read "the rest of the story."

Notes

PROLOGUE

[1] After I retired from the court, I associated with the Baker, Donelson, Bearman, Caldwell & Berkowitz law firm at its Jackson offices as senior counsel on a part-time basis. I hasten to add that the views expressed in this book are mine alone.

CHAPTER ONE

[1] "Fresh Air," National Public Radio, 16 February 2005.

[2] Denis Steven Rutkus and Mitchell A. Sollenberger, "Judicial Nomination Statistics: U.S. District and Circuit Courts, 1977–2003," *CRS Report,* Congressional Research Service, Library of Congress, updated 23 February 2004, CRS 10.

[3] Denis Steven Rutkus, "Judicial Nominations by President Clinton during the 103rd–106th Congresses," *CRS Report,* Congressional Research Service, Library of Congress, updated 12 March 2002, CRS 9, 17.

[4] Included in this initial group of nominees was John Roberts to the District of Columbia Circuit Court of Appeals. He would later be President Bush's choice to replace Sandra Day O'Connor on the U.S. Supreme Court. His nomination was then changed to that of chief justice of the United States upon the death of William Rehnquist. After a two-year delay, Roberts was ultimately confirmed unanimously by the U.S. Senate to the circuit court. He was confirmed as chief justice by a vote of 78-22 on September 29, 2005.

[5] Todd Gaziano and Rich Tucker, "Justice Delayed," Heritage Foundation, http://www.heritage.org/Press/Commentary/ed040402a.cfm?RenderforPrint=1, 4 April 2002.

[6] "Bush, Gore touted different justices," Associated Press, 11 December 2000.

[7] Gaziano and Tucker, "Justice Delayed."

[8] American Bar Association: "The ABA and the Judicial Confirmation Process," *The Compleat Lawyer* (Summer 1997). As Senator Hatch indicated, the first involvement of the ABA in evaluating judicial nominees was in 1947 at the invitation of Senator Alexander Wiley, a Wisconsin Republican. In 1952, the U.S. attorney general requested the ABA Standing Committee on the Federal Judiciary to express its views on a prospective nominee before the administration submitted the name of the nominee to the Senate. In the 1980s, the ABA committee sought comments from prospective nominees from various interest groups on the Left, but turned down a request from a

conservative foundation to furnish names of prospective nominees. The standing committee then discontinued the formal practice of consulting with outside groups. President Reagan did not seek ABA evaluation of Supreme Court nominees before he submitted their nominations to the Senate. However, neither President Reagan nor President George H. W. Bush would send a nominee for appellate or district court vacancies to the Senate if the ABA committee deemed the prospective nominee "not qualified." In effect, the ABA committee possessed a veto over nominees to the lower courts. But the first President Bush refused to submit his nominees for evaluation by the ABA committee until the committee had deleted from its standards the consideration of political or ideological factors.

Considerable controversy erupted in 1987 when a substantial minority of the ABA committee indicated Judge Robert Bork was "not qualified" because of his judicial temperament, which the ABA defined as "his compassion, open-mindedness, his sensitivity to the rights of women and minority persons, and comparatively extreme views respecting constitutional principles or their application, particularly within the ambient of the Fourteenth Amendment." Conservatives thought this inappropriate and biased.

[9] Senator Tom Daschle, press conference, 22 March 2001.

[10] Bennett Roth, "Bush Won't Use ABA to Evaluate His Judicial Picks," *Houston Chronicle*, 23 March 2001.

[11] Rhonda McMillion, "A 48-Hour Day: Bar Leaders Lobby on Capitol Hill Regarding Key Justice System Issues," *American Bar Association Journal*, July 2001.

[12] Thomas J. Jipping, "Bush Bites Sharks," *Washington Times*, 22 March 2001.

[13] Audrey Hudson, "GOP Set to End Judicial Backlog," *Washington Times*, 11 November 2002.

[14] Ibid.

[15] Ibid.

[16] Ibid.

[17] Estrada withdrew his nomination on September 4, 2003. Owen would eventually be confirmed on April 25, 2005, with a vote of 56-43.

[18] Democratic senator Ben Nelson of Nebraska was unavoidably absent from the vote but had publicly said he would have voted for me: making the vote 55 but still shy of the 60 necessary.

[19] U.S. Department of Justice, www.usdoj.gov/olp/judicialnominations108.htm#courtofappeals, 2 August 2005.

CHAPTER TWO

[1] For more discussion on this point, see chapter 10.

[2] U.S. Code, Title 28.

[3] Denis Steven Rutkus and Mitchel A. Sollenberger, "Judicial Nomination Statistics: U.S. District and Circuit Courts, 1977–2002," *CRS Report for Congress*, received through the CRS web, Congressional Research Service, Library of Congress, 23 February 2004, CRS 13.

[4] "U.S. Circuit Court Nominees of President William J. Clinton Who Failed to Receive Senate Confirmation, 1993–2000" and "U.S. District Court Nominees of President William J. Clinton Who Failed to Receive Senate Confirmation, 1993–2000," from Denis Steven Rutkus, "Judicial Nominations by President Clinton During the 103rd-106th Congresses," *CRS Report for Congress*, received through the web, Congressional Research Service, Library of Congress, CRS 98-510.

[5] Rutkus, "Judicial Nominations by President Clinton during the 103rd-106th Congresses," updated 12 March 2002. During President Clinton's final two years (106th Congress: 1999–2000), only fifteen of his thirty-four nominees to the courts of appeals were confirmed: one was withdrawn and eighteen were returned to him. The Senate did not confirm 56 percent of President Clinton's appellate nominees during that time. Even more frustrating to the Democrats, sixteen of the nominees who were not confirmed failed to receive committee hearings.

[6] These numbers represent individual nominees and do not take into account multiple nominations of the same person to the same position (Rutkus and Sollenberger, "Judicial Nomination Statistics: U.S. District and Circuit Courts, 1977-2002," CRS 13).

[7] While original to James Harrington in the seventeenth century, this principle became familiar to Americans with its use by John Adams under the pseudonym "Novanglus" in the *Boston Gazette* (1774) and incorporated by Adams into the Massachusetts Constitution (1780).

[8] Paul Johnson, *A History of the American People* (New York: HarperCollins Publishers, 1998), 117.

[9] See generally David Limbaugh, *Persecution: How Liberals Are Waging War Against Christianity* (Washington DC: Regnery, 2003).

[10] John Emerich Edward Dalberg Acton ("Lord Acton"), later professor of modern history at Cambridge, to Bishop Mandell Creighton, 5 April 1887.

CHAPTER THREE

[1] Material and quotes from James Davidson Hunter, *Culture Wars: The Struggle to Define America* (New York: Basic Books, 1991), 33-35.

[2] Ibid.

[3] Material and quotes from Louis Bolce and Gerald De Maio, "Our Secularist Democratic Party," *Public Interest* (Fall 2002).

[4] Dennis Prager, "The second American civil war: What it's about," Creators Syndicate, Inc., 14 October 2003; and Dennis Prager, "The second American civil war: What it's about: part II," Creators Syndicate, Inc., 21 October 2003.

[5] Noah Feldman, "A Church-State Solution," *New York Times Magazine*, 3 July 2005.

[6] NBC, *Today Show*, 20 July 2005.

[7] *Roe v. Wade*, 410 U.S. 113, 93 S.Ct. 705, 35 L.Ed.2d 147 (1973).

[8] Nat Hentoff, "The Indivisible Fight for Life," presented at AUL Forum, 19 October 1986, Chicago.

[9] Ibid.

[10] Quotes and references from Naomi Wolf, "Our Bodies, Our Souls," *New Republic*, 16 October 1995.

[11] Hentoff, "Indivisible Fight for Life."

[12] Cited by Hentoff, "Indivisible Fight for Life."

[13] *USA Today*, 14 July 2005.

[14] *Romer v. Evans*, 517 U.S. 620 (1996).

[15] B. A. Robinson, "Targeting Gays and Lesbians: Ruling by the U.S. Supreme Court in *Romer v. Evans*," Ontario Consultants on Religious Tolerance, updated 16 September 2004.

[16] *Lawrence v. Texas*, 539 U.S. 558 (2003).

[17] Jamin B. Raskin, "Yes, Liberals, You Won the Culture War," TomPaine.com (27 June 2003).

[18] When the case was submitted to the jury, I instructed them, your "verdict is not to be affected by bias, prejudice, nor sympathy. Homosexuals are as much entitled to be protected from fraud as are any other human beings, but not any more so. The fact that the alleged victims in this case are homosexuals shall not affect your verdict any way whatsoever."

[19] Charles W. Pickering Jr., "The Federal Marriage Amendment," 28 May 2004.

[20] All citations to the Massachusetts case are found in *Goodridge v. Dept. of Public Health*, 440 Mass. 309, 798 Northeast Second 941 (Mass. 2003)

[21] Dan Ring, "Gay couples challenge old state law," *Republican*, 7 October 2005.

[22] Article IV, Section 1, Constitution.

[23] Pickering, "Federal Marriage Amendment."

[24] In October 2005, Connecticut's new law allowing same-sex civil unions went into effect, conferring the same rights as marriage but defining "marriage" as between "a man and a woman." Under the law, Connecticut will recognize civil unions and domestic partnerships from other states, but not same-sex marriages.

[25] In September 2005, California's state legislature became the first in the nation without court pressure to approve same-sex marriages. California governor Arnold Schwarzenegger—citing Proposition 22 that passed on a statewide vote in 2000 and bans same-sex marriage in the state of California—vetoed the legislation.

[26] Charisse Jones, "Gay marriage on the ballot in 11 states," *USA Today*, 15 October 2004.

[27] CNN.com, 2004 Election Results,

http://www.cnn.com/ELECTION/2004/pages/results/ballot.measures/.

[28] Chip Reid, "Democrats push for age limit on Web porn," NBC *Nightly News* with Brian Williams, 27 July 2005.

[29] Theresa Chmara, http://www.ala.org/ala/washoff/WOissues/civilliberties/cipaweb/legalhistory/remarksch mara.htm.

[30] Charles E. Beggs, Associated Press, 29 September 2005, Spokesman–Review.com.

[31] Ibid.

[32] David Reinhard, *Oregonian*, Sunday, 9 October 2005.

[33] "Oregon justices defeat efforts to limit sex shows," *Oregonian*, 30 September 2005.

[34] Reinhard, *Oregonian*, 9 October 2005.

[35] Ibid.

[36] Irving Kristol, "Pornography, Obscenity, and the Case for Censorship," *New York Times Magazine*, 28 March 1971.

[37] For more see "The Case for Censorship," ch. 8 in Robert H. Bork's *Slouching Towards Gomorrah: Modern Liberalism and the American Decline* (New York: ReaganBooks, 1996).

[38] David Amsden, "Not Tonight, Honey. I'm Logging On," *New York Magazine*, 20 October 2003.

[39] Naomi Wolf, "The Porn Myth," *New York Magazine*, 20 October 2003.

CHAPTER FOUR

[1] Joe Belz, "The great divide," *World Magazine*, 5 February 2005.

[2] Noah Feldman, "A Church-State Solution," *New York Times Magazine*, 6 July 2005.

[3] Claudia Winkler, "The Party of Unbelievers," *Weekly Standard*, 8 January 2003.

[4] Material cited from Bolce and De Maio from Louis Bolce and Gerald De Maio, "Our Secularist Democratic Party," *Public Interest* (Fall 2002).

[5] Ibid, 11.

[6] George J. Olszewski, "A History of the Washington Monument," United States Department of the Interior (1971).

[7] For this and more on the subject, I am indebted to David Limbaugh's *Persecution: How Liberals Are Waging War Against Christianity* (Washington DC: Regnery, 2003).

[8] Thomas Paine, *Common Sense*, quoted in *The Founders' Constitution*, vol. 1, ch. 4, 106.

[9] *Time*, 14 February 1954, 49.

[10] Encyclopedia Britannica, Inc., *1784–1796: Organizing the New Nation*, vol. 3 of *The Annals of America* (William Benton, 1968).

[11] David S. Lutz, *The Origins of American Constitutionalism* (Baton Rouge: Louisiana State University Press, 1988), 142.

[12] Benjamin Franklin, address to the Constitutional Convention on 28 June 1787.

[13] "Washington's Inaugural Address of 1789," *American Originals,* www.archives.gov/exhibithall/americanorignals.

[14] *Newdow,* 124 S. Ct. 2301 at 2317.

[15] James D. Richardson, *A Compilation of the Messages and Prayers of the Presidents, 1789–1887,* vol. 1 (Washington: Bureau of National Literature, 1899), 220.

[16] John Jay to Jedidiah Morse, 1797.

[17] Dee Wampler, "Never Hostile to Religion," *Liberty* (July-August 2005): 10.

[18] Daniel L. Dreisbach, "Religion and Legal Reforms in Revolutionary Virginia," in *Religion and Political Culture in Jefferson's Virginia,* ed. G. W. Sheldon and D. L. Dreisbach (Lanham MD: Rowman and Littlefield Publishers, Inc., 2000).

[19] Jefferson's First Inaugural, 1801.

[20] Discussion of De Tocqueville from Matt Kaufman, "Foundations of Freedom," *Citizen Magazine,* March 2004.

[21] John Adams, address to the military on 11 October 1798.

[22] Letter to Jasper Adams (14 May 1833) Dreisbach 19, quoted by Justice Stevens in *Van Orden v. Perry,* 545 U.S. (2005), Stevens dissent, slip opinion, p. 22.

[23] *Van Orden,* Stevens dissent, slip opinion, page 22. Internal quotations omitted.

[24] *Church of the Holy Trinity v. U.S.* 143 U.S. 457.

[25] Theodore Roosevelt, *The Strenuous Life* (New York: The Century Co., 1900).

[26] Roger Lundin and Mark Knoll, *Voices from the Heart: Four Centuries of America* (Grand Rapids: Eerdmans, 1987), 237.

[27] *Zorach v. Clauson,* 343 U.S. 306, 313 (1952).

[28] *Time* (15 February 1954).

[29] Warren L. Jones, "First Amendment Religious Liberty guarantees neutrality not hostility," *Liberty* (July-August 2005).

[30] William J. Federer, "Separation of God and State?," www.WorldNetDaily.com, posted 11 October 2003.

[31] *Engel v. Vitale,* U.S. Citation, 370 U.S. 421 (1962).

[32] James L. Buckley, "The Constitution and the Courts: A Question of Legitimacy," 24 Harv. J.L. & Pub. Pol'y 189, 194 (2000).

[33] Jeff Brady, "Air Force Academy Embroiled in Religious Controversy," *Morning Edition,* 2 June 2005.

[34] Jeff Brady, "Air Force Says No Religious Discrimination at Academy," *Morning Edition,* 23 June 2005.

[35] "School District Steals 'Christmas in August,'" FOXnews.com, http://www.foxnews.com/story/0,2933,166259,00.html, 20 August 2005.

[36] David Limbaugh, *Persecution: How Liberals Are Waging War Against Christianity* (Washington DC: Regnery, 2003).

37 In September 2005, a federal court in Sacramento, California (under the Ninth Circuit jurisdiction), ruled in another case filed by Newdow that the Pledge of Allegiance is unconstitutional. At publication, this case had yet to be resolved.

38 Larry Schweikart and Michael Allen, *A Patriot's History of the United States* (New York: Sentinel, Penguin Group, 2004), 96, 97.

39 Ibid., 825.

40 David Hampton, "Defining moments in WorldCom saga center on 'choices,'" *Clarion Ledger*, 21 August 2005.

41 Paul M. Weyrich to conservatives, 16 February 1999.

42 Charles Colson, "The Man Who Wouldn't Quit," *Break Point Commentary*, 26 February 1999.

43 George Orwell, "Notes on the Way," *The Collected Essays, Journalism, and Letters of George Orwell* (1968).

CHAPTER FIVE

1 Paul Singer and Lisa Caruso, "The Battle Is Joined," *National Journal* (9 July 2005): 2193, 2194.

2 People for the American Way, http://www.pfaw.org/pfaw/general/default.aspx?oid=9545 (accessed 5 December 2005).

3 People for the American Way, http://www.pfaw.org (accessed 25 April 2005 by RNC Research).

4 Ibid.

5 People for the American Way, press release, 1 October 1999.

6 "People for the American Way and People for the American Way Foundation: A History."

7 Thomas M. Landy, "What is missing from this Picture? Television Producer Norman Lear, Interview," *Commonweal*, 9 October 1992.

8 "People for the American Way and People for the American Way Foundation: A History."

9 Byron York, "Media for the American Way," *National Review Online* (26 April 2002).

10 People for the American Way website, "PFAW on Capitol Hill," http://www.pfaw.org (accessed 4 July 2005).

11 Angie Cannon, "Full-Court Press," *U.S. News & World Report*, 14 February 2005.

12 "Neas's New Orders," *Wall Street Journal*, 24 April 2002.

13 "Chairman Neas," *Wall Street Journal*, 8 February 2002, A18.

14 David E. Rosenbaum and Lynette Clemetson, "In Battle to Confirm a New Justice, Both Sides Get Troops Ready Again," *New York Times*, 3 July 2005.

[15] Matthew Barge, "NARAL Falsely Accuses Supreme Court Nominee Roberts," FactCheck.org (modified 12 August 2005).

[16] Brooks Jackson, "NARAL Falsely Accuses Supreme Court Nominee Roberts," FactCheck.org (modified 12 August 2005).

[17] Ibid.

[18] Web address is http://www.pregnantpause.org/abort/remember-naral.htm.

[19] Web address is http://www.expectantmothercare.org/naral_inside.html (accessed 4 July 2005).

[20] Ibid.

[21] Phyllis Schlafly, "Ashcroft stands up to abortion industry," 8 March 2004.

[22] Center for Responsive Politics.

[23] The National Organization for Women website, http://www.now.org/organization/info.html (accessed 4 July 2005).

[24] Ibid.

[25] Ibid.

[26] Ibid.

[27] As discussed in ch. 1 of this book ("Fresh Air," National Public Radio, 16 February 2005).

[28] The Alliance for Justice website, www.allianceforjustice.org (accessed 4 July 2005).

[29] Ibid.

[30] Ibid.

[31] Ibid.

[32] "Party of No" leader's appearance in Alliance for Justice ad show his principles based on partisanship," www.gop.com, RNC research, accessed 23 May 2005.

[33] Ibid.

[34] Jan LaRue, "The Left's Book on Judicial Warfare: Dismay-Demand-Distort-Defame-Delay," *Citizen Magazine*, 6 June 2005.

[35] "Party of No" leader's appearance in Alliance for Justice ad show his principles based on partisanship," www.gop.com, RNC research, accessed 23 May 2005.

CHAPTER SIX

[1] Manuel Miranda, editorial page, *Wall Street Journal*, Monday, 8 August 2005.

[2] David. S. Lutz, *The Origins of American Constitutionalism* (Baton Rouge: Louisiana State University Press, 1988), 142.

[3] Tony Perkins, "Publicly Honoring God," Family Research Council pamphlet.

[4] James Taranto, *Wall Street Journal*, 9 August 2005.

[5] Ibid.

[6] Roger Clegg, "Politics, Pickering, and Philosophy: The Role of the Political Branches in Judicial Selection," *Nexus, A Journal of Opinion* 7, Chapman University School of Law (2002): 49.

[7] Confirmation hearing on the nomination of Charles W. Pickering Sr. to be circuit judge for the Fifth Circuit, 7 February 2002, serial no. J-107-57, pp. 89, 90.

[8] Clegg, "Politics, Pickering, and Philosophy," 58.

[9] *Colero-Toledo v. Pearson Yacht Leasing Co.*, 416 U.S. 663, 681 n. 17 (1974) (J. Brennan quoting Exodus 21:28); *Memorial Hospital v. Maricopa County*, 415 U.S. 250, 261 (1974) (J. Marshall quoting Leviticus 24:22); *Miranda v. Arizona*, 384 U.S. 436, 459 n. 27 (C. J. Warren citing book of Judges),

[10] Clegg, "Politics, Pickering, and Philosophy," 56.

[11] *United States v. Halat*, no. 2:96cr30 pg (22 September 1997), sentencing hearing.

[12] Confirmation hearing on the nomination of Charles W. Pickering Sr., 7 February 2002, 89, 90.

[13] *United States v. Gillich*, no. 1:90 cr77pr (23 September 1977), hearing on motion for reduction of sentence.

[14] Clegg, "Politics, Pickering, and Philosophy," 56.

[15] Confirmation hearing on the nomination of Charles W. Pickering Sr., 7 February 2002, 89, 90.

[16] Editorial, *Clarion Ledger* (Jackson MI), 26 January 2002.

[17] Letter to Senators Hatch and Leahy, 5 June 2003.

[18] Confirmation hearing on the nomination of William Pryor to be circuit judge for the Eleventh Circuit, 11 June 2003, 85, 86.

[19] National Organization for Women press release, 8 June 2005, http://www.now.org/press/06-05/06-08.html.

[20] Kay Daley, *Wall Street Journal*, 25 July 2003.

[21] Log Cabin Republicans at www.lcr.org (accessed 11 March 2002).

[22] Brendan Miniter, *Wall Street Journal*, 22 April 2003.

[23] Congressional Record, 6 July 2004, S7540, S7541

[24] Congressional Record, 6 July 2004, S7562.

[25] Congressional Record, 6 July 2004.

[26] Manuel Miranda, "Judging While Catholic—II, Democrats Attack Christian Judges, Defeat Themselves," *Wall Street Journal*, 8 August 2005.

CHAPTER SEVEN

[1] Pew Research Center for the People & the Press, "Public More Critical of Press, But Goodwill Persists," 26 June 2005.

[2] Lori Robertson, "Confronting the Culture," *American Journalism Review* (August/September 2005): 37.

[3] Pew Research Center, "Public More Critical of Press, But Goodwill Persists."

[4] Pew Research Center for the People & the Press, "How Journalists See Journalists in 2004," 2004.

[5] Rachel Smolkin, "A Source of Encouragement," *American Journalism Review* (August/September 2005): 31, 32.

[6] Pew Research Center for the People & the Press, "Media Consumption and Believability Study," 2004.

[7] Smolkin, "A Source of Encouragement," 31, 32.

[8] Pew Research Center, "How Journalists See Journalists in 2004."

[9] Pew Research Center, "Public More Critical of Press, But Goodwill Persists."

[10] John Tierney, "Where Cronies Dwell," *New York Times*, 11 October 2005, A27.

[11] Pew Research Center, "How Journalists See Journalists in 2004."

[12] Tom Hess and Karla Dial, "Year of the Values Voter," *Citizen Magazine*, January 2005.

[13] Brian Perry, "Checking religion at the newsroom door," *Madison County Journal*, 6 November 1997.

[14] Louis Bolce and Gerald De Maio, "Our Secularist Democratic Party," *Public Interest* (Fall 2002).

[15] Quotes from Bernard Goldberg, *Bias: A CBS Insider Exposes How the Media Distort the News* (Washington DC: Regnery Publishing, 2001).

[16] Fred Barnes, "The Right Way to Handle the Left," *Citizen Magazine*, August 2003.

[17] Bolce and De Maio, "Our Secularist Democratic Party."

[18] Schumer and Kennedy *National Journal* numbers from Charles Green, "When a Rating Becomes a Talking Point," *National Journal*, 30 August 2004.

[19] Goldberg, *Bias*, p. 63, 66.

[20] Sherry Ricchiardi, "Short Attention Span," *American Journalism Review* (August/September 2005): 59.

[21] Nat Hentoff, "The Ordeal of Charles Pickering: Are Times Editorials Fact-Checked?" *The Village Voice*, 17 October 2003.

[22] Neil Lewis, "A Judge, a Renomination and the Cross-Burning Case That Won't End," *New York Times*, 28 May 2003.

[23] Hentoff, "Ordeal of Charles Pickering."

CHAPTER EIGHT

[1] *Roper v. Simmons*, 125 S. Ct. 1190 (2005).

[2] G. Edward White, "The Constitutional Revolution as a Crisis in Adaptivity," 48 Hastings L. J., July 1997.

[3] Ibid.

[4] Ibid.

[5] Mark R. Levin, *Men in Black: How the Supreme Court Is Destroying America* (Washington DC: Regnery Publishing, Inc., 2005), 1.

[6] *Home Building and Loan Ass'n v. Blaisdell,* 290 U.S. 398, 54 S. Ct. 231 (1934).

[7] *West Coast Hotels Co. v. Parrish,* 300 U.S. 379 at 402, 403, 57 S. Ct., 578 (1937).

[8] Seth Lipsky, "Beyond Brandeis," *New York Sun,* 12 July 2005.

[9] *Justice Black and the Living Constitution,* 76 Harv. L. Rev., 673 at 727, February 1963.

[10] Ibid., 735.

[11] *White v. Weiser,* 412 U.S. 783, 93 S. Ct., 2348 at 798 (1973).

[12] *Rummel v. Estelle,* 445 U.S. 263, at 307, 100 S. Ct., 1133 (1980).

[13] *Roe v. Wade* quotes are from 410 U.S. 113, 93 S.Ct. 705 (1973).

[14] 410 U. S. 179, 93 S. Ct. 762 (1973).

[15] *Barron v. Baltimore,* 32 U.S. 243 (1833).

[16] *Marbury v. Madison.*

[17] Speech of Attorney General Edwin Meese III before the American Bar Association, 9 July 1985, Washington DC, reprinted in *The Great Debate: Interpreting Our Written Constitution,* published by the Federalist Society, November 2005.

[18] Speech of Justice William J. Brennan Jr., Georgetown University, 12 October 1985, Washington DC, reprinted in *The Great Debate: Interpreting Our Written Constitution,* published by the Federalist Society, November 2005.

[19] Speech of Attorney General Edwin Meese III before the D.C. chapter of the Federalist Society, 15 November 1985, Washington D.C., reprinted in *The Great Debate.*

[20] Judge Robert H. Bork speech before the University of San Diego Law School, 18 November 1985, printed originally in the University of San Diego Law Review, reprinted by the Federalist Society, November 2005.

[21] Speech of President Ronald Reagan at the investiture of Chief Justice William H. Rehnquist and Associate Justice Antonin Scalia at the White House, 26 September 1986, Washington D.C., reprinted in *The Great Debate: Interpreting Our Written Constitution,* published by the Federalist Society, November 2005.

[22] *Roper v. Simmons.*

CHAPTER NINE

[1] United States Constitution, Fifth Amendment.

[2] All Kelo citations found in *Kelo v. New London,* 125 S. Ct. 2658, 2660, and 2671, (2005).

[3] Water E. Williams, "Confiscating property," Creators Syndicate, 29 June 2005.

[4] *Elk Grove Unified School District v. Newdow,* 124 S. Ct. 2301 at 2306 (2004).

[5] *Newdow v. ElK Grove Unified School District* et al., 292 Fed. 3ʳᵈ, 597, at 607, 608 (Ninth Circuit, 2002).

[6] Jason Hoppin, "Goodwin Isn't Fazed by Strom Over the Pledge," *Recorder*, 1 July 2002.

[7] 328 Fed. 3rd, 466 at 487, 488,4 90 (Ninth Circuit 2003).

[8] Newdow I, 292 Fed. 3rd, 597 at 613.

[9] Newdow III, 328 Fed. 3rd, 466 at 472.

[10] Newdow filed another case on November 17, 2005, challenging the national motto, "In God We Trust," and seeking to prevent its use on any future coins or paper money.

[11] *McCreary County v. American Civil Liberties Union*, 545 U.S, (2005) (Scalia, dissenting, slip opinion, p. 9).

[12] Quotes from *Goodridge v. Dept. of Public Health*, 440 Mass. 309, 798 Northeast Second 941 (Mass. 2003).

[13] *McCreary County v. American Civil Liberties Union*, Scalia, dissenting, slip opinion, p. 7.

[14] Van Orden, Thomas, J. concurring, p. 6.

[15] Ibid., page 4, citation omitted.

[16] Van Orden, Thomas, concurring, p. 3.

[17] Van Orden, Breyer, J., concurring in judgment, slip opinion, p. 3.

[18] Van Orden, Stevens, dissent, slip opinion at 26.

[19] Van Orden, 545 U.S. (2005), Thomas, J., concurring, slip opinion, p. 2.

[20] Van Orden, 545 U.S. (2005),Thomas, J., concurring, slip opinion, p. 3.

[21] *The Gallup Poll* (13 September 2005).

CHAPTER TEN

[1] For additional information on the filibuster and a formal treatment on the topic, please see "A Proposal: Codification by Statute of the Judicial Confirmation Process," (14 Wm & Mary Bill Rts [2006, forthcoming]), a law journal article coauthored by myself and Bradley S. Clanton of Baker, Donelson, Bearman, Caldwell, & Berkowitz, P.C., of Jackson, Mississippi, the Southeast, and Washington DC. Much of the material for this chapter is drawn from that article.

[2] E. Martin Enriquez, "Tyranny of the Minority: The Unconstitutional Filibuster and the Superimposed Supermajority on the Advice and Consent Clause of the Constitution," 21 T. M. Cooley L Rev. 215 (2004).

[3] Ibid. at 223-24 and quoting Robert Luce, "Legislative Procedure: Parliamentary Practices and the Course of Business in the Framing of Statutes," 283 (1922).

[4] Steven Calabresi, professor of law at Northwestern University Law School, in his testimony before the Senate Judiciary Committee's Subcommittee on the Constitution,

Civil Rights, and Property Rights, 6 May 2003,
http://judiciary.senate.gov/testimony.cfm.

[5] Enriquez, "Tyranny of the Minority."

[6] Bruce D. Hausknecht, "De-bunking the Myths about Judicial-Nominee Filibusters," 26 May 2005, www.family.org/cforum/fosi/government/ congress/senate.

[7] Calabresi, testimony before the Senate Judiciary Committee's Subcommittee on the Constitution, Civil Rights, and Property Rights.

[8] "Filibuster and Cloture," historical minutes on U.S. Senate website, 8 August 2005, http://www.senate.gov/artandhistory/history/common/briefing/Filibuster_Cloture.htm.

[9] "March 8, 1917: Cloture Rule," historical minutes on U.S. Senate website, 8 August 2005, http://www.senate.gov/artandhistory/history/minute/Cloture_Rule.htm.

[10] Ibid.

[11] Ibid.

[12] "June 12-13, 1935: Huey Long Filibusters," historical minutes on U.S. Senate website, 8 August 2005, http://www.senate.gov/artandhistory/history/minute/Huey_Long_Filibusters.htm.

[13] "October 17, 1939: 'Mr. Smith' Comes to Washington," historical minutes on U.S. Senate website, 8 August 2005, http://www.senate.gov/artandhistory/minute/Mr_Smith_Comes_To_Washington.htm.

[14] 109th Congress, S. Res. 39—passed by unanimous consent on June 13, 2005.

[15] Calabresi, testimony before the Senate Judiciary Committee's Subcommittee on the Constitution, Civil Rights, and Property Rights.

[16] "The Last, Hoarse Gasp," *Time*, 9 September 1957.

[17] CongressLink.com, historical notes, Dirksen Congressional Center, 9 August 2005, http://www.congresslink.org/print_teaching_historicalnotes.htm.

[18] The ten filibustered Bush nominees: Janice Rogers Brown, Miguel Estrada, Richard Griffin, Carolyn Kuhl, David McKeague, William Myers, Priscilla Owen, Charles Pickering, William Pryor, and Henry Saad. The six threatened: Claude Allen, Terrence Boyle, Thomas Griffith, William Haynes, Brett Kavanaugh, and Susan Neilson.

[19] Steven G. Calabresi, "Pirates We Be," *Wall Street Journal*, 14 May 2003, A-14.

[20] Congressional Record, 20 February 1975, 3847-50.

[21] Lyndon B. Johnson during the 89th Congress with 68 Democrats—at the time 67 votes were required to invoke cloture; Jimmy Carter during the 95th Congress with 61 Democrats—at that time as now 60 votes were required to invoke cloture.

[22] Presidential filibuster proof material derived from U.S. Senate web page, http://www.senate.gov.

[23] Some individual Republicans did make an attempt during the Clinton administration to filibuster two nominees, but they did not receive the necessary support from even their own party. The attempt to filibuster failed.

[24] U.S. Constitution, Article I, Section 5.

[25] Karen Hosler, "Senators vote 76-19 to maintain filibuster," *Baltimore Sun*, 6 January 1995.

[26] 108th Congress, S. Res. 138.

[27] Hausknecht, "De-bunking the Myths."

[28] From Robert C. Byrd, *The Senate, 1789–1989: Addresses on the History of the United States Senate*, vol. 2, 151, 153—quoted at CongressLink.com, historical notes, Dirksen Congressional Center, 9 August 2005, http://www.congresslink.org/print_teaching_historicalnotes.htm.

[29] Congressional Record, 8 April 2003.

[30] Gerald Walpin, "Take Obstructionism Out of the Judicial Nominations Confirmation Process," 8 Tex. Rev. L. & Pol. (2003).

[31] *The Federalist Papers* 386 (Bantam ed. 1982). As Madison wrote in Federalist 51, "The primary consideration [for the confirmation of judges'] ought to be qualifications" (ibid. at 262).

[32] Speech, American Bar Association, 5 August 1997.

[33] Joseph P. Harrison, *The Advice and Consent of the Senate* (1968): 376.

[34] "The Pickering Precedent," *Wall Street Journal*, 12 March 2002.

[35] Floor statement, 3 October 2000.

[36] Congressional Record, 18 June 1998.

[37] Congressional Record, 2 April 1998.

[38] Floor statement, 16 June 1997.

[39] "The Pickering Precedent."

[40] Press release, "The 105th Congress," 2 December 1997.

[41] Congressional Record, 1 August 1996.

[42] Congressional Record, 3 February 1998, S295.

[43] Betsy Palmer, "Changing Senate Rules: The 'Constitutional' or 'Nuclear' Option," 1 December 2004, CRS 6.

[44] Trent Lott, *Herding Cats: A Life in Politics* (New York: ReganBooks, 2005), 289.

[45] Senator Robert Byrd, Congressional Record, 15 January 1979.

[46] Congressional Record, 20 February 1975, 3847-50.

[47] Senator Harry Reid to Senator Bill Frist, 15 March 2005.

[48] *Washington Post*, 13 December 2004.

[49] David S. Broder, "Nuclear Cloud Over The Senate," *Washington Post*, 19 May 2005, A27.

[50] "Leading Constitutional Scholars Discuss Ramifications if Rumors of U.S. Supreme Court Retirements Prove True," FindLaw.com, press release, 30 June 2003.

[51] John Cornyn, *Our Broken Judicial Confirmation Process and the Need for Filibuster Reform*, 27 Harv. J.L. & Pub. Pol'y (2003).

[52] Ibid.

[53] The Confirmation Improvement Act I advocate would include a provision protecting a request for additional time for similar purposes.

[54] U.S. Senate history minute, "October 1, 1968: Filibuster Derails Supreme Court Appointment," U.S. Senate web site (12 August 2005), http://www.senate.gov/artandhistory/history/minute/Filibuster_Derails_Supreme_Court_Appointment.htm.

[55] "The White House: The President in Motion," *Time Magazine*, 11 October 1971. Poff was not actually submitted to the Senate and so is not considered to have been rejected.

[56] Beth, Richard S., "Cloture Attempts on Nominations." CRS Report for Congress. (Updated 11 December 2002.)

[57] Walpin, "Take Obstruction Out of the Judicial Nominations Confirmation Process."

[58] *The New Criterion* (Notes & Comments, January 2003) suggests this similar definition.

[59] Byron York, "The Record—What sort of filibustering has taken place in the Senate, where judicial nominations are concerned?" *National Review*, 6 June 2005.

[60] Paez's cloture vote passed 85-14 and he was confirmed 59-39. Berzon's cloture vote passed 86-13 and she was confirmed 64-34.

CHAPTER ELEVEN

[1] Kathryn Jean Lopez, "Bench Memos," *National Review* online (20 May 2005).

[2] It should be noted that Senator Robert Byrd supported the filibusters of the Bush nominees and that he rejected that his past actions constituted either a precedent or a justification for the "Constitutional/nuclear/Byrd" option.

[3] Charles Babington, "Filibuster Vote Will Be Hard to Predict," *Washington Post* 28 April 2005.

[4] Janet Hook, "Activists to Senate: 'No deal' on judges," *Los Angeles Times*, 19 May 2005.

[5] Chad Groening and Judy Brown, "Dobson: Lott Has Brokered Deal on Filibuster," Agape Press, 10 May 2005.

[6] Ana Radelat, "Senate filibuster compromise was Lott's idea, not McCain's," *Clarion-Ledger Washington Bureau*, 29 May 2005.

[7] Senator John Cornyn, "An Admission of Guilt," *National Review* online, 24 May 2005.

[8] Alexander Bolton, ". . . but Frist hangs tough on 'nuclear,'" *The Hill*, 25 May 2005.

[9] National Organization for Women, press release, 8 June 2005.

[10] Bolton, "Frist hangs tough."

CHAPTER TWELVE

[1] William Kristol, "O'Connor, Not Rehnquist?" *Weekly Standard*, 22 June 2005.

[2] "Bush nominates Roberts to Supreme Court," CNN.com, 20 July 2005.

[3] As an example of just how far the press would go to attack John Roberts's nomination, the *Washington Post* Style Section criticized Jane Roberts's choice of outfits for herself and the children. And the *New York Times* pried into the adoption records for Josie and Jack to look for anything they could use during the confirmation.

[4] "Bush nominates Roberts to Supreme Court."

[5] Eliezer Zuckerman, "Liberal opposition to Roberts," Committee for Justice, 28 August 2005.

[6] Eliezer Zuckerman, "Liberal opposition to Roberts," Committee for Justice, 9 August 2005.

[7] Ibid.

[8] Charles Hurt, "Contentious start to Roberts hearings," *Washington Times*, 12 September 2005.

[9] "Bush nominates Roberts as chief justice," CNN.com, 6 September 2005.

[10] Jay T. Jorgensen, "Precedent from the Confirmation Hearings of Ruth Bader Ginsburg for the Conduct of Judicial Nominees," *Federalist Society for Law and Public Policy Studies*, 2005.

[11] Edwin Meese III and Todd Gaziano, "The Ginsburg Rule," 25 July 2005.

[12] Robert Novak, "The Ginsburg standard," 25 July 2005.

[13] "I come with 'no agenda,' Roberts tells hearing," CNN.com, 13 September 2005.

[14] Liza Porteus, "Roberts Picks and Chooses Questions to Answer," Fox News, 14 September 2005.

[15] Tom Brune, "Probing to find Roberts' softer side," Newsday.com, 15 September 2005.

[16] Sheryl Gay Stolberg and David D. Kirkpatrick, "Top Democrat Says He'll Vote No on Roberts," *New York Times*, 21 September 2005.

[17] Mark Memmott, "Battle lines may be drawn in new spot," *USA Today*, 4 October 2005.

[18] Judy Keen and Kathy Kiely, "Court pick rewrites script," *USA Today*, 4 October 2005.

[19] Charles Hurt, "Some Republicans balk, but confirmation expected," *Washington Times*, 4 October 2005.

[20] Charles Babington and Thomas B. Edsall, "Conservative Republicans Divided Over Nominee," *Washington Post*, 4 October 2005.

[21] Joseph Curl, "Bush taps Harriet Miers for court," *Washington Times*, 4 October 2005.

[22] Ibid.

[23] *Bloomberg News*, 12 October 2005.

[24] Associated Press, Tuscaloosa AL, Friday, 11 November 2005.

[25] NBC News, *Today Show*, 10 October 2005.

[26] Jim Wooten, associate editorial page editor, "Best nominees don't reach slaughterhouse," *Atlanta Journal-Constitution*, 9 October 2005.

[27] Peter Baker, "Alito Nomination Sets Stage for Ideological Battle," *Washington Post*, 1 November 2005.

[28] Jim Drinkard, Judy Keen, and Kathy Kiely, "Bush nominates Alito for Supreme Court," *USA Today*, 31 October 2005.

[29] Ibid.

[30] Mark Wegner, "Foes of Alito Nomination Launching National Ad Campaign," *Congress Daily AM*, 17 November 2005.

[31] Basil Talbott, "Filibuster Question Slips into Discussions of Alito Nomination," *Congress Daily AM*, 17 November 2005.

[32] Seth Stern and Keith Perine, "Alito Comment in 1985 a Quandary for Abortion Rights Supporters in Senate," *CQ Today*, 15 November 2005.

[33] "Biden: Chance of Alito Filibuster Higher," Associated Press, 20 November 2005.

[34] Talbott, "Filibuster Question Slips into Discussions of Alito Nomination."

[35] Alison Vekshin, "Pryor meets Supreme Court nominee," *Arkansas News*, 4 November 2005.

[36] "Cracks in 'Gang of 14,'" *Associated Press*, 3 November 2005.

[37] Charles Babington and Michael A. Fletcher, "Alito Signals Reluctance to Overturn Roe v. Wade," *Washington Post*, 9 November 2005.

[38] Edward Whelan, "The Right Justice," *National Review*, 5 December 2005.

EPILOGUE

[1] Rudolph Giuliani, "An Ugly Stall," *New York Post*, online ed., 10 February 2003.

[2] Personal conversation with Miguel Estrada.

[3] Melanie Kirkpatrick, "Memogate: Why won't the Senate GOP stand up to Democratic Judiciary Committee shenanigans?" *Wall Street Journal*, 5 March 2004.

[4] Giuliani, "An Ugly Stall."

[5] Thomas Jipping, WorldNetDaily.com, Friday, 7 February 2003.

[6] Giuliani, *National Review* online, 10 February 2003.

[7] George Weigel, "Dancing Around the Issue," Ethics and Public Policy Center, posted Wednesday, 9 November 2005.